Performance Based Supervisory Development

PERFORMANCE BASED SUPERVISORY DEVELOPMENT

Adapted from a Major AT&T Study

CHARLES R. MACDONALD

in collaboration with
Charles Youngblood and Kerry Glum
of the American Telephone and Telegraph Company

Human Resource Development Press
Amherst, Massachusetts

This book is based on supervisory job studies conducted within the Bell System by AT&T personnel. The book was written with the permission and cooperation of the American Telephone and Telegraph Company.

In the course of translating the AT&T internal job study reports into a working guide for training managers in industry generally, any errors or misinterpretations that may have occurred are solely the responsibility of the author and publisher.

Neither AT&T nor Bell System companies can respond to inquiries or requests for information about the material in this book. Any such inquiries or requests should be addressed to the publisher.

Library of Congress Cataloging in Publication Data

Macdonald, Charles R.
   Performance based supervisory development.

   1. Supervision of employees—United States.   2. American Telephone and Telegraph Company—Personnel management.   I. Youngblood, Charles.   II. Glum, Kerry.
III. American Telephone and Telegraph Company.   IV. Title.
HF5549.2.U5M3   658.4'07124   82-3001
ISBN 0-914234-58-7   AACR2

First Printing

Manufactured in the United States of America

Contents

About the Author

Charles R. Macdonald has been on the world headquarters staff of ITT as Director of Planning for North America. Also, he was vice president of marketing and planning for Western Union. He is author of *MBO Can Work: How to Manage by Contract*, McGraw-Hill, and *24 Ways to Greater Business Productivity*, Prentice-Hall—Institute for Business Planning.

Introduction

As the level of concern rises about sagging productivity in American industry and the urgent need to regain the nation's lost prestige and power in the world's markets, science and technology have been singled out as the "driving forces" that can restore America's competitiveness. Other factors have also been identified as major contributors to the restoration of our productivity: the necessity for new capital generation to finance investment in new production facilities; removal of government's heavy hand from the private economy through deregulation of major industries; and the pressing need to correct inflation, which has debased not only our currency but our ability to measure performance of our organizations.

All these factors are correctly called out for attention; each can contribute significantly to the recovery of America's lost preeminence in the industrial world. It seems, however, that amid the furor about low productivity, remarkably little attention is being focused on another factor that may have an even more important influence on the issue.

That factor is *management.*

Advancing the frontiers of science and technology can make new achievements possible, but it does not necessarily make them happen. Massive investments in capital facilities create *potential* for high productivity, but do not automatically put these facilities into productive motion. And improving our capability to account accurately for costs, expenses, and profitability can take much uncertainty out of our business operations, but it will not ensure profitability.

Management is the factor that can transform technology into new products and services that benefit users; that can convert plant investment into useful output of goods; and that can marshal and control the human resources that make it happen. Conversely, management is the factor that can *inhibit* the productivity of technology, capital, and people if it fails to employ these resources with enterprise and skill.

FIRST-LEVEL SUPERVISION IS THE KEY

Within the broad term *management* are many elements and several levels, of course, and each is crucial in its own way to the productivity of our institutions. It is the basic premise of this book, however, that none is more vital to our mission than the level of management that deals directly with the fundamental work groups of the organization—that is, *first-level supervision.*

This presentation proposes first to demonstrate that this is so, and then to offer a prescription for making this key element of management more effective and more productive in the demanding decade ahead. Part of this prescription is a redefining of the role of another member of management who has the greatest influence on performance of the first-level supervisor—the supervisor's direct superior on the second level of the organization.

This prescription is founded upon massive job studies of first- and second-level supervision conducted within the Bell System in the late 1970s. These job studies are among the most comprehensive and penetrating examinations ever made of the lower levels of supervision. They are based on direct observation of a select group of supervisors—those identified as *master performers* by the Bell operating companies for which they work. The prescription, therefore, is *performance-based.*

PURPOSE OF THE AT&T SUPERVISORY JOB STUDIES

The essential purpose of these landmark job studies was to identify the contemporary training needs of new first- and second-level supervisors within the Bell System. AT&T is the world's largest private employer, with over one million people on its payrolls. Some 170,000 of these are first-level supervisors, and 60,000 more are on the second level of management. Each year, nearly 18,000 men and women are promoted or appointed to first-level supervisor; some 5,000 advance to the second level.

Simply to train these people in their new duties and responsibilities is an enormous task. Additionally, advances in telecommunications technology, coupled with changing conditions in the workplace, have placed new demands on management. Training must be kept in phase with these new conditions if the company is to retain its vitality and competitiveness.

These AT&T studies represent a highly disciplined approach to defining the company's everchanging training needs. It is a process of building a data base of up-to-date, valid information out of which to develop training programs that are cost-effective and genuinely responsive to company needs.

OUTPUT OF THE JOB STUDIES

The primary product of these studies was a set of recommendations for training and other remedial action to correct deficiencies in job performance of supervisors. These recommendations were based on many months of intensive data collection and analysis of supervisory job performance by teams of AT&T training and development specialists.

Supporting the recommendations were unique "Skill/Knowledge Mastery Models" of first- and second-level supervisory performance, derived from interviews and observation of hundreds of Bell System *master performers*—a select group of highly proficient supervisors in a variety of job situations. Also included in the study reports were comprehensive Diagnostic Test instruments designed to match up the skills and knowledge of new supervisors with the Mastery Model, thereby revealing deficiencies for remedial actions. The recommendations resulting from the two job studies have since been implemented in the Bell System, and supervisors at both levels are receiving training and using job aids developed from them.

BASIS OF THIS BOOK

This book is based on the final Job Study Reports prepared by the AT&T supervisory job study groups, and discussions with key Bell System participants in the studies. Principal among these are Charles J. Sherrard, division manager, training administration, in AT&T's Human Resources Development department in Morristown, New Jersey; Charles (Buck) Youngblood, project manager of the second-level job studies; and Kerry Glum, who monitored the first-level job study and report for the HRD department.

These studies represent a considerable investment of time and professional effort by Bell System personnel. The job study reports and the training programs that were developed as a result of the recommendations contained in the reports are proprietary to the Bell System. They are being published in this form with the permission and cooperation of AT&T in the belief that the knowledge gained through these intensive studies of first- and second-level supervision can be useful to other organizations.

The American Telephone and Telegraph Company occupies a unique position on the U.S. industrial scene, not only as the principal provider of essential communications services to the nation, but as a major factor of the American economy. Accordingly, AT&T management believes that its responsibilities to the public go beyond its charter to provide telephone service—that it has an obligation to share important knowledge gained through its personnel development efforts with others. This is particularly true of knowledge that can help American industry to increase productivity at this critical time in our history.

PURPOSE OF THIS BOOK

This book is intended primarily as a *resource* for practicing managers of training and training development. The presentation is concerned principally with the job study of *first-level supervision;* the second-level job study is of interest, however, because it was the first comprehensive study of generic managerial duties, tasks, skills, and knowledge made in the Bell System. As such, this study broke new ground and set the pattern for the subsequent study of the first-level job.

The centerpiece of this presentation and discussion is the first-level Skill/Knowledge Mastery Model. This is a highly detailed description of the supervisor's job in terms of *principal duties, major tasks, specific skills required, and knowledge needed.* A better word than description, perhaps, is *prescription*, because the Mastery Model constitutes a design or a profile of an "ideal" first-level supervisor toward which the training and development of supervisors should be directed, *within the constraints of costs and valid organizational needs.* Not a theoretical ideal, it is important to note, but a practical "performance-based" prescription based on intensive observation of sizable numbers of working supervisors identified as *superior performers* in a wide range of job functions and work locations throughout the Bell System.

ORGANIZATION OF THE PRESENTATION

The book is in three major parts. Part I discusses the urgent need for improved productivity throughout our American institutions and the key role of first-level supervision in this effort. New demands on supervision in the decade ahead are cited, and the urgent need for intensified training to cope with these demands is discussed.

The Bell System studies of supervisory jobs are briefly described, and the derivation of the 14 principal managerial duties of the first-level supervisor—the basic framework of the Mastery model—is traced.

Part I concludes with a brief summary description of the first-level Skill/Mastery Model. A simple diagnostic test for knowledge of the 14 duties and their relative importance is provided, as well as a means to identify new supervisors' perceived training needs in respect to these principal managerial duties.

Part II is designed as a resource and a working tool for the practicing manager of training or training development. This section describes the 14 principal duties in several levels of detail, ranging from a general discussion of the need for each activity in the contemporary organization and the role of the first-level supervisor, to the fully detailed Skill/Knowledge Mastery Model and the associated Diagnostic Test instrument.

Each of the 14 processes is covered in a separate chapter; each chapter is in six sections. The intention is that the training manager can select the specific process and/or the specific level of detail appropriate to the particular training need—whether initial training for a brand-new supervisor promoted from the ranks (or a candidate for the first-level job), or retrain-

ing for experienced supervisors to help them cope with new conditions in the workplace.

Part III is a discussion of the study process and the methodology used by the AT&T Job Study task force. This section is intended for the human resources development professional who is interested in the highly disciplined approach to training needs analysis and training development employed by the Bell System.

Part III also presents a brief outline of the actual training courses developed for first- and second-level supervisors in the Bell System as a result of the recommendations by the Job Study Task Forces. (These training courses are proprietary to AT&T; they cannot be made available to non–Bell System companies.)

Also presented in Part III is an appraisal of the significance of the AT&T Supervisory Job Study by noted social scientist, Robert R. Carkhuff.

WHAT THIS BOOK CAN DO FOR YOU

This book has been prepared as a guide and a resource for managers of training and training program development. It will be useful whether you are an experienced training manager or new to the job. The purpose of the book is to help you develop, improve, and maintain the management skills and knowledge of the first-level supervisors in your organization.

More specifically, the book is designed to help you:

1. Determine the overall training needs of your

supervisory force and its individual members.
2. Develop total training programs for new supervisors.
3. Prepare courses of training to remedy specific performance deficiencies.
4. Develop refresher training for experienced supervisors.

In addition, the book can provide guidance in resolving spot problems involving supervisors and supervision.

ASSUMPTIONS

This book is based on several assumptions about you, the reader:

- You are involved, either directly or indirectly, with human resources training and development, and have a strong interest in improving the productivity of your organization.
- You are a member of an organization that employs a dozen or more first-level supervisors—and has a need to replace and/or add three or four (or more) new supervisors each year.

- The nature of work and content of jobs in your company are constantly changing with new technology, organizational growth, competition, and changing customer needs.
- Your supervisors are already trained in the basic *technical* aspects of their jobs and the work they supervise; whether pouring concrete foundations for buildings, selling the company's products, maintaining and repairing production machinery, or programming computers. Furthermore, there is an active effort under way to keep

supervisors' technical skills and knowledge current through periodic retraining.

- You feel some concern—based either on hard data or hunch—that, despite your selection and training efforts, many of your supervisors are deficient in certain basic management skills and knowledge.

- You also may have an uneasy feeling that your *training needs* are not as well defined as they might be and that some of your training programs are not really responsive to the valid needs of your organization.

DEFINITION OF TERMS

The term *supervisor,* as used here, applies to the individual who is directly in charge of a basic work group of two or more persons, regardless of job title or job function.

The term *basic management skills and knowledge* covers the *generic* managerial aspects of supervision. That is, the principal duties, major tasks, specific skills, and points of knowledge common to virtually *all* supervisory jobs, irrespective of the kind of work supervised, the size of the work group, or the type of organization of which the supervisor is a member.

These generic managerial job functions are:

- Planning the work
- Controlling work
- Problem solving
- Providing performance feedback
- Coaching subordinates
- Creating/maintaining a motivative atmosphere
- Communication
- Informal oral communication
- Conducting/attending meetings
- Written communication and documentation
- Career counseling subordinates
- Self-development
- Representing the company
- Managing time

SURVIVAL SKILLS FOR NEW SUPERVISORS

The first four of these managerial functions are identified in the Job Study reports as "survival skills" for newly appointed first-level supervisors. In the words of the final study report, "It is most critical that deficiencies in these four managerial processes be treated immediately (through training) as they provide the *survival skills* needed to be effective on the job and produce results."

Putting these principal duties into narrative form for the sake of emphasis, we can say that super-

visory effectiveness requires the capability to first *plan the work* and then *control the work* while it is in progress. Inevitably obstacles are encountered and things go wrong—supervisors must *solve problems* that arise in the course of doing the work. In order to achieve high productivity and quality output, supervisors must ensure that subordinates are kept informed about their progress through *feedback reports on performance.*

FACILITATIVE FUNCTIONS

The next five managerial processes on the list are labeled "facilitative." In the course of doing the work assigned to the work group, supervisors are required to *coach individuals* whose performance is not up

to standard. They must also strive to keep a *motivative atmosphere* in the workplace at all times. These two processes call upon supervisors' *communication* skills, especially the most common *informal oral* kind used to convey information and ensure understanding.

While guiding and directing the activities of subordinates, supervisors must manage their own daily activities. They must constantly set and reset priorities as they handle paper work, phone calls, and other transactions. This is the process of *managing time*.

The Job Study report states that these processes facilitate the first four survival processes; it is important, therefore, to remedy deficient skills and knowledge in these functions through training.

JOB OR PERFORMANCE AIDS

The remaining five supervisory functions are considered less critical to survival of the newly appointed supervisor, but they are still important to effective performance on the job. The study report recommended that these be treated through the means of job or performance aids, rather than training.

Supervisors are required on occasion to *counsel subordinates* who have potential for career advancement and who seek more challenging work. The capability to *communicate* well with subordinate, peers,

and superiors *formally in meetings* and *in writing* is important to supervisory performance. Increasingly, supervisors are expected to *represent the company knowledgeably* in dealings with people both within and outside the organization.

All the while, of course, supervisors should be aware that their own job skills and knowledge must keep up with changing technology and company circumstances through *self development*.

HOW TO USE THIS BOOK

In the process of adapting the AT&T supervisory job studies for use by training people outside of the Bell System—and outside of the telecommunications industry—the author was required to select from an almost overwhelming amount of data that which was thought to be most relevant to the most people. Obviously, this was a judgment call. I have also taken the liberty to suggest ways in which information can be put to practical use in organizations generally.

This is not to suggest that these are the best—or

the only—ways to use the material for training supervisors; nor to imply that AT&T uses it in this way. I am sure, in fact, that readers will find other and better ways to apply this information to specific needs and circumstances. Above all, it should be kept in mind that the detailed listings of steps in each process, and the accompanying flowcharts that illustrate these listings, are intended as guides and training aids—not as inflexible procedures that must be followed by supervisors in every situation.

EIGHT GUIDES TO SUPERVISORY DEVELOPMENT

1. First and foremost, you need top management recognition and support for your supervisory development efforts. This book is intended to help you gain that support—either to install a supervisory training program if your organization does not now have one, or to upgrade your existing training effort.

The opening chapters, in which the critical need for supervisory training is discussed, can help you build a case for such top-level support. Certainly the

success of the Bell System, with its strong emphasis on supervisory training and development, should be cited. In this connection you are referred to the discussion of the AT&T *Mastery Model* in Chapter 4, in which the enormous (and little appreciated) complexity of the supervisor's job is shown in graphic form.

Use this material to prepare a "selling" presentation to your management group, or simply to persuade your CEO of the need on an informal basis; use it as well with your boss and with your organizational peers and associates to build a base of support.

Where to find it: Chapters 1 to 4.

2. The AT&T job studies identified and defined 14 principal duties, or managerial job functions, considered by their own "master performers" as most important to supervisory effectiveness, and most in need of reinforcement through training and/or job aids. These are presented and discussed at length.

Use this material with new supervisors to emphasize that the job of supervisor is not just that of a "super-technician," but rather is made up of totally different kinds of duties and responsibilities—that it is composed of *managerial duties* such as planning work, controlling, providing feedback, solving problems, and communicating with others.

A proven diagnostic questionnaire is provided which you can use to determine your supervisors' understanding of their managerial duties, the relative importance of each, and their perceived need for training in these vital managerial functions.

Where to find it: Chapter 4.

3. In Part II each of these principal supervisory job functions is presented in various levels of detail, in order that you may select the one that suits your particular needs at any given time. First, each is discussed in *general terms* of its contribution to the contemporary organization, regardless of size or nature of business. These "overviews" were derived from authoritative published sources, plus the author's own experience as a manager and management consultant for many years.

Use this material as pre-reading for new supervisors or candidates before classroom training. They can be easily reproduced and packaged for this purpose.

Where to find it: Section A of each chapter in Part II.

4. Next, each of the 14 supervisory duties is defined and described in summary or "capsule" fashion as a *managerial process.* This is actually a highly condensed interpretation by the author of the AT&T Mastery Model of the function in narrative form, designed for easy reading and quick comprehension.

Use this material to give new supervisors a quick basic understanding of each supervisory duty as a *series of steps* that should be performed in a prescribed sequence in order to accomplish a desired result—that is to say, a *managerial process.*

Where to find it: Section B of each chapter in Part II.

5. Next, each of the 14 supervisory duties is detailed into the specific steps—tasks and decision points—of the process. Each step is described briefly and keyed by number to a *flowchart* that graphically depicts the flow and relationships of tasks and decision points.

Use this material to give supervisors, both new and experienced, a better comprehension of each supervisory duty as a managerial process, and a better perception of the flow and relationships of tasks and decision points in the process.

The lists of steps can be reproduced as classroom discussion material. The flowcharts can easily be made into transparencies or slides for projection on a screen to groups. Both can be modified, of course, to fit your training needs and company circumstances. Or if you wish, you can highlight certain more critical steps in each process and confine the discussion to these points.

Where to find it: Section C of each chapter in Part II.

6. Next, each principal supervisory duty is shown in terms of outputs and results of tasks. A performance measurements chart for each principal duty gives the *outputs* of the various steps, the *standards of performance* for each output, and the *methods used* to measure the supervisor's performance.

Use this material to give supervisors an understanding of the need to view the job in terms of output and results, not simply activity. This can help to orient the supervisor to management by objectives, as well as to broaden the managerial outlook.

You can also use the performance measurements chart with second-level managers, to show them what they should be looking at as output from their first-level subordinates, and how they should measure performance. These performance measurements charts can be made into transparencies for overhead projection, or reproduced as discussion handouts.

Where to find it: Section D of each chapter in Part II.

7. For each of the 14 principal supervisory job functions a *diagnostic test* is provided. Each consists of a list of questions for which answers are given. Questions are keyed to steps in the process and to specific skills and knowledge associated with these steps. The purpose of the diagnostic is to identify areas in which your supervisors, both new and experienced, may be deficient in certain managerial aspects of their jobs, that is, in *generic* skills and knowledge.

Use this diagnostic test to determine your training needs for the total supervisory force and for individual supervisors. It can be reproduced and used as either a classroom or mail questionnaire (instructions and blank answer sheets should be provided, of course). This diagnostic test can be modified to suit your particular needs, if desired. This diagnostic test can also be used as a basis for structured interviews.

Where to find it: Section F in each chapter in Part II, plus Exhibits A, B, and C.

8. Finally, the fully detailed AT&T Skill/Knowledge Mastery Model of each principal supervisory duty is provided. This is needed as a reference for the specific skills and knowledge tested by the diagnostic (Exhibit C, referred to above, keys each diagnostic test question to the Mastery Model by number).

Use the Mastery Model as a reference and a training resource. It represents a prescription for a kind of *ultimate* supervisory performance—the "ideal" toward which all supervisory training and development should be directed within the constraints of costs and organizational needs.

The Model can be used to develop your own objective tests, simulations, and role play situations for training supervisors. The Mastery Model may also be useful as a reference guide for managers to whom first-level supervisors report, to diagnose supervisory problems in their organizations.

Where to find it: Section E of each chapter in Part II.

1 Productivity and the Supervisor

1 New Demands on Supervision

During the past generation or so the job of the first-level supervisor—the individual in direct charge of a basic work group—has undergone many changes. It seems certain that during the 1980s the role and responsibilities of this key manager will be altered even further.

To be sure, the job of the supervisor has been changing since the beginnings of the Industrial Revolution some two to three centuries ago. Early in the industrialization of the western world, the "foreman" was most often the bully of the group, who earned his rank and demonstrated his authority with his fists. In later, more enlightened times, supervisors were appointed on the grounds that they were the most skillful, the hardest workers, or had the most service. Their authority resided in their technical know-how and superior skill in performing the work. They normally had power to hire and fire, to reward and to discipline. The supervisor was, above all, *the boss*.

In earlier times, of course, supervisors neither needed nor expected to receive any training for the job, having already demonstrated skill and knowledge of the work, the nature of which was unchanging over long periods of time. Supervisors were often expected, even required, to pitch in and actually *do* the work whenever necessary.

The years since the end of World War II have witnessed a further evolution of the job of first-level supervisors. Increasingly they are not expected to perform the actual work for which the group was formed, but to function as group leaders. In this role supervisors' technical skills and actual work experience are less important to job performance; their most valuable skills are those involved in communicating to members of the work group what the work requirements are in terms of quantity, quality, and cost, and controlling the work in a way that meets those requirements.

DECLINE OF SUPERVISORY POWER

Before World War II, and for a time afterward, supervisors generally had authority to hire, fire, and discipline subordinates. Frequently the job carried responsibility for employee training, quality of output, safety, job design to the extent this was practiced, and many other activities. With the spread of professional management, however, companies added supporting staff functions until first-level supervisors' authority to hire, train, reward, and discipline subordinates was taken over by personnel specialists. Supervisors' responsibilities were further diminished as quality control specialists, industrial engineers, production and material control managers, safety managers, and a host of other professional managers assumed responsibility for their specialties. The remaining authority of supervisors to manage was further undercut by labor union agreements.

Increasingly, members of basic work groups were counseled, trained, interviewed, hired and fired, pro-moted and awarded pay raises by persons other than their direct supervisors. In large numbers, too, subordinates turned to staff specialists for guidance and assistance, bypassing their supervisors. And more and more frequently, workers went to their shop stewards with problems and grievances.

Stripped of authority, and with little of the job left except the purely supervisory function, the typical first-level supervisor felt like the forgotten person—almost invisible to subordinates and superiors alike. These management actions and changes diminished supervisors in the eyes of those they were appointed to oversee. They have at the same time rendered supervisors ineffective in dealings with peers and counterparts in staff and service functions—the very people whose jobs are to serve the line function. As a consequence it has become increasingly difficult for supervisors to meet the cost and quality requirements of the work for which they are responsible and accountable.

LOST POWER AND LOST PRODUCTIVITY

The extent to which this condition prevailed during the past couple of decades, and to which the condition exists in our institutions today, may be one of the principal causes of low and declining productivity. For clearly, when quality of output is the declared responsibility of staff quality control specialists, first-level supervisors of work groups, as well as members of these groups, can disclaim accountability for sub-standard output. Similarly, when supervisors are simply "handed" people whom the personnel department has interviewed and qualified, and in whose selection the supervisor has no voice, supervisors are unlikely to feel any real accountability for subordinates' failure or any real concern for their development as individuals. By the same token, when supervisors have no part in the design of the work or the workplace, there is little incentive for them to ensure that these designs work efficiently.

All of these factors are vital to high productivity. Some five decades of research and experimentation in the workplace have proved that workers and their supervisors can contribute substantially to the quality and productivity of the enterprise when they are actively involved in all matters relating to the work and the workplace. The Japanese, with their famous "quality circles," are presently driving home the point, to our discomfort and dismay.

The quality of output is an essential element of productivity, of course. For it benefits no one to turn out great quantities of a product that contains visible defects or will fail in use. Whenever members of work groups and their first-level supervisors are held directly accountable for defective product—with guidance from quality assurance specialists—the quality of output tends to be high.

The design of the work and the workplace are crucial to high output; it has been found repeatedly that whenever workers and first-level supervisors of the work group are involved in their design at the outset, they more readily tend to accept new work methods and to use them more productively.

Members of a group normally want and need leadership. They prefer it to come from a member of their own group, but if their supervisors fail to provide it they will turn to others—either to an informal leader within the group, a union official, or someone outside. By stripping first-level supervisors of power to manage, business management has deprived its workers of the strong leadership so essential to product quality and high group output.

THE NEW BREED OF SUPERVISOR

The changes that have taken place in the job content of the first-level supervisor up to now may come to seem inconsequential compared with the changes that are likely to occur during the period ahead. Most of these changes will better the lot of the supervisor, but many will complicate his or her life.

One change almost certain to happen (indeed is already under way) is a transfer *back* to supervisors of responsibility for results of their work groups, together with a redefinition of the roles of staff specialists to that of guidance and support. Another change is the restoration of their lost authority to manage, as top management becomes increasingly aware of first-level supervisors' value and contribution to the productivity of the organization. A third is a diminution of labor union strength as union membership and bargaining power decline through factory closings and company failures brought on in large part by competition from countries with lower labor costs.

One important change supervisors can expect is a more precise definition of their organizational role and their relationships with other members of the organization. The supervisor's role has tended in the past to be ill-defined and ambiguous; as a consequence, the job has been perceived in very different ways by managers on different levels and in different functions, creating the potential for misunderstandings and communication problems.

The job content is almost certain to become more complex. Unfortunately, the job is even now more complex and demanding than most managers appreciate. Unless others can be made to realize this, first-level supervisors will continue to be regarded (and treated) as subordinates who simply carry out the commands of higher-level superiors, instead of being viewed as full-fledged members of the management team. Until first-level supervisors are correctly perceived as managers who plan and control work; motivate subordinates; solve problems and make decisions; provide feedback, coaching, and counseling to all members of their work groups; communicate information up, down, and across organizational lines; develop subordinates and self; manage time; and act as knowledgeable representatives of the firm, their power to influence productivity will be limited.

Not only is the job of the first-level supervisor undergoing profound change, supervisors themselves are changing in ways that will affect the organization and administration of the enterprise. For one, supervisors increasingly seek job satisfaction, not simply an income. This is especially true of those younger, college-trained members of the famous post-war "baby crop." For most of these, the supervisory job is an entry point, an initial career step, not an end objective. They often have vastly different expectations from those of older colleagues and organizational superiors—and even higher expectations from the company and the job.

Many of these new supervisors have inherited a distaste for and distrust of authoritarian structure. They want and expect a strong voice in decisions that affect them and genuine participation in setting the goals to which their efforts contribute. Their loyalty to the organization tends to be weaker than that of older supervisors, as evidenced by the refusal of many young managers to accept transfers that involve dislocation. They tend to tune out executive exhortations to work for the good of the company; they are turned on by challenging goals and the opportunity to make a real contribution to a cause they believe in.

THE CHANGING WORK FORCE

Workers too are changing in similar ways and for many of the same reasons. They tend to be less amenable to authoritative methods of management; they want a more gratifying work life and more satisfying work to perform. Their loyalties are directed more toward the group of which they are part than to "the company." This new breed of worker, like their supervisors, want to know "why," and are demanding a voice in issues that affect them, such as new work arrangements and new processes. Not incidentally, more than a few workers are refusing promotion to supervisory levels, seeing little to gain from taking a job that pays so little more for all the headaches involved.

The work force is changing in other respects, as well. Militant minority groups and civil rights legislation have opened up jobs formerly closed to minorities, the disadvantaged, and the handicapped. As a result of earlier discrimination and restrictions, many of these persons are poorly prepared for entry. Women are in the work force in increasing numbers, performing traditional "men's work" and becoming valued members of management. And not only younger workers are changing. Many older, experienced employees have become dissatisfied with the routine, disillusioned and alienated from the "establishment." Retiring "on the job" is commonplace.

The workplace is undergoing as radical a change as the work itself. New worker safety and job environmental requirements are altering the face of the workplace dramatically. The design and manufacture of virtually every product are being modified to meet new energy-efficiency standards and new safety and health requirements in production and in use. New technology is creating new products and processes at an increasing rate. Mechanization, automation, computer-aided design and manufacture (CAD-CAM), and robotics are displacing human drudgery from production operations, and creating new jobs with higher skill and knowledge requirements. More and more work is concerned with symbols and software—information instead of hardware—and people deal daily more with words, numbers, and concepts than with materials and products.

Job enrichment is a genuine movement that cannot be stopped or turned back. Quality circles, an American invention the Japanese are using against us in world markets, are now penetrating U.S. companies and are spreading faster than a recently-formed association can keep count.

MULTIPLE ROLES OF THE NEW SUPERVISOR

In our increasingly fast-paced world, rapid changes in consumer needs and desires call for frequent modifications in styles and models, resulting in shorter production runs of any one particular product type. Consequently, the conventional measures of productivity have become less and less meaningful. New tools and measurements are called for. Meanwhile, the changed economics of energy have created a need to upgrade or replace practically every energy-using and energy-consuming machine, vehicle, appliance, building, and device in use today with new energy-efficient types. This need places an incredible burden on American industry at a time when other demands are also taxing the capabilities of management. Unquestionably, a large share of this burden will fall upon the shoulders of the nation's first-level supervisors.

These changes will frequently be accompanied by faster industrial growth coupled with more frequent organizational changes to adapt them to new market opportunities and changing economic conditions. All of these add up to more uncertainty and less routine, more frequent obsolescence of everything in use, and a more frenetic pace of work life. Supervisors can expect to deal with new, unprogrammed problems never encountered before, often in new situations for which past experience offers little guidance.

It is known that constant exposure to new and unfamiliar problems and situations can cause severe stress and anxiety in supervisors and workers alike. Supervisors will have to learn to cope with increasing uncertainty and to resist stress, as well as to function as absorbers of "future shock" for their work groups.

What is more, the new breed of supervisors of the '80s can be expected to play many roles at various times and in various circumstances. They must be *administrators, leaders, entrepreneurs,* and *decision makers.* They must also become *synthesizers* and *catalysts.* Perhaps above all, they must be *planners* and *resource allocators.*

SUPERVISORY TRAINING—AN IMPERATIVE, NOT AN OPTION

The transition from worker to supervisor is perhaps the most momentous change in a person's career. No experience prior to this event, and few afterward, can compare with this change in its impact on an individual's work life. Earlier switches in jobs from company to company—or from one type of work to another—may require the learning of new work skills, and can cause a degree of stress and anxiety, to be sure;

later promotions to higher levels of management may demand the making of decisions with far-reaching consequences and the assumption of weightier responsibilities. Nevertheless, the elevation from worker to supervisor of workers, or from technician to supervisor of technicians, can have such a profound effect on the individual's outlook, attitudes, and actions that the change should not be made without careful consideration of its implications for the person and for the organization.

The advancement from worker or technician to supervisor of workers or technicians is more than a step upward, as are most subsequent moves up the management ladder. The shift from nonmanagement to management represents a quantum jump in organizational role and relations with others—subordinates, peers, and superiors. Nor does the change signify simply the grafting on of a new set of duties and responsibilities to those already possessed. The move signifies a passage from a world of *doing* to a new and very different world of managing the activities of others in the performance of work. This event can profoundly and irreversibly alter an individual's attitudes and actions, and requires the learning of a whole new repertoire of skills and knowledge unrelated to past experience.

Very little of a person's earlier work experience (or education), unfortunately, prepares him or her for the transition from member of a work group to supervisor of a work group. The differences in job content can be enormous; the gap between the two functions can be both wide and deep; and the change can be traumatic to some individuals. It is even more unfortunate that many company managements fail to recognize these factors, and frequently promote people into supervisory positions with little or no conditioning or preparation, not infrequently turning a competent technician into a mediocre supervisor in the process.

Newly appointed supervisors generally have a great deal to learn—and much to unlearn. They must learn to let others do the work that they have only recently been doing, and put aside all thoughts about how much better and faster they could do it themselves. They must learn to plan and schedule work formerly laid out for them and not wait for their bosses to tell them what to do next. They must learn how the work of the group fits into the work flow of the total organization and how it relates to the processes that go before and after. They must learn about the company resources that are available to service the work group and how to get a fitting share of these services. And they must become familiar with the policies, procedures, and standard practices that guide the activities and govern the relationships of the work group.

Newly appointed supervisors must learn, as well, to derive satisfaction from the accomplishments of others, rather than from the output of their own technical know-how and manual skills. Earlier in our industrial history—before constant, unrelenting change became the norm—we would have had less cause to be concerned about the need to condition and train first-level supervisors. Most supervisors, as noted earlier, neither wanted nor needed training. The person elevated to the job was, as a rule, the worker who had demonstrated the highest competence in performing the work or who had the greatest length of service (leaving aside, of course, those promoted on the basis of favoritism or nepotism). The goods produced were relatively simple and enjoyed long lives in the marketplace; consequently the work itself was unchanging over long periods of time. Thus technical skill and knowledge of the work were primary requisites for success as a supervisor.

Into this world of stability technology intruded with an increasingly rapid flow of new products, new processes, new methods, and new equipment. The life cycle of products in the marketplace became brief, as did their life on the production line. Products and processes became more and more complex, and a person's skill in performing a particular job became less and less important as a supervisory trait.

The characteristics to be valued most in a supervisor came to be flexibility and adaptability to new situations; the capability to cope with change. This quality exhibits itself in the supervisor's ability to *plan* new kinds of work, to identify in advance what resources will be required and make provision for them, and to anticipate problems that may arise and set up alternative actions to cope with them.

Other desirable characteristics are the interpersonal skills of communicating, coaching, counseling, and providing feedback to subordinates on their performance. These are qualities that do not come naturally to most people. Fortunately, however, the skills and knowledge needed to cope with these new conditions can be acquired by sincere, intelligent individuals. These vital skills and knowledge can be imparted to newly appointed supervisors through *training*.

These new and demanding conditions make supervisory training and development mandatory. No longer is training of supervisors optional for management—it is imperative if the organization is to grow and prosper, and essential for the very survival of the enterprise.

2 The Bell System and Its People

One American institution that is intensely concerned about the productivity of people is the Bell System, not because the productivity of its workers is low—on the contrary, it is generally quite high—but simply because the company employs more people than any other nongovernment organization on earth.

At last count, AT&T employed 1,050,000 people in its operating companies and departments. Of this total, some 250,000 are members of management; of this group, 170,000 are first-level supervisors and over 60,000 are second-level supervisors. (These numbers diminish, of course, at each successively higher level of the organizational pyramid, until we find a single individual, Charles L. Brown, at level 10, with the title of chairman of the board.)

The Bell System is enormous in other respects, of course. The corporation controls assets of $114 billion, a sum greater than the gross national product of all but a handful of sovereign nations—more than the combined assets of the three major auto producers plus IBM and General Electric. These assets are growing, as the enterprise invests upwards of $15 billion· annually in new plants and equipment. A portion of those assets are represented by 24,000 buildings of assorted sizes and types and 177,000 vehicles.

The company's network of nearly 20,000 switching offices and millions of miles of lines interconnect 160 million telephones in U.S. households and offices. Some 140 million (85 percent) of these phones belong to the Bell System; the other 20 million are owned by about 1600 independent telephone operating companies scattered throughout the United States. Three million people share ownership of the corporation's common stock—twice as many as any other private enterprise in the world.

Despite its great size in population and assets, though, AT&T's annual revenues are substantially less than those of the top petroleum and automobile companies. Its profits, too, rank well below those of Exxon and Mobil. Unlike these other corporate giants, however, AT&T has never had a loss in any quarter throughout its 100-year history—and very possibly never will. The Bell System is, of course, a regulated public utility whose service rates and earnings are subject to approval by state and federal regulatory agencies.

STILL GROWING AFTER 100 YEARS

Surprisingly, in the light of its advanced age and great size, the Bell System is growing rapidly. The company's revenues, while not as great as those of the giant oil companies, amount to about 1.8 percent of the U.S. gross national product and are growing twice as fast. America has 40 percent of the world's telephones and the highest ratio of phones to people. Americans also tend to talk a lot. Telephone usage in the United States is increasing at a rate of eight percent a year, a rate far in excess of the country's population growth or its economic growth rate. Every working day, 100,000 more telephones are hooked up to the Bell network—although subscribers are so mobile that seven phones must be installed to gain one. By the year 2000, the number of telephones in service is expected to approach 240 million, and assets will triple as new electronic switching offices, microwave towers, coaxial cables, and communications satellites are put in place to meet the insatiable demand for communications by individuals and businesses.

(It should be pointed out that in the process of growing, the Bell System is also changing, largely under the pressures of changing technology. Chief among these technological forces is the merger of communication and data processing.

Since the late 1960s, the Bell System has been undergoing a transition from a regulated monopoly to a partially deregulated corporation operating in an almost fully competitive industry. With Congress considering legislation to formalize this trend in national telecommunications policy and with the Federal Communications Commission continuing its string of procompetitive, deregulatory decisions, the transition probably will continue for a few years more. The result may well be a new operating environment for the Bell System, encompassing all parts of the information industry.

At the time the supervisory job studies discussed in this book were made—indeed, even as this book is written—the American Telephone and Telegraph Company is a single entity; the Bell System of 23 telephone operating companies, AT&T Long Lines department, Western Electric, and Bell Laboratories. As a consequence of the new environment, however, the structure of the company may be somewhat different by the time this guide is being used. Exactly what shape the new organization will take is beyond anyone's ability to predict, of course.)

TECHNOLOGY AND COMMUNICATIONS GROWTH

The years since the end of World War II have witnessed unprecedented change in the way we live and work. The jet aircraft has made intercontinental travel commonplace, our dwellings and vehicles are vastly more efficient, television has brought the world into our living rooms, and the electronic computer has profoundly altered the jobs of millions, mostly for the better. The American population has become widely dispersed and highly mobile, breaking the intimate bonds of family and neighborhood in the process, and creating an enormous demand for communication over distance.

The telecommunications industry, of which the Bell System is far and away the foremost element, has responded by wiring American society together with an incredibly complex network of cables, switching centers, microwave beams, and communications satellites. This network has made it possible to communi-cate almost instantly with any other resident of the nation, and much of the world, simply by touching ten buttons on a telephone handset.

We tend to take this astounding capability for granted, yet it is a modern wonder of the world. It is altering our lives in ways we do not yet appreciate or understand. Because even as the telecommunications industry has responded to sociocultural demands, the industry itself, AT&T in particular, has been a predominant agent for change and an important shaper of the new society.

Advances in technology, many of them products of the Bell Laboratories, continue to improve the capabilities of the telecommunications network to handle information faster and more accurately. These advances directly affect the equipment in place in the system, either altering it or replacing it with new, more efficient devices. Most generally, the equipment changes are to replace electromechanical types with electronic, and to change the technology from analog to digital; both represent a sharp break with the past.

These advances also have transferred to the telecommunications system increasing amounts of information formerly moved by other means—mail or face-to-face contact. They have also added to the network a great deal of data formerly not communicated at all because of economic constraints. Effectively, technology tends to increase communication among people by making it easier and cheaper to communicate.

PEOPLE—SOURCE OF STRENGTH

The Bell System's growth and vitality is due to more than technological innovation. Author John Brooks, in a book titled *Telephone: The First 100 Years*,[1] made this observation:

Compared with other American corporations of exceptional age, size, and power, AT&T has weathered the years strikingly well—has, indeed, come through a century with a remarkable vitality intact. Experience has shown that great size and power in corporations generally leads sooner or later to case-hardening, to a deterioration of imagination, to a blind following of old forms that results in decline and decay. Railroading, the first great American industry, has degenerated into bankruptcies and passenger service that is appalling or nonexistent; automobile manufacture, the industrial miracle of a half century ago, has become increasingly unresponsive to public needs. Yet telephony, scarcely younger than railroading and considerably older than the automobile, presses on with ever more rapid technical innovation as if it were in the bloom of youth.

Why? Perhaps the answer lies in the fact that the telephone business by its nature enforces constant, daily contact with the customer, not just through his representatives in Washington but face to face and voice to voice, through talk with the local service representative or through installation and repair of equipment by the man on the truck from the local equipment garage. The railroads have escaped the public by concentrating on shipping freight rather than moving passengers; the automobile makers have interposed between themselves and the public a vast network of dealers. But telephony has no users except people, and no middleman dealers. Talking to customers tends to counteract the most self-destructive habit of great corporations, that of talking to themselves. The century-old telephone business—Bell and independent—may have been saved from hardening of the arteries by the necessary discipline of direct, everyday contact with the millions of people it serves.

The Bell System appears to have succeeded, as well, in retaining a tradition of service to customers that transcends the loyalties of employees to a specific craft or job description. Certainly the company has exhibited through the years a concern for employees that is shared by few other corporations. Lifetime employment is virtually assured for workers and managers alike. Until recently, all management above the first level was home-grown—it was almost unknown for anyone to enter the middle or upper levels of the organization from the outside. In the 1970s, however, AT&T imported some high-level marketing types in response to competitive threats by RCA, IBM, ITT, and a host of entrepreneurs.

It is through its overriding preoccupation with personnel training and development, though, that the Bell System has built its unique strengths. Few organizations on earth devote so much time and effort to the continued development of workers and managers. It can be argued with some justification, of course, that AT&T's monopoly status and assured return on investment transfer the costs of this effort to the corporation's customer base; nevertheless, the same money could just as well be dissipated on executive perquisites or frivolities with little benefit to the well-being of the organization or the great bulk of its members.

The Bell System's belief that people are its greatest source of strength goes back to its beginnings. Theodore Vail set the tone during AT&T's formative years, with policies that emphasized "the best possible service to the public at the most reasonable rates consistent with the risk, investment, and the continued improvement of the property," and consideration by all telephone employees of the needs and wishes of telephone users. Later company leaders reasserted that good and considerate service can be rendered only by employees who believe their own needs are being considered; who feel they are fairly treated as individuals, and who believe the company can be trusted to "do the right thing" by them. These employees' work environment, moreover, must provide opportunities for personal growth. Beyond this, training is required,

[1]Harper & Row, New York, 1975.

because such attitudes and behavior do not always come naturally to individuals.

Bell employees are unfailingly courteous and respectful, in my experience, when dealing with customers, and exhibit unusual patience with complainants who tend to become abusive toward service personnel. I believe this to be a result of training, but in part, it must reflect a sincere belief by these employees that they work for a "good company."

It is amusing to contrast this customer-service orientation with the attitude of the French Poste et Telegraphe (P&T), the government-operated telephone system of France. The French journalist, Jean-

Jacque Servan-Schreiber, wrote in the late 1960s that despite the deplorable service provided by the system—with two-year waits for installation of a telephone, and trunklines so overloaded that people had given up making long-distance calls—

. . . the French bureaucracy continued to display its unfathomable suspicion of telephone subscribers in a brochure written in pure penitentiary style: In case of offensive behavior or insulting speech toward telephone personnel the company may suspend use of the instrument . . . if the subscriber's behavior is exceptionally serious, the company may . . . cancel the service of said subscriber.

ADAPTABILITY TO CHANGE

Even as the Bell System has, through the years, retained its vigor and sensitivity to those it serves, the organization has also managed to avoid the bureaucratic paralysis, the internal rigidity of form, that so often seems to settle on a business enterprise when it reaches a certain age and size.

Nowhere is this demonstrated more dramatically than in the remarkable transfer to subscribers of responsibility for installing, disconnecting, and even servicing their telephones. Only a few years ago, when a subscriber moved his or her place of residence, a phone company technician disconnected the telephone at the one location and another technician wired in a new one at the subscriber's new home or apartment. This made it necessary for the new occupant of the former residence to have his or her telephone installed by yet another phone company installer. Today, residential customers see telephone installers much less frequently; more often than not, they simply unplug the phone at one end and plug in the same instrument at the other, or else they pick out a new telephone at the local "Phone Center," where dozens of styles and colors are displayed in a retail setting.

A recent advisory accompanying the monthly bill of New Jersey Bell subscribers informed them that it was no longer necessary to call in a trained repair technician should their telephone malfunction. If they would simply carry the offending instrument to their neighborhood phone center, it would be exchanged for a brand new set.

Possibly in no other telephone company in the world could such a remarkable transfer of work take place with so little bureaucratic foot-dragging. Even supposing the new technology would be allowed, one can hardly imagine the affected technicians of a government-operated P&T in Europe, or a Latin American operating company, giving up their prerogatives to stand watch over homeowners as they unplugged the instrument from the jack and, at the other end, insisting that official representatives of the company be present while the phone is plugged in and tested. All the while, of course, the proceedings would be recorded on official forms that would thereupon pass through countless bureaucratic hands back at company headquarters.

Even in this country such elimination of work is not common. American railroads continue to carry hundreds, if not thousands, of firemen on their payrolls, despite the absence of steam boilers for a generation or more. And it is not unknown for unionized electricians and plumbers to disassemble factory-built equipment at the work site and reassemble it before it can be installed.

It may be argued that competition has forced the Bell System to change its ways. Subscribers, after all, can now own their telephone instruments, a practice strictly forbidden by AT&T until the momentous Carterfone decision. Even so, this sort of responsiveness to the customer does demonstrate a degree of adaptability to change that is quite rare in large organizations.

PIONEERS IN HUMAN RESOURCE DEVELOPMENT

The Bell System was an early visitor to college campuses to recruit bright young graduates of engineering and other schools. As early as the 1920s the company conducted research on the relationship of college achievement and later success in business life. These studies demonstrated that rank in college graduating class was a valid predictor of success—defined as reaching the upper third in salary versus others in the group with equal service. The studies also tended to confirm that achievement in nonscholastic activities

was a good indicator of rapid progress in management.

These studies were repeated on a larger scale after World War II, with similar results. This landmark research was thought important enough to report in a book called *Business Purposes and Performance*, written by Frederick R. Kappel, chairman of AT&T from 1961 to 1967. A consequence of these studies is that the Bell System concentrates its recruiting efforts on the top half of the graduating classes of colleges and universities.

THE HAWTHORNE STUDIES

Other pioneering human relations programs within the Bell System have been important enough to have become the subjects of books. Nearly 60 years ago, the Hawthorne, Illinois, manufacturing plant of Western Electric was the site of a ground-breaking study of work and working conditions. Conducted in cooperation with the National Research Council, the National Academy of Science, and the Harvard Business School, the work resulted in a book, *Management and the Worker*. These classic Hawthorne studies, directed by psychologist Elton Mayo and conducted over a period of nearly a decade, represented a major shift in emphasis from the Taylor school of "scientific" management, in which jobs were broken down into their simplest repetitive elements, to a concern for the attitudes and relationships of people in the workplace.

These studies led to what is still known as the "Hawthorne effect," the phenomenon that workers

under study tend to increase their output regardless of whether workplace illumination is raised or lowered, whether rest periods are lengthened or shortened, or whether hours of work are increased or cut. The Hawthorne effect suggests that increases in productivity may be caused less by the nature of the change than by the change itself; by the very fact that the workers involved are "in the spotlight."

AT&T's concern with human resource development became institutionalized in the years following the war. Some highly-promising young managers were sent to major universities for an entire academic year. Internal development programs of several weeks duration were routinely attended by department heads. Training programs and packages of two to five days in length were administered to thousands of first-, second-, and third-level supervisors and managers.

JOB ENRICHMENT IN THE BELL SYSTEM

The landmark Hawthorne studies almost certainly had an influence on Frederick Herzberg's later theory of motivation, in which he proposed that the factors related to the work itself—job content factors—have a much more pronounced effect on people's output than factors related to the work environment—what he called the "hygiene"factors.

This classic theory was put to the test by the Bell System in a notable series of experiments during the 1960s. Robert N. Ford, then personnel director for manpower utilization, has described this work in a book titled *Motivation Through the Work Itself,*[2]

[2]American Management Association, New York, 1969.

which he dedicated to Professor Herzberg. In it, Ford described a set of 19 experiments in *job enrichment* which he directed in AT&T headquarters departments and operating companies. These studies were precipitated by indications of rising employee discontent throughout the System; discontent that signalled itself by increasing turnover, particularly among people in their first few months with the company. Ford reasoned that the work itself might be the cause of the problem, inasmuch as wages and benefits were high, working conditions were excellent, and job security was superior to most other firms.

The experiments involved "loading" the jobs of selected employees in a vertical manner—that is, adding responsibility and challenge to their work. (Horizontal loading simply enlarges a job without making it more satisfying to the worker.) No important changes were made in hygiene factors, and to avoid the Hawthorne effect, the participants were not told they were the subjects of experiments. This isolation was carried to the extreme of excluding the workers' first-level supervisors from the experiments, an omission Ford admitted later was a serious mistake.

Several thousand employees were involved in these job enrichment projects, which were conducted over a prolonged period of time. Ford's conclusions, presented "as beliefs, not proof positive, but based on more evidence than we have ever had before," were that employees gained deeper satisfaction from work that had been loaded with the real motivators identified by Herzberg—recognition, opportunity for achievement, more responsibility, a higher order of task, and growth in personal competence. Ford also

noted better attitudes and real improvements in job performance. He observed greater group enthusiasm and concern about group problems, as well, although these were plus factors not predicted by Herzberg's theory.

Some other important conclusions from these job enrichment experiments were that:

- Good performance and high productivity *lead to* good attitudes, not the other way around.
- Work simplification, which involves taking the job apart and removing content, reduces the work to the ability level of the lowest performer and thus can cause demotivation in the workplace.
- A job ideally should have somewhat elastic boundaries and potential for learning and psychological growth.
- Group performance indexes do not motivate individual members of the work group. They are the supervisor's motivator, not the worker's.
- To be motivative, feedback on individual's performance should be to the individual.
- Attempts to change the boss's "management style" may not cause much real or lasting improvement in productivity. The real issue seems to be the work itself.

Eighteen months later Robert Ford followed up the job enrichment experiments conducted in certain departments. His conclusion was that gains from genuine job enrichment tend to be permanent and that the costs of the program are self-liquidating *plus*.

A LONG-TERM STUDY OF BELL MANAGERS

A third important study of jobs and work within the Bell System is still going on, although one book has already been written about it and more are expected to be written before it ends. This program, called the Management Progress Study, involves management only. The study was initiated in 1956 by Robert K. Greenleaf, then AT&T's director of management development. Douglas W. Bray, a company psychologist, has been following the careers of several hundred managers ever since, starting from the day they entered the company. Dr. Bray's book, *Formative Years in Business*,[3] is subtitled " A Long-Term AT&T Study of

[3]Douglas W. Bray; Richard J. Campbell; and Donald L. Grant (New York: John Wiley & Sons, 1974).

Managerial Lives," and is described as a first report drawn from the Study.

In summing up the results of the first eight years of this most penetrating study of managers at work, Bray and his co-authors discussed the implications of the study to large organizations. Their major finding is the extreme importance of *initial selection* of individuals entering management, the "pool" from which will come the executives and senior officers who will one day manage the enterprise.

The study, they report, provides no support for the long-held notion that "experience is the best teacher." (In this connection, a Conference Board survey of supervisory training concludes that experience is more often an inefficient and expensive teacher, from which the student may learn the wrong lessons well.) The study provides no support, either, for the belief that mediocre students entering business will catch fire on the job and turn out to be world beaters in management.

Another significant finding demolished the myth that the first year on the job will weed out the unfit—that the testing ground of early experience will discourage those individuals without real potential and they will quit. "The separation route," the authors say, "is not a viable corrective for employment errors."

ESSENTIAL QUALITIES OF MANAGERS

The study revealed some managerial characteristics that are of significance to the present discussion of supervisory duties, tasks, skills, and knowledge. Six primary characteristics were identified as essential to advancement upward through the management hierarchy. The two most important of these are leadership skills in face-to-face situations and administrative ability, in that order.

Leadership skills are defined as the interpersonal skills needed to make a forceful and likable impression on others, good oral communication and presentation skills, and ability to get others to perform (plus flexibility to modify behavior when necessary to reach a goal). *Administrative ability* is the capability to plan and organize work effectively, to make decisions willingly, and the skill to make high quality decisions. The other four clusters of characteristics have rather equal value. They are:

- intellectual ability (that is, the possession of a wide range of interests and the ability to learn quickly);
- stability of performance in the face of stress and uncertainty;
- work motivation (the desire to do a good job for its own sake); and
- an active career orientation.

These six factors are not independent of one another, of course. Administrative skills are correlated with intellectual ability, and leadership skills with stability of performance.

Important findings of the eight-year study are the need for good forward management planning by the organization and the extreme importance of stimulation and challenge in the work itself. With regard to the first, to bring trainees into an organization in which the number of future promotions to higher-level jobs will be few can only build up false expectations that inevitably lead to disappointment and morale problems. In connection with the second point, the need is great for work experiences that "sustain the motivation high quality recruits bring with them" into the organization.

The assessment centers and assessment techniques developed through the Management Progress Study have since been institutionalized within the Bell System. People being considered for promotion to supervisor and newly recruited managers routinely attend them; to date more than 200,000 managers and candidates have been assessed. At this writing Dr. Bray's study is in its twenty-fifth year and is almost certain to produce more valuable insights into the qualities that make managers—and is almost certain, as well, to produce important additions to the management literature.

3 The AT&T Supervisory Job Studies

The human relations programs, studies, and experiments described in the preceding chapter have a tendency to capture people's interest, but to divert attention away from the important personnel training and development work being done throughout the Bell System on a routine, day-by-day basis. This is unfortunate, because this on-going effort often has more lasting value than highly visible one-shot projects.

Every year, Bell System companies and departments, including Long Lines, must hire some 70,000 to 75,000 people to accommodate normal attrition, to take care of growth in telephone usage and expansion of the subscriber base, and to replace about 20,000 retirees. Almost all of these new employees need some initial training. In addition, work and jobs are constantly changing as new technology, new customer needs, and changing market circumstances impact the organization. AT&T spends over one billion dollars

annually (exclusive of salaries) on the effort to maintain and improve the job skills and knowledge of its million employees, much of this to teach new skills necessitated by technological change.

Into the ranks of management each year come about 18,000 men and women. Two-thirds of these become managers through promotion from the worker level; the other one-third come from the campuses of American colleges and universities. In both instances, the appointment is generally that of first-level supervisor, although not all who attain this rank actually have subordinates reporting to them. Whether through promotion or college recruitment, the new managers must be trained in their new managerial responsibilities. Existing members of management, as well, routinely attend in-house and outside training and development courses to sharpen their managerial skills and acquire new knowledge.

NEW DEMANDS FOR TRAINING

Advances in communications technology have a profound effect on the way people work, not only within the telecommunications carriers' own operations but throughout the industrial and commercial economy. Increasing numbers of jobs are involved with information—manipulating, moving, or transforming data in some manner. Today some 50 million people, half the total work force, are doing this sort of work and the number is rising. Indeed, even in industries that are product-oriented, fewer individuals are involved with hardware, and more and more people deal with software knowledge and information.

Within the Bell System itself, the nature of work is constantly changing in concert with the changing technological and market environment. Of necessity the content of many jobs, of workers and managers alike, must be adapted to the changing work and output requirements. To cope with this demand,

AT&T has over the years built up a training organization that is almost certainly the largest, and may well be the finest, in the world.

Quite naturally, in an organization with a population exceeding one million people, the great majority of jobs are at the so-called worker level; in the case of AT&T some 750,000 jobs, or three-fourths of the total. Naturally, too, the work performed by members of this group is heavily impacted by changes in equipment and processes. Thus the bulk of the training effort in the Bell System—perhaps 70 percent—is directed toward keeping workers up with new technology. Much of the remaining effort has been aimed at training new workers entering the company's work force.

A much smaller fraction (although an increasing one) of the training effort has been concerned with management training and development.

NEW CONCERNS ABOUT SUPERVISION

The 1970s was not a particularly auspicious decade for American industry, for the general economy, or for the U.S. as a society, as noted in the introduction to this book. The Bell System has not been untouched by the malaise. Early in the decade, the System company serving the city of New York suffered severe service problems, which only a Herculean effort by the company and a rescue effort by other System companies overcame. At the same time, the social deterioration and sagging economies of many Northeastern cities have impacted the operating companies serving them. At the geographic extreme, unanticipated growth of Sunbelt areas has strained the managerial capabilities and finances of other Bell companies. Through it all, government insistence that large employers like AT&T set examples of Equal Employment Opportunity for minorities and women through Affirmative Action posed heavy demands on personnel and training staffs.

As the decade wore on, people at high levels of the organization became concerned that the training of management people, especially at the first and second levels of supervision, might be inadequate to meet the demands being placed on them by growth of volume, advances in the state of the art, societal

change, and new customer demands. Added to these were the uncertainties of competition in the telecommunications marketplace—a factor that company management had not experienced since the early days of the Bell System—and a strong trend toward deregulation of certain aspects of the business.

There was a feeling, in brief, that a brand-new ballgame was being played on the company's own field, and management, especially on the lower levels of the organization, didn't know the rules of the game.

Accordingly, the AT&T executive office directed that studies be made of supervisory job requirements, and that deficiencies in supervisory performance be identified for training or other remedial action. Management's response was to call upon the professionals and training development specialists in the Human Resources Development department (then situated in the suburban hills of Basking Ridge, New Jersey, but since relocated to a new building on the historic "green" of Morristown, New Jersey). This department undertook the assignment to perform a preliminary study of first- and second-level supervisory job requirements and performance deficiencies throughout the Bell System.

INITIAL FOCUS ON SECOND-LEVEL SUPERVISION

In Bell System terminology such a preliminary study is called a Phase 1 Preproject Study. It is the initial phase of a multi-phase training development procedure, a highly disciplined *process* for determining the organization's valid training needs through intensive data collection and analysis, and then developing training programs that are cost-effective and responsive to the real needs of the organization. Understandably, in an organization as vast as AT&T, there are enormous demands and pressures for training at all levels and from all directions. The procedure is designed to sort out the *genuine needs* from the merely *felt* needs, and respond to them in a cost-effective manner.

The Phase 1 study of first- and second-level supervision was primarily a "content analysis" of all relevant studies made earlier within the company. The report that resulted from this particular study recommended a continuing study on a larger scale, with emphasis on managerial responsibilities, duties, tasks, skills, and knowledge. That is to say, the study should focus on the *generic aspects of supervision* common to most if not all supervisory jobs, rather than on the technical factors specific to certain supervisory jobs.

The Phase 1 Study Report identified four generic duties as the primary areas for further study. They were:

● organizing and planning;
● directing, controlling, and delegating;
● supervisor/subordinate relations; and
● communications and coordination.

The Phase 1 Study Report was accepted by AT&T's advisory group on training, the Management Training and Development Advisory Board (MTDAB),

with a recommendation that the work be given priority. This decision moved the project to Phase 2, a definitive Job Study. An indication of the importance given to this work is that it was presented for consideration at the 1977 annual Presidents' Conference, a meeting of the presidents of all Bell System operating telephone companies.

By decision of the MTDAB, the first supervisory job study to be undertaken was of *second-level* supervisors. This study, conducted by a task force assembled and directed by Charles (Buck) Youngblood, a career Bell System manager on rotational assignment from the Chesapeake and Potomac Telephone Company, produced a Skill/Knowledge Mastery Model of the second-level job, as well as a diagnostic test instrument and a set of recommendations for training and other action to remedy deficiencies revealed by the diagnostic tests of second-level managers in place.

This landmark job study also set a pattern in several ways for the subsequent job study of first-level supervisors with which this book is primarily concerned. First, Youngblood's study identified 14 principal management duties of a second-level supervisor, duties that the later study found to be generally applicable to the job of the first-level supervisor as well. Second, the study process developed by the earlier task force, which broke new ground in some respects, was followed by the first-level study group.

(The process followed by the two job study groups would require too much space to describe properly at this point in the presentation. It may, however, be of interest to other training and development professionals, so the process is discussed at length in Part III. The second-level Mastery Model itself may be described in detail in a separate volume at a later time.)

THE 14 PRINCIPAL SUPERVISORY DUTIES

At this point in the presentation, it is appropriate to discuss the 14 principal management duties of a supervisor as they were developed by the second-level job study. This is necessary because these duties were applied later to the first-level supervisory job (in somewhat modified form) to become the framework for the first-level Mastery Model which is the heart of this discussion.

A significant finding of the second-level job study is that the job of the second-level supervisor was not as clear and specific as it was thought to be. It was, moreover, not as clear as that of some other levels of management. Firm performance standards were found lacking, and the definition of the job itself was not well documented.

To the study group it seemed that an important

factor contributing to the effective performance of any manager is a clear understanding of his or her role and function in the organization. It also seemed important that the manager's subordinates view the job of their boss in the same way, so that they will carry out their duties in a manner that will support the defined role. It is equally important that higher-level managers in the reporting chain also perceive the second-level job in the same way as the incumbent so that their expectations will match reality.

The concern aroused in the study group by the lack of firm role definition led to an investigation of the job aimed at defining the role and identifying associated skills. The approach taken was to interview second-level supervisors on the job and compare their perceptions with those of managers at other levels. Additionally, the views of experienced (master) performers were compared to those of supervisors new to the job (less than two years).

The primary objectives of the investigation were to (1) define the role of the second-level supervisor and (2) determine whether the perceptions of the target population matched the expectations of their superiors and subordinates. A secondary benefit was to focus the job study on the most critical features of the second-level supervisor's job.

Interviews were conducted with 47 second-level supervisors and 35 managers at other levels, using open-ended questions such as these:

- What do you think is the primary role of the second levels in your organization (planner, controller, supervisor, interfacer)?
- From your experience, do you think this is also true in other departments?
- Is it different for line vs. staff?
- Do you think changes are occurring or coming in the second level's role? What kind?
- How is the second level different from the first?
- In terms of outputs, standards, inputs, what expectations do you have of a second level that you don't have of a first?
- How is the second level different from third level? What skills are needed at second level that are needed at third? What expectations do you have of a third level that you don't have of a second? (Outputs? Standards? Inputs?)
- What would happen if all second levels suddenly disappeared?
- Which of the duties in the lefthand column of Table 3-1 do you think is most important to the company? Why? Which is next? Why? Rank order them.
- Look at the outputs listed next to each duty, group by group. Which output in the first group is most important to the company? Why? Which is next? Why? Rank order them. (Cycle through the next three groups of duties.)

Table 3–1.

Rank	Duty	Freq.	Rank	Tasks
_____	Organizing and planning	_____	_____	Plan and organize jobs and resources:
		_____	_____	Define job responsibilities:
		_____	_____	Set objectives, goals, and targets:
		_____	_____	Set performance standards:
		_____	_____	Manage time:
_____	Directing, controlling, and delegating	_____	_____	Assign and follow up work:
		_____	_____	Appraise subordinate's performance:
		_____	_____	Delegate tasks:
		_____	_____	Make decisions:
		_____	_____	Solve problems:
_____	Supervisor/subordinate relations	_____	_____	Motivate subordinates:
		_____	_____	Develop subordinates:
		_____	_____	Career-path subordinates:
		_____	_____	Discipline subordinates:
		_____	_____	Give performance feedback:
_____	Communication	_____	_____	Maintain downward communications:
		_____	_____	Maintain upward communications:
		_____	_____	Maintain interdepartmental communications:
		_____	_____	Make presentations:
		_____	_____	Hold meetings:

- What about frequency? How often is each performed?
- Look at each output separately. What does it look like? What form does it take? Who wants it? Who gets it? How? Why?
- What does each contribute to achieving the company's purpose?

This phase of the job study succeeded significantly in defining the second-level supervisor's role in terms of duties and associated tasks. As the study progressed, this initial list of 20 tasks was successively refined until it became 15 principal managerial duties (later cut to 14 by combining decision making and problem solving) that form the basic structure of the second-level Mastery Model. As part of the refinement process, the list was given to a mixed group of second-level supervisors who were requested to put them into rank order, first in importance to their job performance, and second in order of their perceived need for further training. The survey group was composed of 19 master performers (experienced supervisors selected by their organizations on the basis of their superior performance on the job), and 29 newly appointed (less than 18 months experience) supervisors.

Table 3–2 shows how these two groups viewed the 15 duties in terms of their importance to job performance.

With respect to the need for additional in-depth training, the survey showed few significant differences between master performers and newly appointed supervisors. A greater number of master performers indicated need for training in "developing subordi-nates" and "community relations," while new supervisors tended to call for more training in "written communications" and "upward communications."

The final order of the managerial duties of second-level supervisors was determined through interviews with subject matter experts (SMEs are experienced, highly knowledgeable Bell System managers), and higher-level managers. Although different levels of management tended to perceive these duties in varying orders of priority, the study found confirmation that these fourteen *are* the critical duties of second-level supervisors—and that certain of them are considerably more crucial to the organization than others.

Here is the list of 14 second-level duties in rank order as finally derived:

1. Planning the job
2. Controlling the job
3. Providing performance feedback
4. Managing time
5. Decision making/Problem solving
6. Maintaining upward communications
7. Maintaining downward communications
8. Maintaining peer/coordinate communications
9. Creating a motivative atmosphere
10. Developing subordinates
11. Self-development
12. Providing written communications
13. Involvement with meetings
14. Community relations

This list served as initial input to the job study of first-level supervision, described in the next chapter.

Table 3–2.   Second-level duties ranked in order of importance to job performance

	As ranked by 19 master performers	*The same duties as ranked by 29 newly appointed supervisors*
1. Planning		1
2. Developing subordinates		4
3. Providing performance feedback		7
4. Decision making		4
5. Downward communications		14
6. Problem solving		2
7. Managing time		10
8. Controlling		6
9. Creating a motivative atmosphere		4
10. Peer communications		9
11. Upward communications		8
12. Self-development		11
13. Written communications		12
14. Meetings		13
15. Community relations		15

4 Principal Duties of the First-Level Supervisor

The work of the first-level job study team was in two principal parts:

1. Construction of a Mastery Model that details the principal managerial duties into their sequential steps, and then into the associated skills and knowledge required to perform these duties;
2. Development and administration of a Diagnostic Test designed to measure the actual performance of the target population against the Mastery Model, thereby identifying any deficiencies in skill or knowledge.

The Mastery Model—The actual task of constructing the Mastery Model required the study group to perform these major actions:

- Develop a plan for gathering data; that is, ensure that the data would be representative of the target population in terms of such variables as sex, racial origin, educational level, work type, etc.
- Gather data by observing and interviewing first-level supervisors identified as "master performers" (and interviewing the second-level bosses of these selected highly competent supervisors). These observations and interviews analyzed each of the 14 managerial duties (identified in the earlier study as significant to supervisory performance) into its component tasks and identified the skills and knowledge associated with each. In the course of this, the make-up and rank order of the 14 duties changed to some extent, and they became "managerial processes."

- Summarize and analyze the data collected to
    determine the importance of each process,
    chart the flow of tasks and decision points (contingencies) in each process,
    develop output standards for each process, and
    derive the specific skill and knowledge required to perform each process.
- Put the Mastery Model together; have the prototype reviewed by "subject matter experts"; and construct the final model.

The Diagnostic Test—Development and administration of the Diagnostic Test required the following principal tasks:

- determine *who* to test,
- determine *what* to test, and
- determine *how* to test.

The first task required the task force to select first-level supervisors representative of the variables and company departments (job functions) identified

19

in the data-gathering plan, and spread over 20 operating companies across the United States. This "target population" of 460 first-level supervisors was in two groups—master performers and newly appointed supervisors. Testing both groups enabled the study team to determine the skill and knowledge level of each. This permitted performance deficiencies to be diagnosed more accurately, thereby leading to better design of training for new supervisors. This first task also enabled the Mastery Model to be verified by testing a large group of master performers against it.

The second task involved first deciding which of the 200 skills and 380 knowledge items contained in the Mastery Model needed to be tested, and which were not consequential to the study results.

The third task was to determine how best to design and apply the diagnostic instrument for the most valid results. The output of this task was a diagnostic test in three basic parts:

1. *Objective tests* in writing (essay, multiple choice, true or false) to test participants' knowledge of all 14 processes.
2. *Simulation*, such as in-basket type exercises, to test participants' skills in applying the processes of planning and controlling.
3. *Role play*, to test participants' skill to coach subordinates, communicate orally and in writing, provide feedback on performance, and control work.

RANKING OF THE 14 PRINCIPAL DUTIES

The job study task force found that the principal managerial duties of a supervisor at the first level are somewhat different, but not greatly so, from those identified earlier as applicable to the job of the second-level supervisor. Starting with the final list of 14 duties identified earlier (see page 18), the task force proceeded to refine and modify the list through surveys and structured interviews with selected first-level supervisors and with second-level superiors. (The process followed, and the data collection instruments used by the study group to refine and define the list of

generic managerial processes is rather too involved to discuss here. Details and examples of forms used will be found in Part 3).

It was found that the 14 duties, or *managerial processes*, of the supervisor can be put into rank order in several different ways, depending on their relative level of difficulty, frequency of use, need for training, and the manner in which they are perceived by various people. The newly appointed supervisor, for instance, often has a very different view of the importance of certain activities from that of the experienced master

Table 4–1.

Rank order	Process	Percent of time spent on the process	Frequency of performance
1	Controlling the work	17	Every day
2	Problem solving	13	Every day
3	Planning the work	12	Every day
4	Informal oral communication	12	Every day
5	Communication	12	Every day
6	Providing performance feedback	10	Every day
7	Coaching a subordinate	10	Every day
8	Written communication/documentation	7	Every day
9	Create/maintain motivative atmosphere	6	Every day
10	Time management	4	Every day
11	Meetings	4	Twice monthly
12	Self-development	2	Weekly
13	Career counseling a subordinate	2	Bi-monthly
14	Representing the company	1	Monthly

performer. The second-level manager, as well, may rank certain functions higher or lower than his or her first-level subordinate.

The study group spent considerable time and effort to develop a ranking process that would represent realistic priorities for remedial training and job aids. To do this they looked at the 14 processes in several ways. One ranking was done by first-level members of the target population in terms of the amount of time spent performing each duty and the frequency with which it was performed. This resulted in the listing shown in Table 4-1.

LEVEL OF DIFFICULTY

A second order of ranking is by the relative level of difficulty, or complexity, of each duty as a managerial process. In this regard, the 14 duties fall into three groups—high complexity, moderate complexity, and low complexity—as follows:

- *High Complexity Processes*
  Planning the work
  Controlling the work
- *Moderate Complexity Processes*
  Problem solving
  Providing performance feedback

  Coaching a subordinate
  Create/Maintain a motivative atmosphere
  Time management
  Communication
  Informal oral communication
  Written communication/Documentation
  Career counseling
- *Low Complexity Processes*
  Self-development
  Representing the company
  Meetings

NEED FOR REMEDIAL ACTION

The several importance rankings developed by the job study task group served as input to the development of the final Mastery Model rankings. These final rankings are based on the criticality of the need for remedial action, either training or job aids. This ranking of the 14 processes is derived from a formula that incorporates the following eight factors:

- the relative amount of time spent on each process;
- how often each duty is performed;
- the relative complexity of each process;
- importance ranking by test population master performers;
- importance ranking by second-level supervisors;
- criticality ranking by first-level master performers in the initial stage of the study;
- deficiencies in skills and knowledge revealed by the diagnostic test;
- key decision points in each process.

Study data on these eight factors were translated into a weighting formula that gives each process a point weight based on a possible total of 48 points. The final ranking of the 14 processes in order of

critical need to take remedial action is given in Table 4-2:

Table 4-2.

Rank	Process	Point weight
1	Planning the work	45
2	Controlling the work	45
3	Problem solving	40
4	Providing performance feedback	36
5	Coaching a subordinate	34
6	Create motivative atmosphere	33
7	Time management	32
8	Communication	31
9	Informal oral communication	31
10	Self development	21
11	Written communication/documentation	21
12	Representing the company	15
13	Career counseling	12
14	Meetings	8

The four managerial processes with the highest point weight are labeled in the Job Study report as critical "survival skills" for newly appointed supervisors.

They should be given highest priority with respect to developing remedial training.

The next five processes are identified as "facilitative processes," for which deficiencies should also be remedied through training.

The five lowest-rated processes, while important, are not considered to be critical to survival on the job for new supervisors. For these managerial duties, deficiencies can usually be remedied through job or performance aids.

DIAGNOSTIC TEST—PROCESS RANKING

A newly appointed first-level supervisor (or a candidate for the position) should have a basic understanding of these 14 principal duties of the job—or *managerial processes*, as they are called in the job study report—as a preliminary to further training in supervision. Definitions of the 14 processes are given next, as developed by the job study task force and used in the Mastery Model. It was noted in the job study report that these definitions differ in some respects from the conventional textbook definitions; nevertheless they are believed to be valid, having been developed through an intensive set of interviews

and observations of first-level master performers, and subsequently reviewed by subject matter experts and higher-level managers in a wide range of job functions.

Following the list of definitions, a *diagnostic test* form is provided. This form can be used together with the definition sheet and the accompanying instructions to test supervisors' understanding of the relative importance of the 14 processes, and to determine the training needs of first-level supervisors as perceived by supervisors themselves.

Definition of first-level managerial processes

Career Counseling is helping subordinates achieve realistic personal job goals. It includes the planning of activities to help place subordinates in appropriate jobs.

Coaching Subordinates is the process which includes activities to help subordinates learn to do a job correctly.

The *Communication* process includes such activities as face-to-face contact, writing letters or memos, formal meetings, and telephone conversations. Communication is the exchange of opinions, ideas, facts, and/or feelings.

Controlling the Work is applying the results of Planning to the people who will be doing the work and to the materials they will use. This includes assigning the work, checking its progress, and measuring the work.

Creating/Maintaining a Motivative Atmosphere includes activities which may help a supervisor and subordinate work together, and activities which may lead to an environment conducive to efficient work.

Providing Performance Feedback is informing subordinates how their job performance compares with job requirements so that future job requirements can be met or exceeded.

Meetings (Formal Oral Communication) includes one-to-one encounters or meetings with more than one person. It requires some preparation beforehand and/or some structure during the communication.

Informal Oral Communication is the kind of communication that takes place in an unstructured situation and requires little or no preparation.

Knowledgeable Representative of (company name): As a manager within the _____, you are perceived as a representative of the _____ by customers, neighbors, civic groups, and your subordinates. This process involves representing and sharing knowledge of _____ when appropriate.

Planning the Work is the process performed by the supervisor individually before implementing a course of action. The end result of the Planning process provides all the information needed to begin to manage an area of responsibility.

Problem Solving is a process used by a supervisor to solve day-to-day problems while managing the work.

Self-Development is identifying own requirements for producing better results on the current job and implementing plans to meet those requirements.

Time Management is the scheduling of administrative responsibilities. It includes handling telephone calls, office
    paper flow, and work activities most efficiently.
Written Communication/Documentation includes activities such as writing letters, reports, or memos, and com-
    pleting forms, or maintaining local documentation.

Process ranking sheet Instructions

Importance Ranking.   On the attached PROCESS RANKING SHEET we would like you to rank order the
fourteen different processes you perform on the job. Rank them in order of their importance to your effectiveness
on the job. The process you feel is *most* important would be #1, and the next most important #2, and so on. If
there are several processes you feel are equally important, you can use the same number to rank them all. For
instance, if two of the processes are the *most* important to you, and you cannot rank one as more important than
the other, then rank them both as #1. You might find it easier to rank, by starting with the processes that are most
important, then skipping down to the least important. Those processes in the middle range of your importance
ranking would be done last. You can rank them numerically in the "Importance Ranking" column. Definitions
of these different processes are included in this section on a separate page.

Process ranking sheet	Importance ranking	Types of training needed		
		In-depth	Overview	None
Written communication				
Career counseling				
Time management				
Coaching				
Knowledgeable representative of the Bell System				
Planning				
Formal oral communication				
Feedback				
Creating/maintaining a motivative atmosphere				
Problem solving				
Communication				
Self-development				
Controlling				
Informal oral communication				

Type of Training.   The next three columns on the PROCESS RANKING SHEET deal with the type of training
you need to perform a particular process on your job.
      Read the definitions below and place an "X" in the box associated with the type of training you feel you
need to perform that process.

In-depth Training: This type of training is extensive training that provides you with all of the skills/knowledge to perform the process and use what was learned back on the job.

Overview Training: This type of training consists of basic concepts or theories on a particular process without going into detail.

None: This term means you feel you *do not* need any training in a particular process.

Note: On this diagnostic test form, the listing of the 14 processes is deliberately given in different rank order, so as not to influence the respondent.

THE FIRST-LEVEL MASTERY MODEL IN BRIEF

The AT&T Skill/Knowledge Mastery Model is a comprehensive, in-depth *prescription* for the job of a first-level supervisor. This model is performance-based and is constructed on a framework of the 14 principal duties of a supervisor, developed through the process just described, and in the sequence shown in the final listing (see Table 4-3).

Each duty is viewed and presented as a *managerial process*—a series of steps to be followed for mastery of the duty. The number of steps in a given process—tasks and decision points—varies with the complexity of the process. The number of steps can range from as few as six to as many as twenty-eight. The complete model contains a total of 229 separate and distinct tasks and decision points (contingencies).

Under each step in each process are listed the specific skills and points of knowledge associated with the task or decision. The total model contains 196 skills and 383 items of knowledge; the number per task and per process again depends on the complexity of the task or process. This number can range from as few as three skills and knowledge for the process *Representing the Company*, to as many as 88 for the complex process *Providing Performance Feedback*.

These numbers begin to give an indication of the scope and complexity of the first-level supervisor's job. Just how intricate and wide-ranging the job is can be seen from Table 4-3, which details the duties, tasks, skills, and knowledge of the model in numerical form—in effect, a symbolic model of the job.

Thus the first-level supervisor's job—in terms of managerial processes—is composed of over 800 indi-

Table 4-3. First-level duties, tasks, skills, and knowledge

Principal duties	Major tasks	Decision points	Skills	Knowledge	Total items
1. Planning the work	15	6	12	32	65
2. Controlling the work	9	6	13	36	64
3. Problem solving	11	4	14	17	46
4. Performance feedback	24	4	28	60	116
5. Coaching subordinates	22	1	22	25	70
6. Motivative atmosphere	13	3	10	19	45
7. Managing time	9	2	17	44	72
8. Communication	6	1	1	16	24
9. Informal oral comm.	19	5	21	20	65
10. Self-development	8	1	7	17	33
11. Written comm.	11	3	21	23	58
12. Representing company	5	1	—	3	9
13. Career counseling	17	3	2	32	54
14. Meetings	18	2	28	39	87
TOTAL	187	42	196	383	808

vidual tasks, decision points, skills, and knowledge items, to which must be added the 14 principal duties themselves. This represents a grand total of 822 separate and distinct managerial elements in the management repertoire of a first-level master performer. To these must be added considerable *enabling knowledge* of company and local policies, practices, and procedures. This does not include, of course, the many technical and specialty skills and knowledge the supervisor calls upon to perform the job competently.

In highly simplified schematic form, the Mastery Model looks like the diagram in Figure 4-1. Obviously this diagram is oversimplified, because it does not show the differences in complexity and learning difficulty of each process, task, decision, skill, and knowledge. This representation also fails to show that certain of the 14 principal duties—planning, controlling, solving problems, and providing performance feedback—were found by the Job Study to be essential to the very survival on the job of the newly appointed first-level supervisor. Nor does it show which skills and points of knowledge relate to specific duties, decision points, and tasks. Only the full Mastery Model can do that—as will be seen in Part 2 of this book, next.

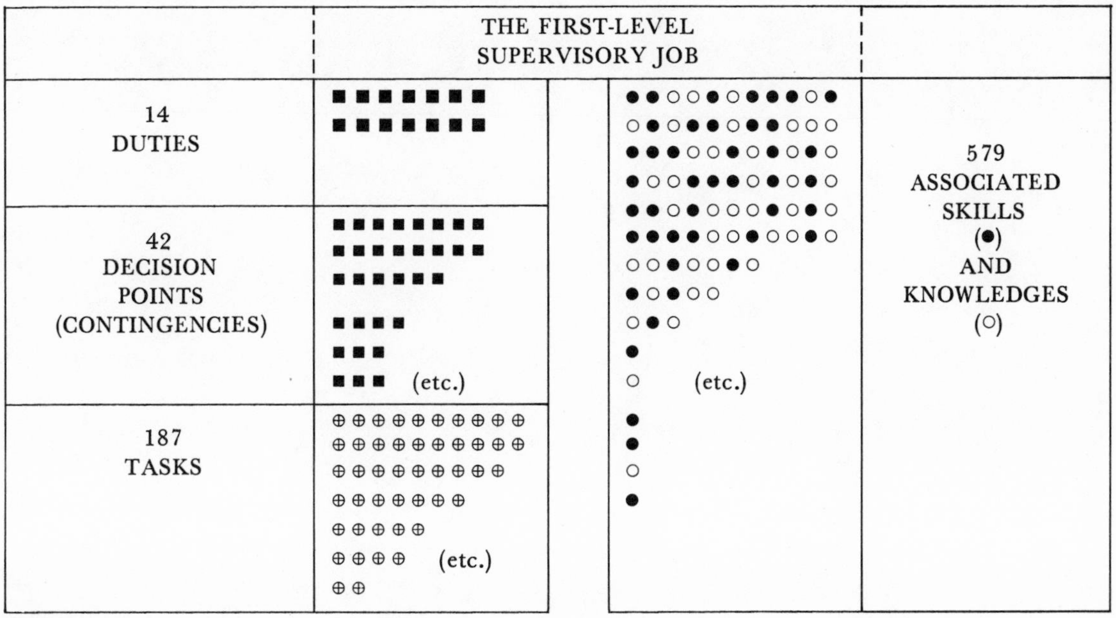

	THE FIRST-LEVEL SUPERVISORY JOB		
14 DUTIES	■ ■ ■ ■ ■ ■ ■ ■ ■ ■ ■ ■ ■ ■	● ● ○ ○ ● ○ ● ● ● ○ ○ ● ○ ● ● ○ ● ● ○ ○ ○ ● ● ● ○ ○ ● ○ ● ○ ● ○ ● ○ ○ ● ● ● ○ ● ○ ● ○ ● ● ○ ● ○ ○ ● ○ ● ○ ○ ● ● ● ● ○ ○ ● ○ ● ○ ● ○	579 ASSOCIATED SKILLS (●) AND KNOWLEDGES (○)
42 DECISION POINTS (CONTINGENCIES)	■ ■ ■ ■ ■ ■ ■ ■ ■ ■ ■ ■ ■ ■ ■ ■ ■ ■ ■ ■ ■ ■ ■ ■ ■ ■ ■ ■ ■ ■ ■ (etc.)	○ ○ ● ○ ○ ● ○ ● ○ ● ○ ○ ○ ● ○ ● ○ (etc.)	
187 TASKS	⊕ ⊕ ⊕ ⊕ ⊕ ⊕ ⊕ ⊕ ⊕ ⊕ ⊕ ⊕ ⊕ ⊕ ⊕ ⊕ ⊕ ⊕ ⊕ ⊕ ⊕ ⊕ ⊕ ⊕ ⊕ ⊕ ⊕ ⊕ ⊕ ⊕ ⊕ ⊕ ⊕ ⊕ ⊕ ⊕ ⊕ ⊕ ⊕ ⊕ ⊕ ⊕ ⊕ ⊕ ⊕ (etc.) ⊕ ⊕	● ● ○ ●	

FIGURE 4-1.

II Supervisory Duties, Tasks, Skills, and Knowledge

HOW TO USE THIS SECTION

The 14 principal duties of the first-level supervisor are described and discussed in the chapters that follow. They are presented in the order determined by the Job Study Task Force, as listed in the preceding chapter.

Each duty is covered in a separate chapter. Essentially, each is described and discussed in increasing levels of detail, ranging from the *basics of the duty* which a new supervisor should know, to the *full Skill/Knowledge Mastery Model* in all its complexity, which represents an "ideal" toward which the training and development of first-level supervisors should be directed.

Each chapter also contains a discussion of Performance Measurements at the first-level, and describes the Diagnostic Test Instrument used by the Job Study Task Force to determine the training needs of the target population.

Each chapter is divided into six sections. The *contents* of each section and the *purpose* of each are given below.

SECTION A.   OVERVIEW OF THE SUPERVISORY DUTY

CONTENTS: This section describes in general terms the need for the job function in the contemporary business organization and the role of the first-level supervisor. This discussion is drawn to some extent from sources other than the Mastery Model; some are from published sources that are acknowledged in footnotes; some come from the author's experience as a manager and consultant. All of it, however, is related to and has been influenced by the AT&T Job Study and the work done by the task force.

PURPOSE: Basic knowledge for the newly appointed supervisor or the candidate for the position.

SECTION B.   HIGHLIGHTS OF THE AT&T STUDY

CONTENTS: *Definition of the duty* as developed by the Job Study Task Force and used in the Mastery Model. *Brief summary description* of the duty abstracted from the Mastery Model.

PURPOSE: This definition and description can help the new supervisor understand the duty as a series of steps that should be performed in a prescribed sequence—that is, a *process of management.*

SECTION C.   TASKS AND DECISION POINTS IN THE PROCESS

CONTENTS: 1. A detailed listing and description of the steps in the process, as a series of tasks and decision points or contingencies, taken directly from the Mastery Model.
             2. A set of flowcharts that depict the sequence and flow of steps in the process in graphic form.

PURPOSE: This section develops the *managerial process* concept in greater detail, in order to give the supervisor an understanding of the sequence, flow, and relationship of the steps in the process, as well as a better appreciation of the complexity of the job.

SECTION D.   PERFORMANCE MEASUREMENTS CHART

CONTENTS: The fourth section describes the way in which the first-level supervisor's performance of each duty is measured by his or her organizational superior. Shown in tabular form are 1) the outputs of the various tasks, 2) the performance standards that apply to these outputs, and 3) the method used by the supervisor's boss to evaluate performance of the duty.

PURPOSE: This section is intended to give the supervisor a better understanding of the need to view the job in terms of *output* and *results,* not simply activity. This can help to orient the supervisor to management by objectives, and to broaden the managerial outlook.

SECTION E.   THE AT&T MASTERY MODEL

CONTENTS: This is the *full Skill/Knowledge Mastery Model* of the duty as a generic managerial process. Each task and decision point is described together with the specific skills and knowledge required. This Model, as noted earlier, was derived from interviews and first-hand observation of "master performers," and thus is performance-based.

PURPOSE: The Skill/Knowledge Mastery Model represents a pattern, an "ideal," toward which the first-level supervisor's development efforts—both self-development and company-provided training—should be directed, within the constraints of costs and valid organizational needs.

SECTION F.   TRAINING NEEDS DIAGNOSTIC

CONTENTS: In the final section of each chapter, the diagnostic test instrument developed by the AT&T Job Study Task Force is described and discussed as it relates to the particular duty, or managerial process, of the first-level supervisor.

PURPOSE: This information can be adapted to the unique characteristics of your organization to serve as a diagnostic to test the skills and knowledge of your supervisors, either newly-appointed or candidates for the position. It can also be used as a "needs analysis" for designing training programs for experienced supervisors who may be deficient in certain skills and knowledge.

It should be noted here that the Mastery Model as presented in this book differs from the published internal AT&T Job Study Report in certain respects. First, Bell System terminology has been modified to make the Model more generally applicable to other companies and other industries. Second, some topics have been revised or expanded to make them more easily understandable to managers outside of the Bell System and the telephone industry. Third, the numbering system for tasks, skills, and knowledge has been simplified. In no case, however, has the meaning of the Job Study and the Mastery Model—or the intent of the Task Force—been knowingly altered.

5 Planning the Work

PROCESS 1

A. OVERVIEW OF PLANNING AT THE SUPERVISORY LEVEL

Planning is a management activity that comes in a variety of types and sizes. It is performed at every level of management and, in one form or another, by every business function. Plans range in scope and range from the broad, long-term strategic plans, which are closely guarded by the executive office, to the individual weekly sales call plan of a field sales representative. In the typical organization, between these extremes will be found a host of business plans, marketing plans, new-product development plans, production plans, etc.

Unfortunately, supervisors in many organizations tend to view planning as a somewhat academic and ritualistic process performed by a corps of "beard strokers" in the front office, remote from the real world of people and problems. Planning, however, is a very real and essential part of every supervisor's job. Planning—and the ability to plan—is one of the principal distinguishing characteristics between a supervisor and those supervised.

Planning is the ability to *look ahead,* to view the work in a context of its longer-range significance to the organization. It is the ability to *look up* from the task at hand and see how the task fits into the larger scheme of things with which the organization is concerned. And it is the capability to *look out* from the confines of the workplace and perceive how the work is affected by events and developments outside.

In his excellent book, *Management-Minded Supervision,*[1] Bradford Boyd observes that each move up the management ladder requires a higher degree of planning skill. If planning ability is lacking at the first level of management—the first-line supervisor—then that individual is not likely to get very far up that ladder. Boyd goes on to identify the benefits of good planning at the supervisory level, as well as the consequences of poor planning. Notable among the adverse effects of inadequate planning are low productivity, high costs, and increased risk of accidents, all of which are harmful to the enterprise. But the adverse impact of poor planning radiates in every direction and causes severe difficulty for supervisors themselves as well. For one effect, it tends to increase

[1]McGraw-Hill Book Company, New York, 1968.

the pressures from higher management, pressures already too high in many organizations. For another, it creates confusion and misunderstanding among subordinates. It also has the effect of lessening coordination and cooperation among the various departments of the organization.

The benefits of good planning, on the other hand, are almost self-evident. For the first-line supervisor, perhaps the most important is his or her enhanced job effectiveness. Supervisors who plan well are perceived by others as being in control of the work, in control of themselves, and in control of the situation despite the problems and adversities that inevitably besiege leaders who are out on the cutting edge of the effort.

Most management authorities agree on the basic list of steps that constitute the planning process. One such list that seems well suited to first-line manage-

ment is given in *Supervision: The Management of Organizational Resources.*[2] It is a short list:

1. Specify the goal or objective.
2. Gather and evaluate relevant data.
3. Determine the individuals involved.
4. Evaluate and test the plan.

This process, it is stated, determines how the organization is structured to accomplish the desired goals.

Others have expanded the list to include such factors as identifying premises and constraints and developing alternative plans. These are important planning factors, to be sure, but they do not alter the need to perform the four basic tasks listed above.

[2]Sterling H. Schoen, and Douglas E. Durand (Englewood Cliffs, N. J.: Prentice-Hall Inc., 1979).

The next section gives the definition of this duty as developed by the Job Study Task Force and as defined in the Mastery Model. Section B also describes Planning in brief summary form, as "Highlights" of the AT&T Job Study.

B.   HIGHLIGHTS OF THE AT&T JOB STUDY

Definition of the process

In the AT&T Mastery Model, planning the work at the first supervisory level is regarded as a very pragmatic and activist kind of management process. It is concerned only with planning the work for which the first-level supervisor is responsible. As defined in the Mastery Model, planning the work is:

The duty performed by the supervisor individually before implementing a course of action. The end result of the planning process provides all information needed to begin to manage an area of responsibility.

There is no conflict here with the conventional definitions of planning. There is no single accepted definition, of course, but one that serves the purpose well reads, "The effort to control one's environment and to reduce the degree to which chance, guesswork, and uncertainty affect the job." The planning process prescribed by the Mastery Model is surely directed toward this purpose.

Summary description of the process

In its simplest terms, this process consists of first identifying the output requirements of the work to be planned—that is, the goals, targets, or final results of the work. Next, the supervisor is required to determine whether or not resources are available to do the work in the prescribed manner to achieve the desired result or output. When the needed resources are *not* available, the supervisor is required to search for an acceptable alternative method to achieve the desired result (and take action to get such alternative approved).

When it has been determined that resources are available to do the work, either in the prescribed manner or by an approved alternative method, then checkpoints, or interim benchmarks of progress, should be identified and recorded on an appropriate control form (in the Bell System this is often called a Master Control List, or something similar).

This task represents a "programming" of the plan; that is, putting in writing the series of steps that will serve as a basis for controlling progress of the work. Too often this planning task is not done or is done poorly—yet unless this task is done well, the supervisor is poorly equipped to control the work during its execution.

The planning process is described in greater detail in the next section. Section C lists the 21 steps in the process—15 tasks and six decision points—and illustrates the process with a set of flowcharts. In this presentation, the process is broken down into three stages: steps 1 through 7; steps 8 through 15; and steps 16 through 21. The three stages are accompanied by a progressive series of charts that depict the *flow* and *relationships* of the 21 tasks and decision points (contingencies) in the process of planning the work.

C. PLANNING TASKS AND DECISION POINTS

Following is a list of steps in the process of planning the work. You will note that later tasks and decisions are dependent upon earlier steps; thus the sequence is important and should be observed for mastery of planning as a managerial process. You will also note that decisions made at certain points in the process affect your subsequent *path* through the process.

STEP 1   The first task is to determine that a "stimulus" exists to initiate the planning process; such as a directive from your boss, a special assignment, a meeting action assignment, an unanticipated event impacting the present plan, etc.

Planning may also be self-initiated to attain personal job objectives.

STEP 2   Identify the output requirements of the work to be planned; that is, the desired result, goal, or target.

STEP 3   Decision point: *Have you had experience performing or managing this kind of work before?*

If your decision is *yes*, skip Step 4 and go to Step 5 and determine whether or not you have the resources you need to do the work.

STEP 4   If your decision is *no*—you lack such experience—your next task is to examine information about this type of work (or comparable work).

STEP 5   Determine what resources—people, skills, materials, equipments, etc.—are *needed* to do the work in the prescribed manner to produce the required outputs.

STEP 6   Identify what resources are *available* and whether they will be adequate to do the work at the time the work must be done.

STEP 7   Decision Point: *Will all required resources be available when needed?*

If your decision is *yes*, bypass the next eight steps and go directly to Step 16 to identify the planning checkpoints needed to control progress of the work.

(Refer to flowchart in Fig. 5-1.)

STEP 8   If your decision in Step 7 was *no*—resources may not be available—then your next task is to look for alternative methods to achieve all or as many of the output requirements as possible.

STEP 9   Decision Point: *Is there an alternative method?*

If your decision is *yes*, go to Step 11.

STEP 10   If your decision is *no*—there is no alternative method—then you should inform the initiator of the planning (and your boss) that a roadblock to further planning exists.

You should also document the situation as required.

STEP 11   Decision point: If an alternative exists, respond to the question: *Does the chosen alternative achieve all output requirements?*

If your decision is *yes*, bypass the next four steps and proceed directly to Step 16 to identify the planning checkpoints for controlling the work using the alternative method.

STEP 12   If your decision is *no*—the alternative does not meet all output requirements—your next task is to present the alternative to the initiator for approval.

STEP 13   Decision point: *Does the initiator agree to accept the alternative method?*

   If your decision is *yes*, go to Step 15.

STEP 14   If your decision is *no*—the alternative is not acceptable—document the rejection and your inability to continue the planning process any further. Also notify your boss.

STEP 15   If the alternative is accepted, document this fact and the ways in which it may deviate from the standard method.

   (Refer to flowchart in Fig. 5-2.)

STEP 16   Identify the planning checkpoints needed to control the work to meet output requirements.

STEP 17   Determine whether local procedures exist for recording (logging) your checkpoints, such as on a Master Control List or similar control document.

STEP 18   Decision Point: *Are there local procedures for logging checkpoints?*

   If your decision is *yes*, go directly to Step 20 and record the checkpoints on the appropriate document.

STEP 19   If your decision is *no*—there are no local procedures—your next task is to construct a control document such as a Master Control List.

STEP 20   Your final step in planning the work is to record (log) your planning checkpoints on the Master Control List or other appropriate control document.

   This control document is input to Process No. 2—Controlling the Work.

STEP 21   END OF PROCESS—GO TO CONTROLLING THE WORK.

   (Refer to flowchart in Fig. 5-3.)

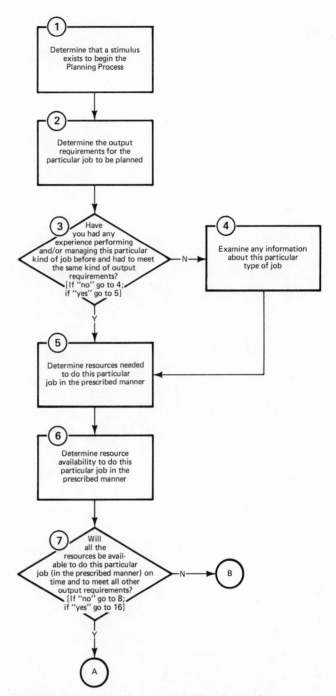

FIGURE 5-1. Flowchart of the First Seven Steps in the Process

Section D, next, describes the way in which the first-level supervisor's performance in planning the work is measured by the higher level manager to whom he or she reports directly. Shown in tabular form are the outputs of the various planning tasks, the performance standards that apply to these outputs, and the method used by the supervisor's boss to evaluate planning performance.

34

SUPERVISORY DUTIES, TASKS, SKILLS, AND KNOWLEDGE

Flowchart of the planning process—first 15 steps

Figure 5-2 depicts the process of planning the work up to this point. Steps 8 through 15 are required if you responded no to the question in Step 7 and it was necessary to look for an alternative method to do the work.

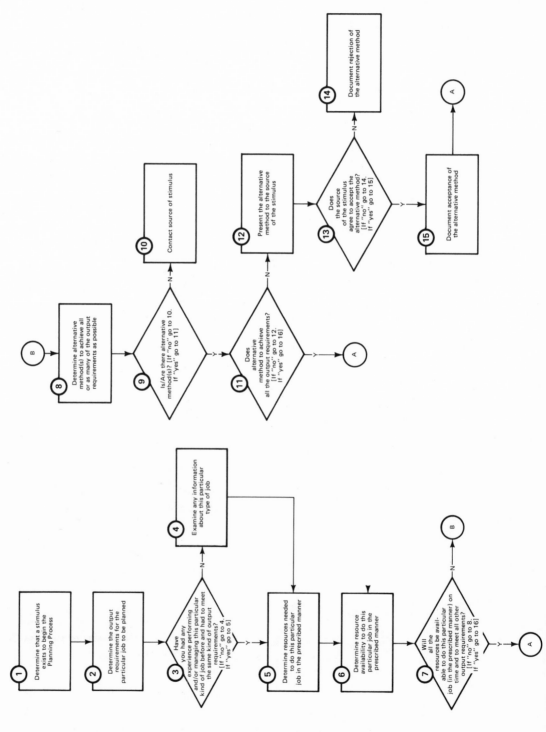

FIGURE 5-2.   The First Fifteen Steps

The flowchart in Figure 5–3 illustrates the total pro-cess of Planning the Work at the first supervisory level.

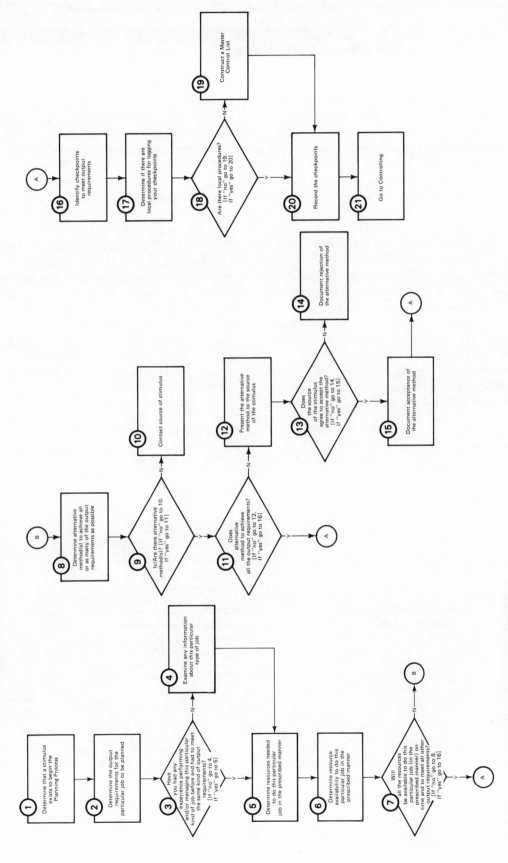

FIGURE 5–3. Flowchart of the Total Process—Planning the Work

D. MEASURING PERFORMANCE OF THE SUPERVISOR IN PLANNING THE WORK

Setting performance standards and measuring performance of subordinates are among the most important activities and responsibilities of the first-line supervisor. These tasks are the essence of control of any operation, and control is a supervisor's primary task. When it comes to measuring the management performance of first-level supervisors themselves, however, it appears that little is known about the performance standards that should be applied to them, or how their performance should be measured.

The AT&T job studies found that many second-level managers did not measure their first-line subordinate's performance in the managerial skills area at all. Of those who do, few used the same standards of measurement for a particular output. It was discovered, in fact, that many second-levels could not even articulate standards for the managerial performance of the supervisors reporting to them.

Most second-level managers tended to measure the output of an entire process rather than the output of the individual steps in the process. This does not mean that they are poor managers. On the contrary, the practice allows a subordinate a chance to correct interim errors and deviations from standards during the performance of their duties—in other words, it represents a desirable practice of measuring end results rather than interim efforts. However, for diagnosing managerial deficiencies in performance and designing remedial training programs, it was found necessary to develop performance standards for all tasks in the managerial process.

The 21 tasks and decision points in the process of Planning the Work fall naturally for performance measurement purposes into seven principal *groups*. Table 5–1 lists the steps in each group, the output of each group, the performance standards that apply to each output, and the method used by the second-level manager to measure the planning performance of first-level subordinates. These standards and outputs were developed through interviews with second-level supervisors.

Table 5–1. Process no. 1—planning the work

Performance Measurements Chart			
Step or group of steps	*Output*	*Performance standards*	*Methods of measurement*
Step 1	Need for planning identified	Areas of responsibility defined Unexpected events are planned for Plans are made for developing subordinates Duplication is eliminated	
Steps 2, 3, 4	Performance standards and goals are defined	Performance standards are set in accordance with consumer requirements, boss's requirements, etc.	
Steps 5, 6, 7	Human and physical resources are defined and aligned to product outputs	Resources and work are aligned so objectives are met Jobs are matched to people's abilities	Supervisor's boss reviews documented plans, master control list, etc., and discusses with the supervisor
Step 8	Alternative ways of completing the work are identified	Work completed despite obstacles, vacations, schedules, etc.	
Steps 10–15	Communication with initiator of planning is maintained and documented	Fewer problems brought to next higher level to resolve	
Step 16	Checkpoints are identified		
Steps 17–21	Completed plan with timeframes Master control list maintained	Documented plan	

E. THE AT&T MASTERY MODEL—PLANNING THE WORK

Each of the tasks and decision points in the process of planning the work at the first supervisory level requires specific skills and knowledge. In addition, certain fundamental skills and knowledge are required for mastering the process. In this section, the 21 steps in the process are listed together with the specific skills and knowledge associated with each one.

Fundamental skills and knowledge required

To plan the work effectively, it is necessary that you *know four fundamentals of management* that relate to planning, and *possess one fundamental planning skill,* as follows:

Knowledge Required	K1	The output of planning is input to the next duty, Controlling the Work.
	K2	Planning the work is done best under quiet, secluded conditions free from distractions.
	K3	Planning the work is necessary in order to accomplish results efficiently; the plan is a medium for obtaining resources, prioritizing and assigning tasks, etc.
	K4	It is necessary to ascertain the scope of your responsibilities by consulting job descriptions, standard practices, your superior, former incumbents, etc.
Skill Required	S1	The fundamental skill needed is the ability to determine what resources—people, equipment, etc.—you are responsible for.

Step 1—Identify the Factor that Stimulates the Planning

Knowledge Required	K5	The planning process may be set in motion (initiated) by one or more of the following events or people: overall job objectives received from boss meeting minutes work generated by boss

special assignments
work generated by other sources (other departments, customers, peers, subordinates, higher-level managers, etc.)
interference by unanticipated events
additional personal objectives (train, develop, and coach subordinates, give performance feedback, community relations, self-development)

	K6	The planning process may be used to develop the management capabilities of one or more subordinates.

Step 2—Determine the Output Requirements of the Work

Skill Required	S2	This requires skill to determine the final results of the work—output requirements, goals, targets, standards—in terms of quantity, quality, or time. If these are not specified by the initiator, you need skill to ascertain what they are by querying your boss, peers, other departments, etc.
Knowledge Required	K7	Output requirements must be established where they do not already exist. These requirements should be based on information derived from subsequent Step 4, Examine Information about This Type of Work.

Step 3—Decision Point: Have You Had Experience Performing or Managing This Specific Type of Work Before, and Meeting the Same Kind of Output Requirements?

Knowledge Required	K8	Know that "experience" means having either supervised or worked all or part of this kind of work before.

	K9	The phrase "same kind of output requirement" means that the same measurements are used but may vary in amount. For example, three equipments installed in ten days as opposed to three equipments installed in 30 days.

(If your decision is *yes*, skip the next step and go to Step 5, Determine Needed Resources.)

Step 4—Examine Information about This Type of Work

If your decision was *no*—you lack such experience—then your next task is to locate and examine available information about this particular type of work.

Knowledge Required	K10	The sources of such information may be company practices, local practices, your boss, peers, subordinates, customers, historical data, etc.
	K11	In the absence of information about this specific job, know to examine information about comparable work.
	K12	If you cannot obtain information about the work (or any comparable work), you should know to ask the initiator of the planning how to continue the process.
Skill Required	S3	This task requires skill to review the references listed and determine: how long the job took what resources were used technical competency and training needed of each subordinate unusual obstacles encountered contingency plans made or actions taken output requirements (objectives, targets) if there is a prescribed manner if standard practices exist

---

Step 5—Identify Needed Resources to Do the Work in the Prescribed Manner

Knowledge Required	K13	The prescribed manner has been defined in Step 3 or 4—by

past experience, research, or the initiator.

Skill Required	S4	This requires skill to compare the work to be done with the information obtained in Step 4, and determine: how many people are needed what kind of skills are needed what kind of materials are needed how much material is needed whether other departments are involved what tools and equipment are needed

---

Step 6—Determine Whether Available Resources Are Adequate

Knowledge Required	K14	Availability of resources may be ascertained from current workload data; that is, who is assigned to what tasks.
	K15	It may be necessary to contact more than one source to ensure that resources are adequate; that is, other than regular suppliers, or borrowing people from other work groups.
	K16	A resource should be considered *unavailable* if a firm determination of its availability cannot be made.
Skills Required	S5	This task requires skill to determine whether the people you need will be available when you need them—that is, at the projected time of the work. This requires checking the vacation schedules, work schedules, sick lists, overtime schedules, upgrade and transfer plans, scheduled retirements, etc.
	S6	You also need skill to determine whether the other resources you need will be available at the projected time of the work. This can be done by checking equipment on hand, equipment out of service, suppliers of equipment, preventive maintenance schedules, the needs of other users of the equipments, etc.

Step 7—Decision Point: Will All Needed Resources Be Available to Do the Work in the Prescribed Manner, on Schedule, and in a Way that Will Meet All Other Output Requirements?

(If your decision is *yes,* bypass the next eight steps and go directly to Step 16, Identify Planning Checkpoints.)

Step 8—Look for Alternative Methods

| Knowledge Required | K17 | Know to look for alternatives that can achieve *all* output requirements before looking for alternatives that can achieve *only some* output requirements. |
| Skill Required | S7 | You need skill to determine whether there may be nonstandard methods to achieve the outputs—by comparing the output requirements with knowledge gained through Step 4. Examples: renting equipment, overtime, etc. |

Step 9—Decision Point: Is There an Alternative Method?

(If your decision is *yes,* skip the next step and go to Step 11.)

Step 10—Contact the Initiator of the Planning

If your decision is *no*—there is no alternative method—your next task is to inform the initiator that a roadblock to further planning exists.

Skill Required	S8	This task requires skill to communicate to the initiator that planning cannot be completed to meet the output requirements, and that no alternative method is available.
Knowledge Required	K18	Know that even if your boss was not the initiator, he or she should be notified.
	K19	Know to use the "Communication Process" (see later) to inform the initiator (and your boss).
	K20	Know to notify people in accor-

dance with custom or standard procedure.

| | K21 | Know to document the following: your inability to continue planning process the transmission of information relating to this inability to whom the information was sent when the information was sent |

Step 11—Decision Point: Does the Alternative Method Achieve All Output Requirements?

(If your decision is *yes,* skip the next four steps, and go directly to Step 16, Identify Planning Checkpoints.)

Step 12—Present the Alternative Method to the Initiator

If your decision is *no*—the alternative does *not* meet all output requirements—then your next task is to present the alternative method to the initiator of the planning for approval.

Knowledge Required	K22	Know to use the Communication Process to inform the initiator.
	K23	Know *not to proceed* until the initiator agrees to the alternative method.
	K24	Know that this contact should be documented.

Step 13—Decision Point: Does the Initiator Agree to Accept the Alternative Method?

(If your decision is *yes,* skip Step 14 and go to Step 15.)

Step 14—Document Rejection of the Alternative Method

If the decision is *no*—the alternative method is not acceptable—your next task is to document this fact.

| Knowledge Required | K25 | Your boss should be notified of the rejection even if the boss is not the initiator of the planning. |
| | K26 | Know to document the same four factors listed in K21. |

Step 15—Document Acceptance of the Alternative Method

Knowledge Required	K27	Know to document the acceptable alternative, which may involve deviations from standard procedure, substitutions of resources, fewer resources, or acceptance of reduced output requirements.

Step 16—Identify Planning Checkpoints

Knowledge Required	K28	Planning checkpoints are predetermined steps in the work flow that must be met if the work is to meet the output requirements. Checkpoints are needed to control progress of the work. For example, is the work on schedule, is quality acceptable, etc.?
Skill Required	S9	You need skill to identify checkpoints based on: specifications given by initiator company practices mandated checkpoints information from boss, peers, subordinates own experience on similar work natural ending points of activities within the task the completion of the work

(Example: annual budget for equipment is $12,000—checkpoints could be actual spending of $1000 a month)

Step 17—Determine Whether Local Procedures Exist for Recording Checkpoints

Knowledge Required	K29	When such procedures exist, they should be followed. Examples are Master Control List, work log, job book, etc.
Skill Required	S10	You need skill to determine whether such procedures exist by consulting your boss, peers, subordinates, etc.

Step 18—Decision Point: Are There Local Procedures?

(If your decision is *yes,* bypass Step 19 and go to Step 20.)

Step 19—Construct a Master Control List (or Similar Control Document)

If your decision is *no*—there are no local procedures—your next task is to construct a Master Control List of planning checklist, tasks, responsibilities, etc.

Knowledge Required	K30	A Master Control List should contain: your plan checkpoints progress/status of the work due dates time frames follow-up dates experience of personnel in producing outputs quantity checks quality checks final output(s) regulations training of personnel roadblocks encountered action taken to clear roadblocks
	K31	A Master Control List may be constructed either as a matrix with tasks listed across the top and due dates shown down the left side, or vice-versa, or as a "laundry list" of tasks, responsibilities, due dates, etc.
Skill Required	S11	You need skill to determine if any appropriate procedures exist to use as a pattern.

Step 20—Record the Checkpoints

Skill Required	S12	You need skill to record your checkpoints in accordance with procedures and practices.
Knowledge Required	K32	This record of checkpoints is input to the next major duty of a supervisor, Controlling the Work.

Flowchart of the total planning process

A flowchart illustrating the total process of Planning the Work is given in the preceding section (see Figure 5-3). To put the Mastery Model process into perspective, it may be helpful to refer to this chart at this point.

F.   TRAINING NEEDS DIAGNOSTIC

This phase of the diagnostic test is in two sections: an *objective test* consisting of 11 questions, and a *planning simulation*. Both are designed to test a supervisor's planning skills and knowledge, as follows:

Objective Test	Skills S1, 3
	Knowledges K1, 3, 4, 5, 7, 10, 11, 12
Simulation	Skills S4, 5, 7, 9
	Knowledges K16, 17, 19, 20, 21, 24, 26, 30

Objective test

The test questions and answers are found in Exhibits A and B. The specific skills and knowledge (and process steps) tested by the 11 questions are shown in Exhibit C.

Planning exercise

The Planning Simulation is designed to measure the first-level supervisor's planning skills and knowledge in relation to

analyzing information,
determining resources,
identifying alternatives, and
documenting plans.

Essentially, the planning exercise simulates a work situation with a broad range of inputs, both relevant and nonrelevant to the situation, several alternative paths, and roadblocks. The exercise consists of three work assignments, background reference information, and a battery of test questions.

The planning exercise is not included in this book for two reasons: first, it is highly specific to a Bell System work situation that might be difficult to adapt to another company in another industry, and second, it is too voluminous to reproduce here.

The skills, knowledge, and process steps covered by the questions in the planning exercise are shown in Exhibit D. You will note that this exercise also tests several skills and knowledges related to Controlling the Work.

Diagnostic test exhibit A: Process 1—planning the work

Planning is the process performed by you individually before implementing a course of action. The end result of the planning process provides you with all the information needed to begin to manage your area of responsibility.

1. From the list below, what are the five activities that should always be performed to plan work successfully? (X-out the *five* activities on the answer sheet.)
   a.   check with the boss
   b.   document plan
   c.   consult with other work groups
   d.   determine alternative methods
   e.   determine resources available
   f.   determine what the work should accomplish
   g.   determine resources needed
   h.   identify checkpoints
2. *Sequence* your *five* choices from question 1 in the order in which they should be performed to plan work successfully. (Write the letter of each statement you selected from question 1 in the correct order on the answer sheet.)

3. How should you go about determining whether a task is your responsibility or not? (X-out the *three* best answers on the answer sheet.)
   a. check with your subordinates
   b. read Bell System Practices and/or local practices
   c. carefully consider the situation and make your own judgement
   d. consult your supervisor
   e. check with the methods group
   f. ask anyone who has previously held your position

4. Good planning is important because it guarantees (X-out the *best* choice to complete the statement on the answer sheet):
   a. meeting objectives for your work or office
   b. subordinate productivity
   c. the availability of information to monitor the progress of a job
   d. that jobs are completed early or on schedule

5. What is the *best* way to ensure that a job is completed efficiently? (X-out the *best* answer on the answer sheet.)
   a. weighing alternatives carefully
   b. discussing plans with your supervisor
   c. preparing a detailed budget
   d. performing the job as in the past
   e. predetermining a course of action

6. It is *necessary* to plan when (X-out the *choice(s)* to complete the statement on the answer sheet):
   a. work is generated by your boss
   b. work is generated by other departments
   c. unanticipated events interfere with current plans
   d. job objectives are received from the boss
   e. you want to achieve personal objectives

7. When you are planning work for which there are no standards (e.g., no quantity or quality measurements), you must develop your own standards. (X-out T for True or F for False on the answer sheet.)

8. No information exists for planning a particular job you have been assigned. What should you do *next*? (X-out the correct answer on the answer sheet.)
   a. document your reasons for stopping the job
   b. go ahead as best you can
   c. consider data on similar types of jobs
   d. give the job back to the person who assigned it
   e. put the job aside and come back to it later

9. You have no information or limited information about a particular task. What are seven *sources* from which you can obtain relevant information? (List *seven* sources on the answer sheet.)

10. You have been given an unfamiliar task. What are eight kinds of information needed to plan the task? (List the *eight* kinds of information on the answer sheet.)

11. Your boss assigns a job to you. You investigate all possible sources of information. You still do not have enough information to plan the job. What should you do next? (Write your answer on the answer sheet.)

Diagnostic test exhibit B—answer sheet: Process 1—planning the work

1. a X c d X X X X
2. 1st __F__ 2nd __G__ 3rd __E__
   4th __H__ 5th __B__
3. a X c X e X
4. a b X d
5. a b c d X
6. X X X X X

7. X F
8. a b X d e
9. (1) BSP'S   (6) S.M.E.
   (2) SUBORDINATES   (7) BOSS
   (3) PRACTICES   (8) PRIOR INCUMBENT
   (4) HISTORICAL DATA (9) CUSTOMERS
   (5) PEERS   (10) METHODS/STAFF

10. (1) HOW LONG JOBS TOOK
    (2) WHAT RESOURCES WERE USED
    (3) TECH. COMPETENCY & TRAINING
        BACKGROUND OF SUBS.
    (4) UNUSUAL OBSTACLES
    (5) CONTINGENCIES TAKEN
    (6) OBJECTIVES-QUALITY, QUANTITY,
        TIME
    (7) TIME AVAILABLE
    (8) SOURCES OF INFORMATION ABOUT
        TASK
11. CONSULT YOUR BOSS ON HOW TO CONTINUE

Diagnostic test exhibit C—items tested by objective test: Process 1—planning the work

Test question number	Items tested		
	Skills	Knowledge	Process steps
1			2, 5,
2			6, 19, 20
3	S1	K4	
4		K1	
5		K3	
6		K5	
7		K7	
8		K11	
9		K10	
10	S3		
11		K12	

Diagnostic test exhibit D: List of skills and knowledge covered in each question in the simulation section of the diagnostic test

Question	Process	Flow chart step	Skills	Knowledge
1	Planning		S4	
2	Planning	5		
3	Planning		S5	
4	Planning		S5	
5	Planning			K17
6	Planning		S7	
6–1	Planning	12		
6–2	Planning			K24
7	Planning		S5	
8	Planning			K30
9	Controlling			K13
10	Controlling			K19
10–1	Planning		S9	
10–11	Controlling		S13	
11	Planning			K16
12	Planning			K19
13	Planning			K20
13–1	Planning			K20
13–2	Planning			K21, K26

Note: The Planning Simulation itself is not included in this presentation for the reasons cited on page 41.

6 Controlling the Work
PROCESS 2

A. OVERVIEW OF CONTROLLING AT THE SUPERVISORY LEVEL

Over the decades during which business management has developed into a professional discipline with its own unique body of knowledge, *control* has been one of management's major concerns. Enormous amounts of energy and effort have been expended in attempts to find the "one best" control system, one that could be superimposed on an organization of any size in almost any industry to provide instantaneous feedback and automatic correction of deviations. In recent years, the computer was thought to be the answer because of its incredible speed and enormous capability to store, process, and display data.

The search for a system solution or an electronic solution to the control problem, however, has been largely in vain. It has become increasingly clear that the answer to control of a process—whether a business process or any other—resides in people. And more often than not, this means *first-line supervisors.*

In most organizations that deal with a product—and in many that provide services—first-line managers are concerned with control of three major elements of operational control. These are:

1. *Control of the work flow.* This involves scheduling, routing, and dispatching work.

2. *Control of the material flow.* In addition to materials that go directly into the product, this involves tools, equipment, and supplies. Processes involved at one stage or another are shipping, receiving, procurement, materials handling and storage.

3. *Control of information flow.* This involves the recordkeeping and other paper work that must accompany the work and the materials.

The role of information in control

In any organization of people, information is the essence of control, although it is clearly subordinate to it. One can have information without control, but control without information is inconceivable. Thus the purpose of information is to facilitate control—and the information source must be work itself. It almost goes without saying that the better the information, the finer and more effective is your control.

This applies equally to the "external" kind of control that is imposed upon people—setting standards, checking actual performance against standards, and directing corrective action—and to the "internal" type of control in which subordinates regulate much of their own performance through self-control. In the first instance,' the supervisor assumes the role of inspector (inspection, observes Peter Drucker, is *not* control!). In the second approach, the supervisor becomes a provider of information, support, and guidance. Most authorities on management favor the second approach to control for supervisors.

Drucker, in fact, says that controlling the work means *control of the work, not control of the worker.*

This is not to imply, of course, that the supervisor does not have to *monitor* the activities of subordinates. Drucker states further that the question to ask about control is not how much control is needed, but how little. "What is the minimum of control needed to maintain the process?" is the right question to ask.[1]

[1]Peter F. Drucker, *Management* (New York: Harper & Row, 1973).

B. HIGHLIGHTS OF THE AT&T JOB STUDY

Definition of the process

In the AT&T Mastery Model, the process of Controlling the Work at the first supervisory level is defined as:

Applying the results of Planning the Work to the people who will be doing the work and to the materials they will use. This includes assigning the work, checking its progress, and measuring the work.

Summary description of the process

In its simplest terms the controlling duty is a process of implementing the plan. It begins with the obvious task of assigning the work to individuals. It should be noted that, while this is an "obvious" task, it is not necessarily an easy one; it requires knowledge of individuals' capabilities and skills, as well as a sensitivity to the needs and aspirations of individual members of

the work force. The supervisor then proceeds to review and log the status (progress) of the work at intervals against the checkpoints that are recorded on the Master Control List or similar control document.

Whenever the work is *not* progressing according to plan, the supervisor is required to utilize the Problem Solving process to remove the roadblocks to progress. (Problem Solving is discussed in the next chapter.) Similarly, should the completed work have to be redone because it fails to meet all output requirements, the Problem Solving process must also be used to identify and correct the causes of the failure to meet output requirements.

Finally, the supervisor is required to document all significant information about the work, for purposes of reference by self or others. This documentation may become the basis for future planning, performance appraisals, personnel information, possible legal or regulatory problems, etc.

C. TASKS AND DECISION POINTS IN THE PROCESS OF CONTROLLING THE WORK

STEP 1 Assign the work, guided by a control document such as a Master Control List.

STEP 2 Review the status of the work periodically against the control documents.

STEP 3 Record (log) the status of the work on the control document.

STEP 4 (Decision) Based on the comparison of actual progress with predetermined checkpoints on the control document, respond to the question: *Is the work progressing satisfactorily according to plan?*

If your decision is *yes,* continue the work and your periodic status reviews as in Step 2; bypass Steps 5 and 6 and go directly to Step 7. (If the work is *ahead of schedule,* or the work group is *exceeding* the work requirements, you should go back to the Planning process and replan the allocation of your resources in order to optimize their use.)

STEP 5 If your decision is *no*—the work is not progressing satisfactorily—you should turn to the Problem Solving process to help determine why this is so.

STEP 6
(Decision)
Respond to the question: *Was the problem resolved successfully?* If not, return to the Problem Solving process until either a successful solution is developed or the problem is deemed to be not solvable under present circumstances (in which case, document the situation and also notify the initiator of the work about the impasse).

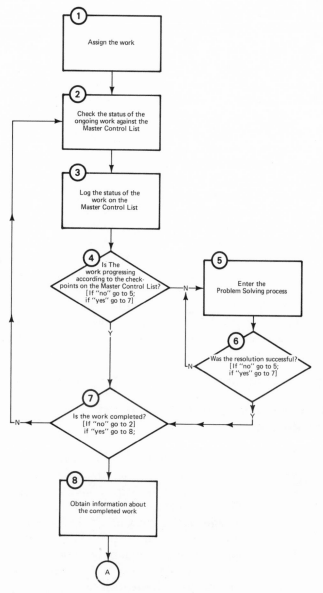

FIGURE 6-1. Controlling Process: Steps 1 through 8

STEP 7
(Decision)
Respond to the question: *Is the work completed?* This decision should be based on a comparison of the work with the final checkpoint on the Master Control, as well as by observation and inspection.

If your decision is *no*, return to Step 2 and continue to review status of the work. If your decision is *yes*, proceed to:

STEP 8
Obtain information from all appropriate knowledgeable sources as a preliminary to evaluating the completed work.

The flowchart in Figure 6-1 illustrates the Controlling process up to this point—Steps 1 through 8.

STEP 9
Evaluate the completed work by matching your information about the completed work with the output requirements of the work.

STEP 10
(Decision)
Respond to the question: *Does the completed work meet all output requirements?*

If your decision is *yes*, bypass the next four tasks and go directly to final Step 15 and document your findings and results.

If your answer is *no*—the completed work fails in some respects to meet all output requirements—then you are faced with another critical decision.

STEP 11
(Decision)
Respond to the question: *Must the work be redone?*

If your decision is *yes*, go to Step 13 and use the Problem Solving process for guidance in proceeding further.

If your decision is *no*—the work does not have to be redone, even though it fails to meet all output requirements—then your next task is to:

STEP 12
Determine causes of failure to meet output requirements. Once this is done, you can proceed to final Step 15 to document these and other findings and results, bypassing Steps 13 and 14.

STEP 13
If the work must be redone, you should turn to the Problem Solving process for guidance before proceeding further. After using this process, you should make the decision:

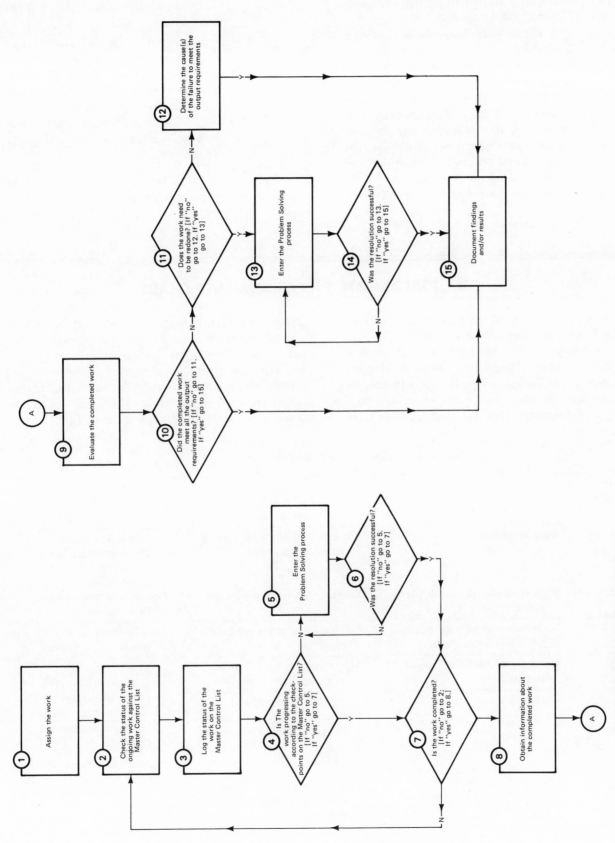

FIGURE 6–2. Controlling the Work: Total Process

STEP 14 (Decision) — Respond to the question: *Was the problem solution successful?*

If your decision is *yes,* document it in Step 15.

If your decision is *no,* return to Step 13 and re-enter the Problem Solving process until either a successful solution is obtained or the problem is deemed to be not solvable under present circumstances (in which case, document the situation and also notify the initiator of the work about the impasse).

STEP 15 — Document your findings and results.

This final task in Controlling the Work is done when:

the completed work meets all output requirements (Step 10); or

you have determined the specific factors that caused failure to meet output requirements (Step 12); or

you have successfully resolved the problem of redoing the work (Steps 11, 13, and 14).

The flowchart in Figure 6–2 illustrates the total process of Controlling the Work.

D. PERFORMANCE MEASUREMENTS CHART

The second ranking duty of the supervisor—Controlling the Work—involves nine tasks and six contingencies or decision points. For purposes of measuring performance, these 15 steps fall naturally into six principal *groups.* Table 6–1 lists the steps in each of the six groups, identifies the output of each group, shows the performance standards that apply to these outputs, and identifies the method used by second-level managers to measure the managerial performance of subordinate first-line supervisors.

These outputs, performance standards, and measurement methods were developed under the constraints recorded earlier in the discussion of performance measurement in Planning the Work.

Table 6–1. Process 2—controlling the work

Step or group of steps	*Output*	*Performance standards*	*Method of measurement*
Step 1	Work assigned	Subordinates of the supervisor know duties and responsibilities	Second-level boss receives few Union grievances or complaints from subordinates
	Work reassigned if unanticipated events occur	Overtime held to a minimum	Second-level boss reviews time reports
Steps 2, 3	Follow-up control maintained— work gets completed	Has information for instant reporting to boss	Second-level boss reviews timeliness of reports
Steps 4, 5	Problems solved if check point is missed	Solves own problems instead of going to the boss	Second-level boss receives few complaints in connection with completing work on time
Step 7	Work completed	Meets 95% of objectives Due dates deadlines met and job completed in alloted time	
Steps 8–14	Completed work evaluated, work redone when necessary	First-level supervisor knows why output requirements were missed	Second-level boss checks due dates and reviews objectives with first-level supervisor
Step 15	Results documented		

E. THE AT&T MASTERY MODEL—CONTROLLING THE WORK

In the AT&T Mastery Model for first-level supervision, the process of Controlling the Work is composed of 15 steps, nine tasks and six contingencies or decision points. Each of these steps is described in the following pages, together with the specific skills and knowledge required to master each. Listed first are three *fundamentals of management* that apply to Controlling.

Fundamental skills and knowledge required

Knowledge Required	K1	Controlling the Work is a process of achieving the designated output requirements by: 1. implementing the items on the Master Control List, 2. checking progress of work, 3. keeping work on schedule, 4. completing work, 5. evaluating completed work, and 6. documenting work.
	K2	This process is necessary for the effective use of resources in achieving output requirements.
	K3	You must first have a good plan.

Step 1—Assign the Work

Knowledge Required	K4	Know to assign work according to the Master Control List developed in Planning Step 19.
	K5	If modifications to output requirements or changes in assignments occur, they should be noted on the Master Control List.
	K6	If modifications or changes cannot be made, reassign work so that output requirements are met.
	K7	Handle reassignments of tasks by using steps from Planning, beginning with Step 6.
Skill Required	S1	This task requires skill to determine the best way to inform subordinates of the work to be done. Use the appropriate communication process, as follows:

1. Assign work orally if assignment is new or complicated, or if subordinate is new to the work.
2. Communicate what has to be done, why, when, and to what quantity and quality standards. If different from standard operating procedure, explain why the work is to be done the way described.
3. Ensure that assignment is understood by questioning subordinate, or by having assignment fed back by subordinate.
4. Ask if there is any information that might change the output requirements or modify the assignment (for example, vacation conflict with work schedule).
5. For regular routine assignments, use normal communication means—bulletin board, work assignment schedules.

Step 2—Check Status of Ongoing Work Against Master Control List

Skills Required	S2	You need skill to detect discrepancies in the Master Control List and to discern patterns which, if continued, may result in missed output requirements.
	S3	Observe actual work of subordinates; single out for attention the most critical work, the work of less experienced people, and the work of those whose past performance was unsatisfactory.
	S4	Offer improvement suggestions, and reinforce effective work with positive comments (praise) when appropriate.

Knowledge Required	K8	Know to make yourself available to subordinates who have questions or need help.
	K9	There may be a mandated way to check progress of the work, such as official measurements.
	K10	Arrangements should be made in your absence either to reschedule the observation or to have another supervisor check the work.
	K11	Information about the work can be provided by customers.
	K12	Your subordinates can report on status of on-going work.

Step 3—Log Status of Work on the Master Control List

Skill Required	S5	This task requires skill to enter onto the Master Control List (MCL) the required information on progress to schedule, work quality, roadblocks encountered, potential roadblocks.
Knowledge Required	K13	Know to log the work status, checkpoints attained, etc., according to the MCL format.
	K14	Know to have items logged after they are checked, either by yourself or by a delegated subordinate.
	K15	The MCL should be kept accessible to your boss, subordinates, peers.
	K16	Keep others informed as to where the MCL is kept.

Step 4—Decision Point: Is the Work Progressing According to the Checkpoints on the Master Control List?

Skill Required	S6	This decision requires skill to determine the progress of the work by comparing the status with the checkpoints on the MCL.
Knowledge Required	K17	If the work is proceeding satisfactorily according to this review, keep the work going and continue to check its status.
	K18	If your work group is attaining

or exceeding the work requirements ahead of schedule, go back to Planning Step 1 and replan the allocation of your resources.

| | K19 | If any checkpoint is not met, use the Problem Solving process. |

If your decision is *yes,* bypass Steps 5 and 6 and go directly to Step 7.

Step 5—Enter the Problem Solving Process

If your decision is *no*—the work is not progressing according to the checkpoints on the MCL—then your next task is to use the Problem Solving process.

Knowledge Required	K20	Know that the Problem Solving process should be used, entering at "Define the Problem."
	K21	If the problem, *as defined above,* affects meeting the output requirements, you should continue the Problem Solving process. If it does not, proceed to Step 7.
	K22	When a possible solution cannot be developed within the Problem Solving process, document the circumstances surrounding the defined problem, the problem itself, and the impact on output requirements. You should also know that the source or initiator of the work should be notified about the situation.

Step 6—Decision Point: Was the Problem Resolution Successful? If Your Decision Is Yes, *Go to Step 7; If No, Return to Step 5 and Re-enter the Problem-Solving Process.*

Step 7—Decision Point: Is the Work Completed?

If your decision is *yes,* go to Step 8; if *no,* return to Step 2 and recheck the status of the work against the Master Control List.

| Skill Required | S7 | This decision requires skill to determine if the work is completed |

by comparing status of the work with the final checkpoint on the MCL.

Knowledge Required	K23	Know that you can learn about the final status of work by querying your boss, peers, subordinates, printouts, etc.

Step 8—Obtain Information about the Completed Work

Skills Required	S8	This task requires skill to gather information about the completed work from peers, customers, subordinates, boss, printouts, etc.
	S9	Determine whether the completed work meets all requirements by collecting all possible data about quantity, quality, time frames, etc.
Knowledge Required	K24	This data will serve as reference for similar work in the future; as basis for estimates, for example.
	K25	The output of this step may be an input to giving Feedback or Career Counseling (see later chapters).
	K26	Someone other than you can gather the required information.
	K27	Local procedures may prescribe how to acquire information about completed work.
	K28	On-site observations may be necessary.
	K29	Complaints about quality of work could result from delay in doing this task.

Step 9—Evaluate the Completed Work

Skill Required	S10	This task requires skill to compare the results of Step 8 with output requirements to determine whether each output requirement was met.
Knowledge Required	K30	Criteria for evaluating work may be contained in company or local procedures.
	K31	It may be necessary to observe only a sample portion of the total work in some cases.

	K32	If you can't evaluate the work, ask others to do it for you (peers or boss).

Step 10—Decision Point: Does the Completed Work Meet All Output Requirements? If Yes, Bypass the Next Four Tasks and Go Directly to Step 15.

Step 11—Decision Point: If Your Decision Is No—the Completed Work Does Not Meet All Output Requirements—then You Should Ask Yourself the Question: Does the Work Need to Be Redone?

If your answer to this question is *yes*, skip Step 12 and go to Step 13.

Knowledge Required	K33	In order to make this decision, you need to *know the criteria* for determining whether work must be redone, such as, for example:

customer complaint
negative impact on objectives of your boss
safety hazard
negative impact on results of another work group
item does not work
minimum technical requirements were not met
mandate from your boss
your own objectives were not met

Skill Required	S11	Based on the above criteria, you need skill to determine whether the work must be redone.

Step 12—Determine Causes of Failure to Meet Output Requirements

If your decision was *no* on Step 11—that is, the work does not have to be redone—then your next task is to identify the factors that caused you not to meet output requirements, so they may be documented.

Skill Required	S12	This task requires skill to identify the specific factors that caused failure to meet output requirements, such as unanticipated

roadblock, absenteeism, illness, weather, equipment failure, subordinate lacked needed skill or knowledge, etc.

After completing this task, you should go to final Step 15 and document findings and results.

Step 13—Enter the Problem-Solving Process

| Knowledge Required | K34 | If your decision in Step 11 was *yes*—the work must be redone—then you should *know* to use the Problem Solving process, entering at "Define the Problem" and exiting after "Implementation." |

Step 14—Decision Point: Was the Problem Solution Successful? *If Your Decision Is Yes, Document It In Step 15; If Not, Return to Step 13 and Re-enter the Problem-Solving Process*

Step 15—Document Findings and Results

This final task in Controlling the Work is done when either (1) the completed work meets all output requirements (see Step 10), (2) you have determined the specific factors that caused failure to meet output requirements (see Step 12), or (3) you have successfully resolved the problem of redoing the work (see Steps 11, 13, and 14).

Knowledge Required	K35	You should *know* to provide feedback if appropriate.
	K36	Documented information may serve many purposes, such as: basis for future planning, appraisals, coaching, counseling, etc. evidence in case of legal problem personnel information
Skill Required	S13	This task requires skill to document findings and results on the MCL, or in accordance with local procedures and practices.

Flowchart of the total process of controlling the work

A flowchart depicting the flow of all tasks and contingency points in this process is given in Figure 6-2. To help put the total process into perspective, it may be useful to refer to that chart at this point.

F. TRAINING NEEDS DIAGNOSTIC

The diagnostic test for Controlling is in two sections: an *objective test* intended to test knowledge of the process, and a *role play* designed to test interpersonal and behavioral skills in applying the process.

Objective test

The objective test of 22 questions is designed to test nine controlling skills and 21 items of controlling knowledge at the first level of supervision. The test questions and answers can be found in Exhibits A and B. The specific skills and knowledge tested by the 22 questions are shown in Exhibit C.

Role play

Included in the diagnostic test is a Role Play section designed to test the behavioral and interpersonal skills and knowledge of first-level supervisors in performing the duties of:

communicating informally by word
providing performance feedback
coaching a subordinate
communicating by writing
controlling the work

The specific task tested by the Controlling part of the Role Play is Controlling *Step 1—Assign the Work.* The specific *skill* tested is *S1—Skill to determine the best way to inform the subordinate about the work to be done;* that is—

what has to be done,
why it has to be done, and
how well it has to be done

and to check for understanding by the subordinate.

Simulation

In addition to the objective test and the role play, the diagnostic test includes a simulation designed principally to test *planning* skills. As noted in the chapter on Planning the Work (Section F, Diagnostic Test), this exercise also tested the subject's skill in documenting findings and results on the Master Control List (S13); knowledge in logging status of work against planning checkpoints (K13); and knowledge in using the Problem Solving process if a checkpoint is not met (K19). (See note on page 56.)

Diagnostic test exhibit A: Process No. 2—controlling the work

This section deals with the Controlling process. When Controlling the work, you apply the results of Planning to the people who will be doing the work and to the materials they will use. Controlling includes assigning the work, checking its progress, and measuring the work.

1. In assigning work, what are the three most important factors to consider about a subordinate? (X-out the *three* most important factors on the answer sheet.)
    a. availability
    b. attitude
    c. current work load
    d. competency level
    e. energy level
    f. leadership qualities
2. If situations occur while work is underway that require changing or modifying assignments, what are the two most *important* actions to take? (X-out the *two* most important actions on the answer sheet.)
    a. reassign the work
    b. tell your boss that changes must be made
    c. postpone the work
    d. modify plans to accomplish the work
    e. notify the persons affected that the job will be delayed
3. In the situations listed below, select the communication method (Oral or Written) that is usually more effective for assigning work to subordinates. (X-out the correct answer(s) on the answer sheet.)

	Situations	Methods	
1.	routine job to experienced subordinate	Oral	Written
2.	unfamiliar assignment to new subordinate	Oral	Written
3.	complicated new assignment to experienced subordinate	Oral	Written

4. What are the three most *important* items to communicate in assigning *routine* work? (X-out the *three* items on the answer sheet.)
    a. who did the job previously
    b. what has to be done
    c. how well it must be done
    d. what resources are needed
    e. who has to do it
    f. when it is to be completed
5. In question 4 you identified the three most important items to communicate in assigning routine work. In addition to those items, what are the *four* most *important* other items you would communicate in assigning *nonroutine* work? (Write your *four* answers on the answer sheet.)
6. After assigning work to a subordinate, what are the two most *important* pieces of information to obtain from the subordinate? (X-out the *two best* choices to complete the statement on the answer sheet.) Determine whether the subordinate:
    a. has information that affects the completion of the assignment

    b.   knows how the completion of the assignment affects other work groups
    c.   understands the assignment
    d.   knows how the work has been done in the past
    e.   understands the value of the work
    f.   accepts the assignment

7. A Master Control List contains your plan for accomplishing work and information about the progress of work. From the items below, what are the four most *important* items to be entered on the Master Control List when work is being monitored? (X-out the *four* correct answers on the answer sheet.)
    a.   subordinate's attitude towards the work
    b.   how long the job is taking
    c.   quality checks on work done
    d.   your boss's comments
    e.   roadblocks encountered that may lead to missed objectives
    f.   inputs from other first-level supervisors
    g.   quantity of work done
    h.   requests by coordinates for future work

8. Half of your work group finished its task significantly ahead of schedule. The other half of your work group is proceeding on schedule. The first thing to do is to check with other supervisors to see if they need any help. (X-out T for True or F for False on the answer sheet.)

9. You evaluated a completed job. But it did not meet all objectives. What should you do *next*? (Write your answer on the answer sheet.)

10. What is the most probable consequence of *not* promptly gathering data about completed work? (Write your answer on the answer sheet.)

11. What is the best way of *evaluating* completed work? (X-out the *best* answer on the answer sheet.)
    a.   Compare finished work to your own standards developed over the years.
    b.   Compare the results of the work against job requirements.
    c.   Compare work results against Company practices or local procedures.

12. Because of the time demands on a first-level supervisor, it is usually not necessary to document a subordinate's results. (X-out T for True or F for False on the answer sheet.)

13. What is the most important reason for gathering information on completed work? (X-out your answer on the answer sheet.)
    a.   because it is requested by your boss or organization
    b.   since all the requirements of the job were not met
    c.   to determine whether the work met job requirements

14. Before implementing your own methods for checking the work, you should always determine whether there are mandated methods. (X-out T for True or F for False on the answer sheet.)

15. A Master Control List contains your plan for accomplishing work and information about the progress of work. What are the two most *important* things to do in using a Master Control List? (X-out the *two* correct answers on the answer sheet.)
    a.   Keep the List in an accessible place for those needing to consult it.
    b.   Log the progress of items after they have been checked.
    c.   Keep copies of filled-out List for your records.
    d.   Forward copies of filled-out List to your boss.

16. What are four uses for data gathered about *completed* work? (Write your *four* answers on the answer sheet.)

17. If the work is not progressing as scheduled, the first thing you should do is notify your boss as soon as possible because results may worsen if the situation is not corrected. (X-out T for True or F for False on the answer sheet.)

18. When your time is limited, check only the work that is considered more critical and the work of less experienced subordinates. (X-out T for True or F for False on the answer sheet.)

19. What are three sources of information about the status or quality of a subordinate's work? (Write your *three* answers on the answer sheet.)

20. If a subordinate is given detailed directions for completing an assignment, you need not be available later for the subordinate's questions about the work. (X-out T for True or F for False on the answer sheet.)

21. You have received the following letter from a customer:

    Installation Supervisor:
    One of your people recently installed a phone in my
    living room. The wires were not installed the way
    they should have been. Fix them!
    A Customer

    Which should you do *first*? (X-out the correct answer on the answer sheet.)
    a. Write a letter to the customer explaining why the job was done the way it was.
    b. Have the work re-done to the customer's satisfaction.
    c. Call and ask the customer to describe the problem.
    d. Ask the person who installed the phone why Bell System Practice was not followed.

22. If you are unable to make a scheduled observation of a subordinate's work, what are the two *best* ways to handle this situation? (X-out the *two* best ways on the answer sheet.)
    a. Reschedule the observation to an appropriate time.
    b. Ask your most experienced subordinate to do it for you.
    c. Ask another supervisor or your boss to do it for you.
    d. Document in detail why the observation could not be made.

Diagnostic test exhibit B—answer sheet: Process 2—controlling the work

1. ⊠ b ⊠ ⊠ e f
2. ⊠ b c ⊠ e
3. (1) oral ~~written~~
   (2) ~~oral~~ *~~written~~
   (3) ~~oral~~ *~~written~~
   *written *alone* is incorrect
4. a ⊠ c d ⊠ ⊠
5. (1) WHY THE WORK MUST BE DONE
   (2) HOW THE WORK MUST BE DONE
   (3) WHY THE WORK MUST BE DONE IN THE DESCRIBED MANNER
   (4) HOW WELL THE WORK MUST BE DONE
6. ⊠ b ⊠ d e f
7. a ⊠ ⊠ d ⊠ f ⊠ h
8. T ⊠
9. DETERMINE THE CAUSES OF THE FAILURE
10. COMPLAINTS/CUSTOMER/PUC/ETC.
11. a ⊠ c
12. T ⊠
13. a b ⊠
14. ⊠ F
15. ⊠ ⊠ c d
16. (1) TO EVALUATE THE WORK   (4) REFERENCE FOR FUTURE PLANNING
    (2) FEEDBACK TO SUBORDINATE   (5) COACHING (TRAINING)
    (3) CAREER COUNSELING OF SUBORDINATE
17. T ⊠
18. ⊠ F
19. (1) OWN OBSERVATIONS   (4) CONSUMERS/CUSTOMERS
    (2) SUBORDINATE'S SELF REPORT   (5) BOSS
    (3) PEERS   (6) MEASUREMENT PLANS/INDEXES
20. T ⊠
21. a b ⊠ d
22. ⊠ b ⊠ d

Diagnostic test exhibit C—Items tested by objective test: process 2—controlling the work

| Test question number | Items tested | | Process steps |
	Skills	Knowledge	
1	S1	K4[*]	
2		K5, K6, K7	
3	S1		
4	S1		
5	S1		
6	S1		
7	S5		
8		K18	
9	S12		
10		K29	
11	S10		
12	S13		
13	S9		
14		K9, K27	
15		K14, K15	
16	S9, S11	K24, K25, K36	
17		K19	
18	S3		
19	S8	K11, K12, K23, K26	
20		K8	
21	S11	K33	
22		K10	

[*]Also tests Planning Knowledge K30.

Note: The Role Play and Simulation sections of the AT&T Diagnostic Test are not included here because (1) they are highly specific to Bell System work practices and (2) they are quite lengthy. The guidance given on pages 52 and 53 should enable an experienced training development manager to develop role plays and simulations specific to his or her organization and circumstances.

7 Problem Solving

PROCESS 3

A. OVERVIEW OF PROBLEM SOLVING AT THE SUPERVISORY LEVEL

Some textbooks on supervisory management tend to combine problem solving with decision making. Schoen and Durand, in *Supervision: The Management of Organizational Resources,*[1] list these five critical steps in their discussion of "decision-making and problem-solving methods":

1. Define the problem.
2. Gather information and develop alternatives.
3. Determine the anticipated positive and negative consequences of each alternative.
4. Select the alternative with the most positive—or least negative—consequences.
5. Determine any new problems resulting from implementing the chosen alternative.

This list is expanded to eight decision-making steps by Eckles, Carmichael, and Sarchet in their *Essentials of Management for First-Line Supervisors.*[2]

[1]Schoen and Durand, *Supervision: The Management of Organizational Resources* (Englewood Cliffs, N. J.: Prentice-Hall, Inc., 1979), p. 200.
[2]Eckles, Carmichael, and Sarchet, *Essentials of Management for First-Line Supervisors* (New York: Wiley & Sons, Inc., 1974), p. 201.

In a chapter titled "Decision-Making and the Supervisory Function," they define decision making as "the process of choosing a course of action designed to solve a specific problem. . . ." To the above basic five steps, they recommend that the first-level supervisor add these three steps:

- Identify the key uncertainties surrounding the problem as defined
- Estimate the value of each workable solution
- Follow up on action taken

It is obvious that both of these approaches to decision making are structured processes for resolving problems.

Schoen and Durand recommend an approach to problem solving that requires the supervisor to think *creatively* first, then to apply *critical judgment* to the alternative solutions surfaced through creative thinking. They describe this as the "principle of suspended judgment," and cite research that showed that the suspension of evaluation or judgment from the process of alternatives development produced twice as many useful ideas as compared with those obtained when judgment was allowed "to jam the imagination." What is more, they state, when *more* ideas are produced, the *quality* of the solutions tends to be higher. This accounts for the popularity of "brainstorming" as an approach to group problem solving.

AT&T employed this principle and process very successfully in a series of *job enrichment* experiments conducted throughout the Bell System in the late 1960s by Robert N. Ford. In his book, *Motivation Through The Work Itself*,[3] Ford describes the brainstorming meetings held to identify opportunities for enriching people's jobs as "green light" sessions. Participants were encouraged to think creatively (green light ideas), and to suspend judgment (red stop lights) in order to produce a long list of prospective ways in which a given job might be enriched. The output of this technique—and the results of the program—were gratifying. Some of the then radical job enrichment changes made in Bell System jobs are now accepted as normal parts of a person's job.

Eckles, Carmichael, and Sarchet have analyzed the problems first-level supervisors must deal with into three basic types:

- Routine or systematized problems on which a predetermined solution is devised that can be repeated whenever the problem surfaces. The critical factor here is accurate identification of the problem.

- Individualized or nonroutine problems encountered in day-to-day work and which affect the work group, individual workers, material to be used, etc.

- New problems that cannot be anticipated. These are less frequent; they usually require the greatest ingenuity on the part of the supervisor to resolve.

[3]Robert N. Ford, *Motivation Through the Work Itself* (New York: American Management Association, 1969).

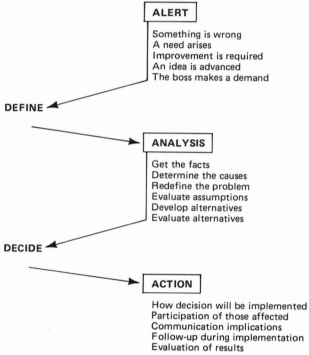

FIGURE 7–1. **The Anatomy of a Decision**

The first two types of problems are the kind first-level supervisors encounter most often. It should be noted that few problem solutions are final. Most solutions contain the seeds of new problems; the capability of supervisors is tested by their ability to anticipate and provide for them in their decisions.

Bradford Boyd, in *Management-Minded Supervision*,[4] sheds some light on the decision-making and problem-solving process with a neat little schematic diagram that he entitles "The Anatomy of a Decision." It is reproduced here with permission (see Figure 7–1).

[4]Bradford Boyd, *Management-Minded Supervision* (New York: McGraw-Hill, 1968).

B. HIGHLIGHTS OF THE AT&T JOB STUDY

Definition of the process

In the AT&T first-level Mastery Model, problem solving is defined as "a process used by a supervisor to solve day-to-day problems while managing the work."

Problem solving, by this definition, cuts across the boundaries of all other supervisory activities, from planning and controlling the work to conducting meetings. This requires the supervisor, whenever a serious roadblock or critical problem arises, to depart from the steps in the particular process being employed at the moment and enter the problem-solving process. Conceivably, the supervisor will do this without being conscious that he or she is interrupting the planning, or the controlling, or the communication process. Because of its primary focus on day-to-day activities, problem solving is most concerned with controlling the work; that is, the day-to-day carrying out of the tasks that are first planned and then assigned.

The importance of this process—and the frequency with which it is used—accounts for its being ranked *third* on the list of supervisory duties. The need for training in this critical process is imperative.

Summary description of the process

The process consists of first determining the source of the problem and defining it, using *facts* to the maximum extent (and identifying data that may be only inference, assumption, or opinion). Next, the supervisor is required to seek a standard operating procedure (SOP) to resolve the problem. If none exists, a process of gathering and sorting out information about the problem follows.

From this organized data, a range of possible solutions is then listed. Judgment is applied to this list in order to select the solutions with the most beneficial, or least harmful, effects on the work and the organization.

The selected solution is then implemented. (If it does not work, the supervisor is directed to go back to "square one"—Define the Problem—and recycle the process.) The process ends with a documentation of the problem solution, if required by circumstances or company procedure. Custom or standard practice may also require the supervisor to notify people involved—the boss, customers, colleagues—about the solution.

C. PROBLEM SOLVING TASKS AND DECISION POINTS

STEP 1   You must first determine that a stimulus exists to solve a problem, such as a serious failure to meet objectives, an equipment malfunction, or the like.

STEP 2   Next you have to define the problem—sorting out facts from inference, assumption, and opinion.

STEP 3 (Decision)   Now respond to the question: *Does a standard operating procedure (SOP) exist to solve the problem?*

If your decision is *no,* go to Step 5.

STEP 4 (Decision)   Respond to the question: *Is the SOP appropriate to use at this time?*

If your decision is *yes,* bypass the next five steps and go directly to Step 10 and implement the solution.

STEP 5   If your answer is *no*—either the SOP does not exist or it is not appropriate to use at this time—then your next task is to identify sources of information about the problem.

STEP 6   After you have identified as many sources as are feasible, determine which ones to use.

STEP 7   Obtain the data. In the absence of data you may be required to make assumptions.

STEP 8   Formulate possible solutions, using the information obtained in Step 7.

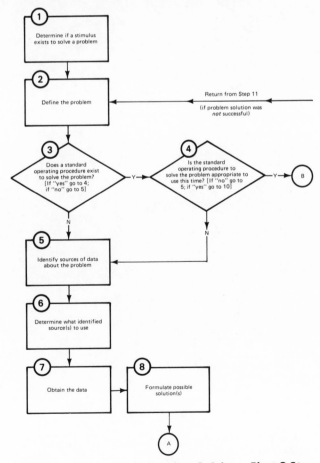

FIGURE 7-2. Process 3: Problem Solving—First 8 Steps

STEP 9   Determine the best solution, considering the pros and cons of each possible solution.

STEP 10   Implement the selected solution.

STEP 11 (Decision)   Now respond to the question: *Was the problem solution successful?* Did it resolve the question as defined in step 2?

      If your decision is *no,* return to Step 2 and redefine the problem.

STEP 12   Determine whether it is necessary to document the solution (and whether the source of the stimulus should be informed about the solution).

STEP 13 (Decision)   Respond to the questions: *Is documentation necessary? Should the source of the stimulus be informed?*

      If your decision is *yes,* go to Step 15 and complete this task as directed.

STEP 14   End the problem-solving process.

STEP 15   Document the solution and inform the source of the stimulus as and if required by custom or local procedure.

Figure 7–3 illustrates the complete process of problem solving at the first-level of supervision.

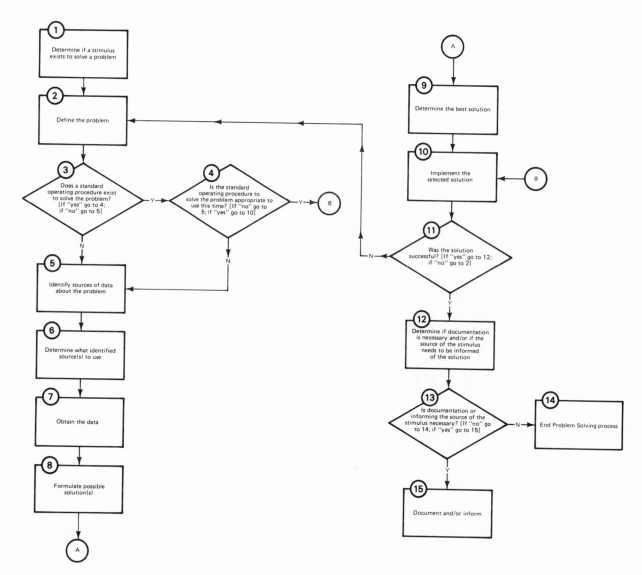

FIGURE 7–3. Flowchart of the Total Problem-Solving Process

D. PERFORMANCE MEASUREMENTS CHART

For measuring performance of the first-level supervisor in problem solving, the 15 major tasks involved in the managerial process have been grouped into seven categories. Table 7-1 shows the steps in each group, identifies the output of each group, shows the performance standards that apply to each output, and identifies the method used by second-level managers to measure the managerial performance of subordinate first-level supervisors.

Table 7-1. Process 3: Problem Solving

Step or group of steps	Output	Performance standards	Method of measurement
Steps 1, 2	Determination made that a problem exists Problem is defined	Supervisor does not defer solving problems Clear definition of problem	
Steps 3, 4	Decisions made in accordance with standard operating procedures	Makes decisions immediately if information is available	
Steps 5, 6, 7	Information obtained to solve problem	Seeks solutions from all sources before coming to boss Makes own decisions Goes to full limit of authority to solve problems	Second-level boss observes that problems are solved, observes that work continues as problems are solved, and does not receive complaints from other departments, etc. about problems not being solved
Steps 8, 9	Solutions selected so that output requirements are met	Solves problems with minimal effect on the workload Solves problems with minimal disruptions Explores consequences of decisions	
Step 10	Solution implemented that will meet output requirements or is acceptable if all output requirements cannot be met	Boss concurs with solution Presents second-level boss with solutions and alternatives	
Step 11	Problem is solved	Resolves problems consistently	
Steps 12–15	When necessary, the solution is documented and sources informed	Communicates solutions to peers and boss	

E. THE AT&T MASTERY MODEL—PROBLEM SOLVING

Problem solving is a complex managerial process that involves 15 steps—11 tasks and four contingencies or decision points. Each of these steps is described in the following, together with the specific skills and knowledge required to master each. Shown first are the three *fundamentals of management* that apply to Problem Solving at the first supervisory level.

Fundamental skills and knowledge required

Knowledge Required	K1	A first-level supervisor is expected to solve problems.
	K2	Postponing the solving of a problem may lead to more problems.
	K3	Problem solving is an algorith-

mic approach that will ensure a rational outcome or conclusion to identified problems.

Step 1—Determine If a Stimulus Exists to Solve a Problem

Skill Required	S1	This task requires skill to determine that a problem exists based on: input from boss, user of services, customers objectives not met budget regulatory situations situations affecting personnel or services situations affecting productivity/ measurements equipment malfunction union grievances other managerial duties, etc.

Step 2—Define the Problem

Skills Required	S2	To define a problem by considering such elements as: seriousness of the problem how soon the problem must be resolved impact on own future work results impact on others' future work results causes of the problem whether there still is a problem to be resolved whether the problem still needs to be resolved by asking the following questions: who, what, where, how, why, when, how much, how often.
	S3	To identify, in defining a problem, what is fact, what is inference, what is assumption.
	S4	When defining problems, to rely on data about the problem according to the following hierarchy: 1. facts 2. inferences 3. assumptions

Step 3—Decision Point: Does a Standard Operating Procedure (SOP) Exist to Solve the Problem?

Knowledge Required	K4	Know that there may be standard practices or procedures that contain the solution to the problem (e.g., company policies or practices, union contract, equipment manuals, etc.)
	K5	If it cannot be determined whether a standard operating procedure exists, treat this case as a *no,* and go to Step 5.

If your decision is *yes,* go to Step 4; if *no,* go to Step 5.

Step 4—Decision Point: Is the Standard Operating Procedure to Solve the Problem Appropriate to Use at This Time?

Skill Required	S5	This decision requires skill to determine if the solution to the problem is contained in the SOP.
Knowledge Required	K6	Know that this step can lead to three possible outcomes: 1. that the SOP is appropriate; 2. you have been through the process already and determined the first time that the SOP was appropriate, but the solution was unsuccessful; 3. that the SOP is appropriate, but does not contain the solution to the problem; e.g., a computer run halts ahead of schedule. A computer run book contains the appropriate SOP, but does not contain the action to take for that halt.

If your decision is *yes,* bypass Steps 5 through 9 and go directly to Step 10.

Step 5—Identify Sources of Information about the Problem

If your answer to Step 3 or Step 4 was *no*—an SOP either does not exist or is not appropriate to use at this time—then you should identify sources of information about the problem.

Skills Required	S6	Determine the sources of information based on the stimulus or definition of the problem (e.g., a union problem may mean that the labor relations staff is a data source). Computer problem data sources might be computer vendor, programmer, computer print-outs, computer operator, etc.
	S7	You need skill to solve problems within the limits of your own authority. Use the boss as a resource sparingly, because your boss expects you to learn and develop by struggling with the problem and making your own decisions. However, at times (short time frames or due dates), it may be prudent to consult the boss as a resource.
Knowledge Required	K7	The data source may be yourself.
	K8	The boss should be used as a resource only after all other sources of information have been consulted.

Step 6—Determine What Identified Source(s) to Use

Skill Required	S8	Determine the feasibility of obtaining data from sources based on time, money, people needed to get the data, usefulness of data, how current the data are, etc.
Knowledge Required	K9	Know to use as many sources identified in Step 5 as feasible; that is, if three sources are identified and are readily available, use all three.

Step 7—Obtain the Data

Knowledge Required	K10	Know that if in Step 3 you could not determine whether an **SOP** existed, the information obtained in Step 7 may tell you whether there is one. If so, go back to Step 4.

	K11	The data sources determined to be used in Step 6 may not be available when the data are actually to be obtained. If so, sources identified as not feasible to use in Step 6 may need to be used. You may need to be a data source yourself; that is, you may have to make *assumptions* in order to formulate solutions.

Step 8—Formulate Possible Solution(s)

Skill Required	S9	This task requires skill to formulate within known constraints (budget, amount of equipment available, numbers of people available, etc.), possible solutions using the information obtained in Step 7.
Knowledge Required	K12	A general solution might be a combination of individual solutions.

Step 9—Determine the Best Solution

Skills Required	S10	This task requires skill to determine possible solution based on the original purpose in problem solving; effects of the solution on quality of work, labor relations, customer relations, boss; feasibility and practicability of implementation, etc.
	S11	This task also requires skill to consider the pros and cons and the positive and negative consequences of each solution. For example, the objective is to complete a job in 10 days with no overtime, possible solutions are: with available manpower, complete the job in 15 days and no overtime, or in 10 days with 40 hours overtime, or complete the job in 10 days with additional borrowed manpower which will negatively impact your productivity index.

Step 10—Implement the Selected Solution

Knowledge Required | K13 | Before some solutions may be implemented, it may be necessary to inform the boss (e.g., a solution will negatively impact the budget, a service index, etc.).

K14 | If the boss rejects a solution because of the negative impact, present alternative solutions developed in Step 8.

K15 | If no solutions are acceptable, but the boss changes the objectives, return to Step 2.

K16 | If no solutions are acceptable and the boss does not change the objectives, work through the Problem Solving process with the boss.

Skill Required | S12 | You need skill to work through roadblocks that may be encountered in implementing the solution.

Step 11—Decision Point: Was the Solution Successful?

Skill Required | S13 | This requires skill to determine if the solution solved the problem as defined in Step 2. If your decision is *no*, return to Step 2 and redefine the problem.

Step 12—Determine if Documentation Is Necessary and/or if the Source of the Stimulus Needs to Be Informed of the Solution

Skill Required | S14 | This task requires skill to make the determination to document the solution, or to inform the source about the resolution. This determination should be based on:
Local procedure
Request by the stimulus
Need to enter solution data on Master Control List
Anticipation of future similar problems
Possible union grievance
Impact of the problem's solution on self, own work force, own objectives, organization

Step 13—Decision Point: Is Documentation or Informing the Source of the Stimulus Necessary? If No, Go to Step 14; If Yes, Go to Step 15.

Step 14—End of Problem Solving Process

Step 15—Document and/or Inform

Knowledge Required | K17 | Know to document and/or inform according to the requirements and formats discovered in Step 12.

F. TRAINING NEEDS DIAGNOSTIC

This is an *objective test* of nine questions, designed principally to test first-level supervisors' knowledge of the problem-solving *process*; that is, understanding of the sequence of tasks and decision points involved in solving problems.

The objective test questions also test *skill* in determining whether and how to document the problem solution (S14); *knowledge* that postponing the

solution of a problem may lead to more problems (K2); and *knowledge* to document and/or inform about the solution (K17).

The questions and answers follow in Exhibits A and B. The specific skills, knowledges, and process steps tested by the nine questions are shown in Exhibit C.

Diagnostic test exhibit A: process 3—problem solving

Problem Solving is the process used to solve day-to-day problems while managing the work.

1. What will most probably happen if you delay solving a problem? (X-out the correct answer on the answer sheet.)
    a. negative feedback from your boss
    b. the problem will go away
    c. more problems
    d. complaints from other work groups
2. The Benefit Group you supervise is having problems because of excess paperwork and duplicate record keeping. Your boss anticipates an increase in the group's work load. The boss asks you to decrease the time required to process a typical claim. You solve the problem.
    a. Would you document how you solved the problem?
    b. Explain your answer.
    (Write your answer on the answer sheet.)
3. The bidding procedure for obtaining safety gloves for line technicians is not working. Gloves are of unreliable quality, costs are too high, and deliveries of gloves are late. Your boss asks you to develop a new method of obtaining the gloves. Listed below are ten possible steps. Identify the five steps that would lead to a *better method* for obtaining gloves. (X-out the *five* steps on the answer sheet.)
    a. Select information sources that will give you information about costs, quality, and prompt delivery.
    b. Find out where you might get data about new methods of obtaining gloves.
    c. Call your coordinate in a nearby Bell Company to learn how they buy gloves.
    d. Ask your co-workers how to find out about buying gloves.
    e. Decide how to obtain gloves, weighing such factors as costs, quality, reliability of delivery.
    f. Rank ways to obtain gloves by convenience and by similarity to past successful procedures.
    g. Locate information about the old method of obtaining gloves.
    h. Obtain necessary information about possible new methods of obtaining gloves.
    i. Prioritize methods of buying gloves as determined by quality, cost, and reliability of delivery.
    j. Present your boss with all your research to see what he or she wants to do.
4. *Sequence* your *five* choices from question 3 in the order in which they should be performed to develop a better method for obtaining gloves. (Write the letter of each step you selected from 3 in the correct order on the answer sheet.)
5. A subordinate had a performance problem with some coin phone repair tasks. You determined the solution was further Coin Phone Repair training at the Repair School. Which of the following is the *best* means of determining whether the solution was successful? (X-out the correct answer on the answer sheet.)
    a. Your boss quits complaining about the subordinate's phone repair work.
    b. The work group's Coin Phone Repair results improve.
    c. The plant school asks the subordinate to return and demonstrate coin phone repair to students.
    d. You discuss what the subordinate learned at the school about Coin Phone Repair with the subordinate.
    e. When the subordinate next repairs a coin phone, you check the work.
6. You are a first-level supervisor. It is summer and many of your subordinates are on vacation. The group's workload is extremely heavy and has been for the last six months. The district head of training has complained to your district head about your group's training schedule. He says in the last two months you have cancelled 62 percent of your subordinates' CPR training. Therefore, instructors are running classes that are only half full. Your district head has contacted your boss and discussed the situation. Your boss has told you about the complaint.
    Describe the problem you have to solve. (Write your answer on the answer sheet.)
7. You have defined the problem in 6. What is the next step you should take to solve the problem? (Write your answer on the answer sheet.)
8. You have identified data sources that may be useful in solving a problem. What six steps should be performed after data sources possibly useful to solving the problem are identified? (X-out the six steps on the answer sheet.)

    a.   Put solution into effect.
    b.   Determine if the problem needs to be redefined.
    c.   Get data.
    d.   Decide which data sources to use or consult.
    e.   Consult boss.
    f.   Determine if solution was successful.
    g.   Document resolution of problem.
    h.   Identify sources of data.
    i.   Inform source of problem that problem is resolved.
    j.   Identify back-up sources of data.
    k.   Return to source of problem.
    l.   Ask peers for advice.
    m.   Determine which solution is best.
    n.   Formulate solutions that may work.
    o.   Determine whether documentation of the problem's resolution is necessary.

9.   Sequence your six choices from question 8 in the order in which they should be performed to successfully solve a problem. (Write the letter of each step you selected from question 8 in the correct order on the answer sheet.)

Diagnostic test exhibit B—answer sheet: process 3—problem solving

1.   a b ~~c~~ d
2.   (a)   YES
        (b)   TO FEEDBACK TO BOSS OR MEASURE ITS IMPACT ON THE TOTAL WORK GROUP OR APPLY SOLUTION TO OTHER WORK ITEMS TO REDUCE TIME REQUIREMENTS
3.   ~~a~~ ~~b~~ c ~~d~~ e f g ~~h~~ ~~i~~ j
4.   1st __B__   2nd __A__   3rd __H__   4th __I__   5th __D__
5.   a b c d ~~e~~
6.   THE PROBLEM IS WHY 62% OF THE CPR TRAINING SEATS HAVE BEEN CANCELLED FOR YOUR GROUP IN THE LAST TWO MONTHS.
7.   DETERMINE WHETHER A SOLUTION IS ALREADY AVAILABLE.
8.   ~~a~~ b ~~c~~ ~~d~~ e ~~f~~ g h i j k l ~~m~~ ~~n~~ o
9.   1st __D__   2nd __C__   3rd __N__   4th __M__   5th __A__   6th __F__

Diagnostic test exhibit C—items tested by objective test: process 3—problem solving

Test question number	Items tested		
	Skills	Knowledge	Process steps
1		K2	
2	S14	K17	
3			5, 6, 7, 8, 9
4			5, 6, 7, 8, 9
5			11
6			2
7			3
8			6, 7, 8, 9, 10, 11
9			6, 7, 8, 9, 10, 11

8 Providing Feedback on Performance

PROCESS 4

A. OVERVIEW OF PERFORMANCE FEEDBACK AT THE SUPERVISORY LEVEL

It was noted earlier that information is essential to control of any task or process. Information is needed before the task can begin—this is the *plan*. Information is needed when the task is completed as well, in order to know whether or not the work is actually finished and to ensure that the work meets all output requirements.

In addition, information is needed during the progress of the work in order to measure actual progress and keep it "on plan." Without such information, there can be no real control. For a supervisor to wait until a task is finished to measure and evaluate it is failure to control.

Information is needed, above all, by the individuals who are actually doing the work, so that they will know whether or not they are performing up to standard. Failure to provide this vital kind of information—feedback on performance—to a worker is akin to issuing a report card to a student at the end of a semester, without providing the student with any information about learning progress during the period. Report card control, it has been said, is the worst kind of control.

Feedback on performance is especially important to a worker (or student) who is learning new skills or knowledge. Reinforcement is necessary for learning to take place, and feedback is an essential ingredient of reinforcement.

Reinforcement and learning

When discussing feedback, the management literature sometimes tends to employ formidable terms such as operant conditioning, aversive conditioning, learning curves, and reinforcement. Much of the mystery is removed from these expressions when they are defined in these everyday terms:

- Reinforcement is simply a response from some outside source to a person doing or learning a task, in the form of acknowledgement, encouragement, support, or praise.
- Operant conditioning is a reward of some sort that follows good performance rather directly and immediately.
- Aversive conditioning is the other side of the conditioning coin—scolding, criticism, or the use of fear.

67

The learning curve and feedback

The learning curve is a complex thing, but it is not mysterious. When analyzed, the learning curve can be seen to contain five distinct stages or periods, each of which requires feedback in varying degrees. For a worker learning a new task, or a student learning a new subject, there is usually an *initial period of frustration*. During this stage, the learner needs lots of reinforcing feedback in the form of encouragement and praise for accomplishment, lest he give up before the task is mastered.

Once past the initial stage, the learner goes through a *period of rapid growth* in skill and knowledge, provided he or she is given adequate feedback on actual performance. During this stage, the learner typically is striving to meet targets or standards for quantity and quality; it is vitally important that these standards are clearly stated and understood, and that they are accepted as meaningful and fair. All feedback should be expressed both in terms of these standards and in terms of variances from them.

There is normally a third stage of *consolidation of gains*—a plateau of proficiency. The worker may meet the standards at this stage. It is sometimes assumed that this period represents peak performance, but this is often wrong. This plateau is frequently followed by another spurt of growth in skill and job knowledge to *peak proficiency*, the fourth stage on the learning curve.

These advanced stages require less and less facilitation from outside sources. There is generally a strong inner sense of accomplishment and progress derived from the work itself during these periods. The best feedback at this time comes directly from the work to the worker, without intervention or interpretation by the supervisor or anyone else.

The final stage is a period of high performance. At this stage, there is danger of the worker becoming bored with a task in which little or no challenge remains. For some workers, a new challenge may be needed, perhaps in the form of job enrichment or a new task to learn. Reward alone will seldom bring about increased output beyond the norm that workers have set for themselves. Reinforcement, however, in the form of positive feedback, is always needed to keep performance levels high and to maintain quality output.

B. HIGHLIGHTS OF THE AT&T JOB STUDY

Definition of the process

The Mastery Model defines the feedback process as one of

Informing subordinates how their job performance compares with job requirements so that future job requirements can be met or exceeded.

There is a distinction between this activity of providing feedback and "coaching," although the dividing line is thin. Providing performance feedback to all members of the work group is a continuous and never-ending process that need not involve the supervisor personally (though it often does). Coaching is one form of corrective action, generally provided by the supervisor on a "one-on-one" basis whenever an individual member needs specific instruction on some phase of the work. (It should be noted, however, that in many situations, this kind of personal on-job training is sometimes delegated to a senior member of the group who possesses particular job skills and knowledge.)

Summary description of the process

The Job Study found the process of providing feedback on performance to be a complex managerial process. It is in two distinct phases: 1) continuous feedback to all subordinates on their day-to-day performance and progress; and 2) periodic "one-on-one" formal reviews of each member's total job performance and progress over a prolonged period of time.

The critical aspect of ongoing feedback is that it must be based on valid actual performance data and clearly defined performance standards. Another important factor in providing feedback—either ongoing or total review—is for the supervisor to set and maintain a constructive tone during discussions with a subordinate. The supervisor must also employ a high degree of communication skill, particularly to draw out from the individual his or her view of the performance being reviewed. It is essential to validate the person's understanding of the feedback and the consequences of substandard performance, both to the individual and the work group of which he or she is a member.

An important aspect of the periodic total performance review and appraisal is a *plan* for improving performance and results during the next review period. The Mastery Model requires the supervisor to prepare a tentative plan based on review of all performance data; this preliminary plan serves as an agenda for discussion and negotiation with the subordinate. The final plan is documented only after the subordinate has been encouraged to express views on his or her own performance, agreement has been reached on the aspects of performance that need attention, and a new set of performance levels and goals for results has been negotiated.

C. TASKS AND DECISION POINTS IN THE PROCESS OF PROVIDING PERFORMANCE FEEDBACK

STEP 1
: The first step is to determine that a stimulus exists for giving feedback to a particular subordinate.

STEP 2
: Next, you must determine whether you have enough job performance data to evaluate performance for purposes of giving feedback to the subordinate. To do this:

STEP 3
(Decision)
: You should respond to the question: *Does sufficient job performance data exist?*

: If your decision is *yes*, skip the next step and go to Step 5.

STEP 4
: If your decision is *no*—not enough job performance data exists—your next task is to collect additional data.

STEP 5
(Decision)
: At this point, you should respond to the question: *Is it necessary to coach your subordinate to perform the job satisfactorily?*

: If your decision is *yes*, go to the Coaching process (see Chapter 9).

STEP 6
(Decision)
: At this point, it is necessary to decide whether the feedback is to be a total performance review or simply ongoing feedback related to the work at hand.

: If your decision is that a "total performance review" is called for, skip the next 11 steps and go to Step 18.

STEP 7
: If your decision is that ongoing performance feedback is required by the situation, you should *prepare* yourself to provide feedback to your subordinate by selecting an appropriate time and place, getting your data together, etc.

The flowchart in Figure 8–1 depicts the flow of steps in the process up to this point, Steps 1 through 7.

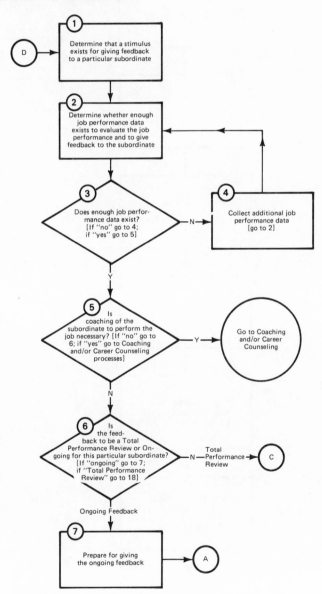

FIGURE 8-1. Flowchart of the Feedback Process— First 7 Steps

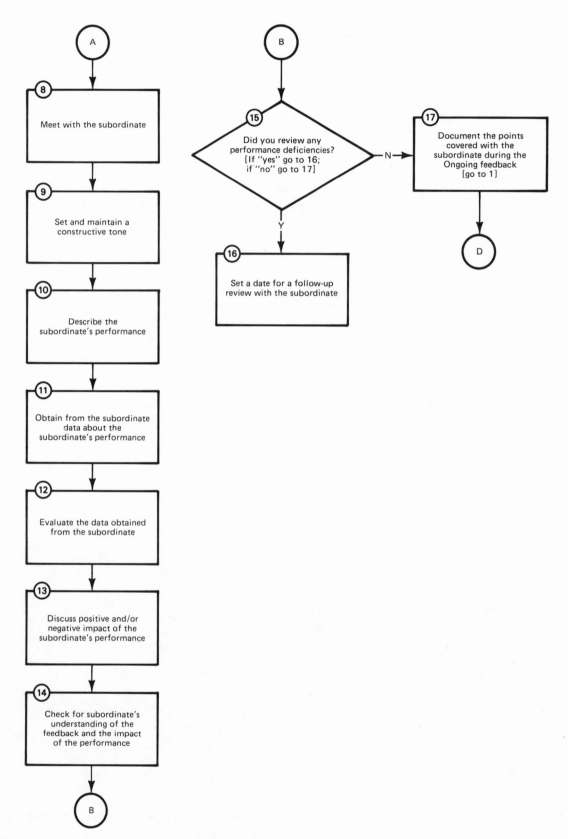

FIGURE 8-2. Steps 8 through 17 of the Feedback Process

STEP 8   When you are adequately prepared to give performance feedback, you can meet with your subordinate.

STEP 9   During the feedback session, you should set and maintain a constructive tone (see Step 8 of the Informal Oral Communication process).

STEP 10   Describe the subordinate's actual performance in terms of its effect on—or how it is affected by—the output requirements of the work.

STEP 11   Obtain your subordinate's view of his or her performance.

STEP 12   Evaluate the information that your subordinate gives you in terms of factors not under his or her control, the possibility that he or she may be following a more current standard practice than yours, etc.

     Note that this input may require you to use the Coaching process (see Process No. 5).

STEP 13   Discuss with your subordinate the consequences of his or her performance to him/herself and the work group.

STEP 14   Verify your subordinate's understanding of the feedback given and its possible consequences through restatement or a demonstration of correct performance by the subordinate.

STEP 15 (Decision)   At this point, you should decide whether your review discovered any deficiencies in your subordinate's performance.

     If your decision is *no,* skip the next step and document the feedback session as in Step 17.

STEP 16   If job deficiencies exist, set a date for a follow-up review with your subordinate.

STEP 17   Document the points covered with subordinate in the ongoing feedback session.

     (Because ongoing feedback is a continuous process, after completing Step 17, return to Step 1.)

The flowchart in Figure 8-2 illustrates the 10 steps in the process of providing ongoing feedback to a subordinate.

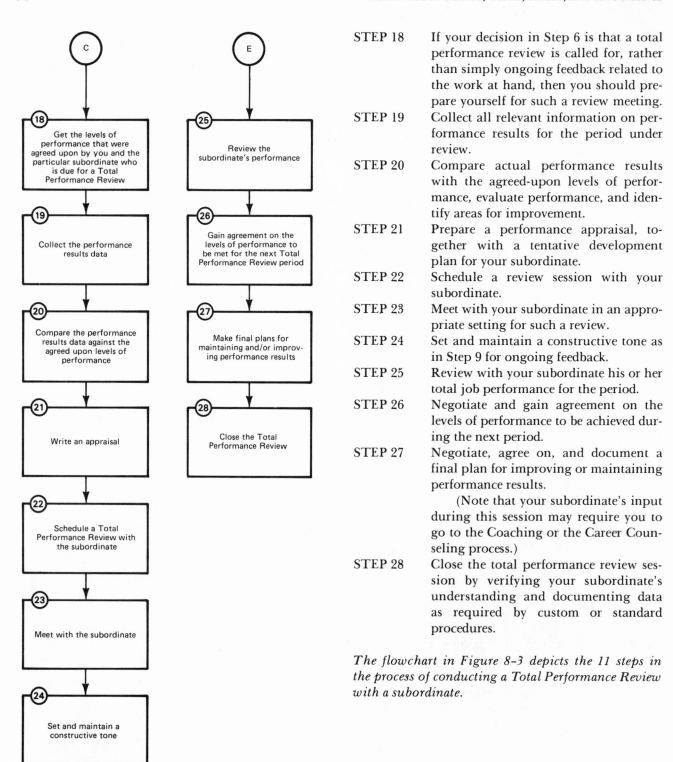

STEP 18	If your decision in Step 6 is that a total performance review is called for, rather than simply ongoing feedback related to the work at hand, then you should prepare yourself for such a review meeting.
STEP 19	Collect all relevant information on performance results for the period under review.
STEP 20	Compare actual performance results with the agreed-upon levels of performance, evaluate performance, and identify areas for improvement.
STEP 21	Prepare a performance appraisal, together with a tentative development plan for your subordinate.
STEP 22	Schedule a review session with your subordinate.
STEP 23	Meet with your subordinate in an appropriate setting for such a review.
STEP 24	Set and maintain a constructive tone as in Step 9 for ongoing feedback.
STEP 25	Review with your subordinate his or her total job performance for the period.
STEP 26	Negotiate and gain agreement on the levels of performance to be achieved during the next period.
STEP 27	Negotiate, agree on, and document a final plan for improving or maintaining performance results. (Note that your subordinate's input during this session may require you to go to the Coaching or the Career Counseling process.)
STEP 28	Close the total performance review session by verifying your subordinate's understanding and documenting data as required by custom or standard procedures.

The flowchart in Figure 8–3 depicts the 11 steps in the process of conducting a Total Performance Review with a subordinate.

FIGURE 8-3. Steps 18 through 28 of the Feedback Process

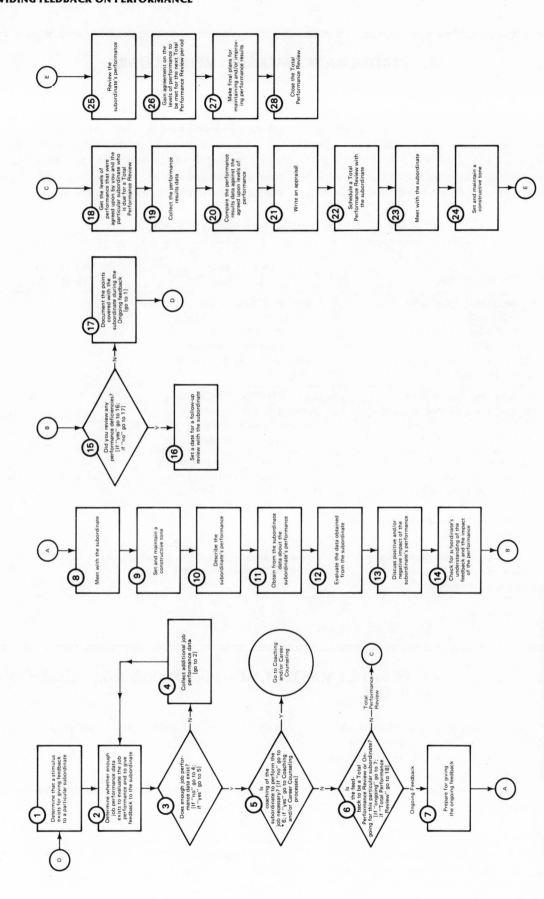

FIGURE 8–4. Flowchart of Providing Performance Feedback—Total Process

D. PERFORMANCE MEASUREMENTS CHART

The fourth ranking duty of the supervisor—Providing Performance Feedback—involves 24 tasks and four contingencies or decision points. For purposes of measuring performance, these 28 steps fall naturally into four principal groups. Table 8-1 lists the steps in each of the four groups, identifies the output of each group, shows the performance standards that apply to each output, and identifies the method used by second-level managers to measure the managerial performance of subordinate first-line supervisors.

These outputs, performance standards, and measurement methods were developed under the constraints recorded earlier, in the discussion of performance measurement in Planning the Work.

Table 8-1. Process 4: Providing performance feedback

Step or group of steps	Output	Performance standards	Method of measurement
Steps 1-6	Subordinates requiring feedback are identified Standards for performance are established Sufficient data are collected to provide feedback	Feedback is given when appropriate Subordinates of the first-level supervisor know the performance standards Feedback is given on time/when due	
Steps 7-17	Ongoing feedback is given Ongoing feedback is documented	Ongoing feedback is objective, based on performance and provides solutions to performance problems	The first-level supervisor's boss reviews the appraisal information and gets feedback from the first-level subordinates
Steps 18-26	Performance data are gathered Appraisal is written The total performance review is given Levels of performance are set for next period	Appraisal contains description of performance and standards. Performance ratings are consistent with the documentation	
Steps 27, 28	Follow-up plans are formulated Appraisal session is closed Items are documented	First-level supervisor follows up on critical performance areas	

E. THE AT&T MASTERY MODEL—PROVIDING PERFORMANCE FEEDBACK

Providing performance feedback is a complex managerial process that involves 28 steps, more than any other single process. The process is in two phases: (1) continuous feedback on a subordinate's day-to-day performance, and (2) regularly scheduled "one-on-one" performance reviews or appraisals which cover a subordinate's performance over a prolonged period of time.

The process is detailed in the following pages, showing each task and contingency point together with the specific skills and knowledge required to master each task.

Fundamental skills and knowledge required

In order for you to give performance feedback effectively, it is necessary that you know four *fundamentals of management* that apply to this managerial process for first-level supervision.

Knowledge Required

K1 It is part of the first-level supervisor's job to provide ongoing feedback and total performance reviews.

K2 Feedback may be motivative and may improve the job performance of subordinates.

K3 The purpose of feedback is to inform subordinates how their job performance compares with total job requirements and with particular output requirements, so these requirements can be met or exceeded.

K4 Giving unfavorable feedback, in some instances, may have labor relations ramifications. In those instances, know to follow the union contract and/or local procedures.

Step 1—Determine that a Stimulus Exists for Giving Feedback to a Particular Subordinate

Skills Required

S1 This task requires skill to determine that one or more of the following stimuli for giving performance feedback exist:
output of controlling Step 15
work observations
information from customers or users of the subordinate's output
information from other supervisors
information from other departments
critical incidents that must be reacted to immediately (e.g., safety violations)
official group results
the output of coaching and career counseling
mandated appraisal time

S2 This task requires skill to identify performance standards by the following:
If the item being tracked is measured . by an official results program, consult the program's standards.
If the item is technical or quali-

tative, consult company practices or technical practices.
If the item is used by clients, customers, or other work groups, consult them.
If no standards exist, consult boss, peers, subordinates, etc., and set your own standards.

Knowledge Required

K5 The stimulus to give feedback contains *job performance data* that will be useful in giving feedback to a particular subordinate.

K6 Job performance data consist of information about the subordinate's actual performance and standards for evaluating the performance.

K7 Job performance standards specify the desired level of performance in terms of quality, quantity, time.

K8 Know to change performance standards when conditions change; such as, changes in official results, technical practices, or organizational goals; or clients and customers request changes in standards.

Step 2—Determine Whether Enough Job Performance Data Exists to Give Feedback

Skills Required

S3 You need skill to evaluate the subordinate's actual job performance by comparing job standards to information about the subordinate's performance.

S4 You need skill to give immediate feedback if there is an emergency incident; such as, for example, a safety violation by a subordinate (failure to wear safety glasses, etc.).

S5 You need skill to determine if enough data exist to evaluate performance and give feedback (e.g., an error by an employee with one month's service warrants feedback; the same error by an experienced, competent employee with twenty years' service does not warrant feedback).

Knowledge Required	K9	If you are entering this step from Coaching Step 23, you should know to evaluate performance by method(s) selected in Coaching Step 19 (see Coaching Process No. 5).
	K10	Know that performance deficiencies may exist in more than one area.
	K11	If entering this step from Career Counseling Step 11, you should know to evaluate performance according to schedules and standards selected in Step 9. (See Career Counseling Process No. 13).

Step 3—Decision Point: Does Enough Job Performance Data Exist? *If Your Decision Is* Yes, *Skip Step 4 and Go to Step 5.*

Step 4—Collect Additional Job Performance Data

Knowledge Required	K12	If your answer to Step 3 is *no*— not enough job performance data exist—you should know to collect additional data in the area of the performance deficiency identified in Step 2 (e.g., performance deficiency in soldering wires— collect data on soldering wires).

Step 5—Decision Point: Is It Necessary to Coach the Subordinate to Perform the Job?

Knowledge Required	K13	This decision requires you to know that coaching is describing, demonstrating, or arranging for the subordinate to learn skills or knowledge necessary to perform the work according to standards.
Skill Required	S6	This decision also requires skill to determine if coaching is necessary, based on lack of improvement in performance to standard levels, despite prior feedback.

If your decision is *yes*, go to the Coaching Process No. 5.

Step 6—Decision Point: Is Feedback to Be a Total Performance Review or Ongoing Feedback for This Particular Subordinate?

Definitions:	*Total performance review:* A formal summarization (annual, semi-annual, or quarterly, etc.) of ongoing feedback that is required by the organization. It is related to the total job and its standards.
	Ongoing performance feedback: An immediate reaction to observed performance. It serves as input to the total performance review.

Knowledge Required	K14	This decision requires you to know *when* the total performance review is due.
Skill Required	S7	This decision requires skill to determine if the subordinate is close enough to the total performance review date to incorporate ongoing feedback into the total performance review.

If your decision is that a "total performance review" is called for, skip the next 11 steps and go to Step 18.

Step 7—Prepare for Giving the Ongoing Feedback

Knowledge Required	K15	If your decision to Step 6 calls for "ongoing feedback," you should know that feedback should be given as soon as appropriate after the incident has occurred.
	K16	Know to give ongoing feedback in private when it might be embarrassing to the subordinate or of a confidential nature; when it would make the work group jealous; when reprimanding a subordinate, etc.
	K17	Know to give feedback in front of your subordinate's peers when the work group can learn from feedback (such as a way to perform a task), when other individuals or the work group would be motivated, etc.

	K18	Know to notify the subordinate in advance of the time and place to receive feedback if it is not to be immediate.
Skills Required	S8	You need skill to determine the appropriate time for giving on-going feedback, based on: workload of the supervisor and subordinate availability of the supervisor and subordinate criticality of the incident the environment (e.g., give feedback immediately if there is a safety violation, or if a particular job cannot be continued without feedback, etc.)
	S9	You need skill to select the location based on the highest payoff to work group, subordinate, boss, and organization, based on the knowledge described in K16 and K17.
	S10	You need skill to prepare the content of the feedback by considering such items as: description of the subordinate's performance standards for the evaluation of performance comparison of performance to standards positive and/or negative impacts of the subordinate's performance objectives of feedback (e.g., continue this sort of performance, change the performance in this way, etc.)

Step 8—Meet with the Subordinate

Step 9—Set and Maintain a Constructive Tone

| Knowledge Required | K19 | Know to use the Informal Oral Communication process (see Step 8 of Process No. 9). |

Step 10—Describe the Subordinate's Performance

| Skill Required | S11 | You need skill to describe the subordinate's performance in terms of how it affects—or is affected by—the output requirements, not in terms of attitudes or personal traits. |

Step 11—Obtain from the Subordinate Data about His or Her Performance

---

| Knowledge Required | K20 | You should know, in order to get all details of information from the subordinate, to listen attentively and not to interrupt the subordinate excessively. |

Step 12—Evaluate the Data Obtained from the Subordinate

Knowledge Required	K21	This task is a mental process that occurs before continuing feedback with the subordinate.
	K22	It may be necessary, at times, to validate the subordinate's input with another source (e.g., the subordinate points out that he or she is following a more updated practice than the one the supervisor is referring to), and it may be necessary to delay or discontinue the feedback session.
	K23	As a result of the subordinate's input, it may be necessary to go to the Coaching Process (e.g., subordinate says he or she does not know how to do the job or lacks the skills).
Skills Required	S12	You need skill to decide what factors affected the subordinate's performance, based on the information received in Step 11.
	S13	You need skill to decide which factors were under the subordinate's control and which were not, by comparing the factors to historical data.

Step 13—Discuss Consequences, Both Positive and Negative, of the Subordinate's Performance

Knowledge Required	K24	Know that personal consequences include: appraisals (poor or good) pay treatment promotions reprimand or demotion, etc.
	K25	Know that job performance affects, for better or worse: performance measurements revenues customer service others in group etc.
	K26	Know to use Informal Oral Communication skills (Set and Maintain Constructive Tone) when explaining the consequences to the subordinate.
Skill Required	S14	You need skill to determine the consequences of behavior according to company policies or practices, union contract, local policies and practices, etc.

Step 14—Check for Subordinate's Understanding of the Feedback and the Impact of the Performance

Skill Required	S15	When giving unfavorable feedback, you need skill to obtain from the subordinate a restatement of the behavior and its consequences and/or a demonstration of correct behavior.

Step 15—Decision Point: Did you review or discover any job performance deficiencies?

Knowledge Required	K27	Know that a job performance deficiency occurs when the subordinate's performance does not meet output requirements.

If your decision is *no*, skip the next task and go to Step 17.

Step 16—Set a Date for a Follow-up Review with the Subordinates

Knowledge Required	K28	Know that job deficiencies may not be corrected without follow-up.

Skills Required	S16	You need skill to determine when the subordinate will perform this task again.
	S17	You need skill to determine the criticality of the behavior (e.g., leads to customer complaints, safety problems, etc.)
	S18	You need skill to schedule follow-up sessions based on the frequency and criticality of the work, considering: how long the subordinate might need to practice before you expect improved performance how critical it is that performance be correct on the next occurrence (if critical, you should check next time task is performed) availability of performance data (e.g., production, indices, service observations)

Step 17—Document the Points Covered with the Subordinate during the Ongoing Feedback

Knowledge Required	K29	Know that ongoing feedback is the basis for the total performance review.
	K30	This task requires you to know the format prescribed by local practice for documenting ongoing feedback.
	K31	Know that ongoing feedback may be input to the Master Control List (see Planning Process) and/or a Bring-Up System (see Time Management Process).
	K32	You should know to document: follow-up dates subordinate's comments the feedback to the subordinate what was agreed upon action to be taken name of receiver date given

(Because ongoing feedback is a continuous process, after completing this step, return to Step 1.)

Step 18—Prepare for Total Performance Review with a Subordinate

Knowledge Required	K33	Know to obtain the agreed-upon levels of performance for the specified period.
	K34	The appraisal should cover performance for the current appraisal period only.
	K35	A Total Performance Review involves *all* goals and objectives that were set with the subordinate (e.g., quality, quantity, safety, attendance, etc.).
	K36	Know where the record of goals and objectives comes from (e.g., Master Control List, initial goal setting session with subordinate, past appraisals, attendance records).

Step 19—Collect the Performance Results Data

| Knowledge Required | K37 | Know to gather data for the specific appraisal period only. |
| | K38 | The data may be contained in the Master Control List, personnel files, etc. |

Step 20—Compare the Performance Results Data Against the Agreed-upon Levels of Performance

---

| Skills Required | S19 | You need skill to determine whether output requirements were met, missed, or exceeded. |
| | S20 | This task also requires skill to identify areas of performance in which to plan for improving and maintaining performance (e.g., if a subordinate has improved in a weak area, make plans to maintain or improve that performance area). |

Step 21—Prepare a Performance Appraisal

| Knowledge Required | K39 | Know to use local practices, forms, and procedures (if they exist), and include a tentative development plan. |
| | K40 | The documentation of the actual performance results is a summary of the ongoing feedback. |

	K41	Know to include performance data, evaluations, and maintenance/improvement plans on safety and EEO/AA, if required by local procedures.
Skills Required	S21	If a local practice, form, or procedure does not exist, you need skill to develop a format that includes: agreed-upon output requirements actual performance results tentative development plan ratings new output requirements
	S22	This task requires skill to establish new individual output requirements that are reasonable, challenging, and attainable, based on the subordinate's current performance and the overall unit goals.

Step 22—Schedule a Total Performance Review with the Subordinate

---

Skill Required	S23	This task requires skill to set an appropriate time for both yourself and your subordinate in terms of workloads, environment, proximity to mandated date, availability and receptiveness of subordinate.
Knowledge Required	K42	A Total Performance Review is always given in private because personal ratings may be involved, personal objectives will be set, etc.
	K43	Know to notify subordinate in advance of the time and place of the Total Performance Review.

Step 23—Meet with the Subordinate

Step 24—Set and Maintain a Constructive Tone

| Knowledge Required | K44 | Know to use Step 8 of the Informal Oral Communication process. |

Step 25—Review the Subordinate's Performance

Knowledge Required	K45	The subordinate may have additional information that may affect the appraisal and tentative developmental plans.
	K46	Know to first discuss the subordinate's performance results and then the agreed-upon levels of performance for each output requirement, one at a time.
	K47	Know to use the Informal Oral Communication process to encourage the subordinate's participation.
Skills Required	S24	This task requires skill to review the subordinate's performance, based on the written appraisal.
	S25	You need skill to encourage the subordinate's participation throughout the discussion.

Step 26—Gain Agreement on the Levels of Performance for the Next Total Performance Review Period

Knowledge Required	K48	This task requires that you know which output requirements are negotiable and which are not, based on: job requirements group's overall objectives union contract boss's mandate, etc.
	K49	Know that you may change planned output requirements based on the subordinate's input.
	K50	Know to document any changes in the output requirements.
	K51	The setting of output requirements and the making of plans to maintain and improve performance are so closely related that sometimes one is done before the other.
	K52	If agreement on performance levels cannot be attained, this fact should be documented.

Step 27—Make Final Plan for Maintaining and/or Improving Performance Results

Knowledge Required	K53	Know to review tentative plan for maintaining and improving performance as stated in Step 21.
	K54	The subordinate's opinions are important input to finalizing the tentative development plan.
	K55	Know to document the final development plan and follow-up dates on Master Control List or per local practices.
	K56	As a result of the subordinate's input, it may be necessary to go to the Coaching or Career Counseling processes (e.g., subordinate says he or she does not know how to perform the job or lacks the skill; subordinate says he or she wants a more challenging assignment; subordinate says he or she has new job interests).
Skill Required	S26	You need skill to negotiate with subordinate to prepare a final plan.

Step 28—Close the Total Performance Review

Skills Required	S27	This task requires skill to ensure mutual understanding by reviewing the critical points in the review.
	S28	You need skill to express appreciation for the subordinate's efforts and confidence in the subordinate's ability.
Knowledge Required	K57	Know to inform the subordinate when the next Total Performance Review is due.
	K58	Know to record the date on the Master Control List or per local procedures.
	K59	The recorded data are input to the managerial processes of Planning, Time Management, and Providing Performance Feedback.
	K60	The output of the Total Performance Review may be input to Career Counseling.

F.   TRAINING NEEDS DIAGNOSTIC

The diagnostic test for providing performance feedback is in two sections; an *objective test* intended to test knowledge of the process, and a *role play* designed to test interpersonal and behavioral skills in applying the process.

Objective test

The objective test of 17 questions is designed to test ten feedback skills and 14 points of knowledge in providing feedback on subordinates' performance at the first level of supervision.

The test questions and answers are found in Exhibits A and B. The specific skills and knowledge tested by the 17 questions are shown in Exhibit C.

Role play

The Role Play section of the diagnostic instrument is designed to test the subject's behavioral and interpersonal skills in performing several duties. Included are:

informal oral communication
providing performance feedback
coaching a subordinate
written communication
controlling the work

The duty of providing performance feedback is given heavy emphasis in this exercise; 12 feedback skills and 10 items of knowledge are tested. (The actual role play instructions and situation background information are too voluminous to include in this book.) The specific skills and knowledge tested are:

Skills: S11, S12, S13, S14, S19, S20, S22, S24, S25, S26, S27, and S28.
Knowledges: K20, K23, K24, K25, K26, K45, K46, K49, K53, and K54.

Diagnostic test exhibit A: process 4—feedback

The purpose of Feedback is to inform subordinates on how their job performance compares with job requirements so that future job requirements can be met or exceeded.

1.   One source of information for giving a subordinate performance feedback is your observation of the subordinate's work. What are five other sources? (Write your *five* sources on the answer sheet.)
2.   What is (are) the *best* source(s) to determine standards for evaluating your subordinates' performance? (X-out the best answer(s) on the answer sheet.)
     a.   Bell System Practices (e.g., for technical work)
     b.   own judgement, based on all available information, if no standards exist
     c.   official results program (e.g., indices)
     d.   specifications by users, customers, or clients
     e.   all of the above
3.   The first error on a routine task by a subordinate with one month's service does not warrant feedback because no error pattern has developed. (X-out T for True or F for False on the answer sheet.)
4.   What are four situations in which you should consider changing a performance standard or objective for a subordinate? (Write your *four* answers on the answer sheet.)
5.   For both informal and formal appraisals, you evaluate subordinates work by comparing what two things? (Complete the statement on the answer sheet.)
6.   One of your subordinates has made the same work error for the third time. You gave feedback on the other two occasions. What should you do *next*? (X-out the *best* answer on the answer sheet.)
     a.   Give feedback to the subordinate.
     b.   Issue a warning to the subordinate.
     c.   Determine if the subordinate needs training.
     d.   Seek assistance from the union delegate.
     e.   Collect additional information and look for error patterns.

7. An experienced, competent employee has made a soldering error. You had no previous reason to give negative feedback to the subordinate. What should you do *next*? (X-out the *best* answer on the answer sheet.)
   a. Give feedback to the subordinate.
   b. Issue a warning to the subordinate.
   c. Determine if the subordinate needs training.
   d. Seek assistance from the union delegate.
   e. Collect additional information and look for error patterns.

8. You are giving negative feedback to a subordinate on the way a job was done. The subordinate tells you that another supervisor said to do it that way. What should you do *next*? (Write your answer on the answer sheet.)

9. Feedback should always be given immediately after a performance incident has occurred. (X-out T for True or F for False on the answer sheet.)

10. What are *four* items that should be documented after an informal feedback session? (Write the *four* items on the answer sheet.)

11. What data should be collected for the formal appraisal of a subordinate? (X-out the correct answer(s) on the answer sheet.)
    a. all objectives originally agreed to at the beginning of the appraisal period which were not changed
    b. any new objectives that were agreed to during the appraisal period
    c. performance results for each of the objectives
    d. any noted circumstances that explain why objectives were not met, were met, or exceeded
    e. performance results from the previous appraisal period

12. What is the *best* source of data for the formal appraisal of a subordinate? (X-out the *best* answer on the answer sheet.)
    a. documentation from ongoing feedback
    b. your boss's opinion
    c. group's monthly results for the year
    d. subordinate's most recent results
    e. group's most recent results
    f. your recall of the subordinate's performance

13. What items should be included in the formal written appraisal of a subordinate? (X-out the correct answer(s) on the answer sheet.)
    a. agreed upon objectives, goals, or targets
    b. prediction of future success
    c. tentative development plans
    d. performance ratings
    e. actual performance results
    f. summary of last appraisal

14 When giving a formal written appraisal, establish new goals, objectives, or targets for your subordinate that are reasonable, challenging, and attainable, based on your feelings about the subordinate's past performance and the overall unit goals. (X-out T for True or F for False on the answer sheet.)

15. You and a subordinate have discussed the coming year's objectives for the subordinate. You and the subordinate cannot reach agreement on an objective. The objective cannot be changed. The *best* thing(s) to do is (are): (X-out the *best* answer(s) on the answer sheet.)
    a. Notify your boss of the disagreement.
    b. Document the disagreement.
    c. Continue to discuss the matter.
    d. Tell the subordinate if the objective is not met, disciplinary action will be taken.
    e. Assign that objective to another subordinate.
    f. Tell the subordinate to think it over.

16. One of the major advantages in giving negative feedback clearly and checking that the subordinate understands is that follow-up will not be necessary. (X-out T for True or F for False on the answer sheet.)

17. You are discussing an unsatisfactory item in a performance review with your subordinate. The subordinate says the unsatisfactory work is due to lack of knowledge. The subordinate also wants a different job. What should you do? (X-out the *best* answer(s) on the answer sheet.)
    a. Change the performance rating.
    b. Determine if training is needed.
    c. Postpone the performance review.
    d. Dismiss the statement as a poor excuse.
    e. Explain that if performance does not improve, disciplinary action will be taken.
    f. Look into other job possibilities for the subordinate.

Diagnostic test exhibit B—answer sheet: process 4—providing performance feedback

1. (1) OUTPUT OF CONTROLLING   (5) OTHER DEPARTMENTS
    (2) CRITICAL INCIDENTS/SAFETY   (6) OFFICIAL RESULTS/INDEXES
    (3) INFORMATION FROM CUSTOMERS   (7) MATERIAL COLLECTED FOR FORMAL
    (4) INFORMATION FROM OTHER SUPVS.   APPRAISAL

2. a   b   c   d   ✗
3. T   ✗
4. (1) OFFICIAL MEASUREMENTS/INDEXES   (3) CLIENT/CUSTOMER REQUESTS CHANGE
          CHANGE   (4) ORGANIZATIONAL GOALS CHANGE
    (2) OFFICIAL TECHNICAL MEASURE-   (5) BOSS MANDATE
          MENTS, BSP'S, PRACTICES CHANGE   (6) STANDARDS UNREALISTIC
5. PERFORMANCE   STANDARDS
6. a   b   ✗   d   e
7. a   b   c   d   ✗
8. STOP GIVING FEEDBACK AND VALIDATE THE NEW INFORMATION
9. T   ✗
10. (1) TOPIC OF FEEDBACK   (5) ACTION TO BE TAKEN
    (2) DATE FEEDBACK GIVEN   (6) SUBORDINATE'S COMMENTS
    (3) WHAT WAS AGREED UPON   (7) NAME OF SUBORDINATE
    (4) FOLLOW-UP DATES
11. ✗   ✗   ✗   ✗   e
12. ✗   b   c   d   e   f
13. ✗   b   ✗   ✗   ✗   f
14. T   ✗
15. a   ✗   c   d   e   ✗
16. T   ✗
17. a   ✗   c   d   e   ✗

Diagnostic test exhibit C—items tested by objective test: process 4—providing performance feedback

Test question number	Items tested		Process steps
	Skills	Knowledge	
1	S1	K5	
2	S2		
3	S5		
4		K8	
5	S3, S19		
6	S6		
7		K12	
8		K22	
9	S8	K15	
10		K32	
11		K33, K34, K35	
12		K29, K40	
13	S21	K41	
14	S22		
15		K52	
16		K28	
17		K56	

9 Coaching Subordinates

PROCESS 5

A. OVERVIEW OF COACHING AT THE SUPERVISORY LEVEL

Coaching subordinates is one of the first-level supervisor's three principal activities specifically intended to contribute to and aid in developing the members of his or her work group. The other two are *career counseling* and *maintaining a motivative environment* in the workplace.

The supervisor also is expected to take an active part in aiding subordinates to develop their skills and knowledge through *self-development*. In this case, the supervisor's role is one of encouraging and supporting the employee's own efforts, rather than providing direct assistance.

Other activities of the first-level supervisor contribute significantly to subordinates' development, although less directly. The *performance feedback* provided to members of the work force by or through the supervisor, whether ongoing feedback on daily activities or periodic performance reviews, can be an important element of employee development, when given with informed awareness of individual capabilities and potential, and genuine sensitivity to individual needs and aspirations.

Specific purpose of coaching

Coaching subordinates is, of course, done with a more specific and a more pragmatic purpose—it is intended to remedy deficiencies in a specific subordinate's work performance and to bring this performance up to the standards of the job. To the extent that the employee gains in job skill and knowledge through the coaching, and to the extent that his or her enhanced skill and knowledge is lasting, the individual has gained in personal development.

Coaching is a highly personalized, one-on-one relationship between the supervisor and a subordinate. The coaching session provides the supervisor with an important opportunity, but it also presents dangers. One *danger* is that only the negative aspects of performance are discussed with the employee, potentially causing resentment of criticism. The *opportunity* is the chance to reinforce the good parts of the subordinate's job performance through praise and encouragement. Done with sincerity and understanding, this can create goodwill and a high degree of job satisfaction.

Another danger is that the supervisor's time and energy may be consumed by coaching the poorest performers in the work group. Accordingly, the supervisor should first ensure that a subordinate has the basic capability (and desire) to improve his or her performance before offering coaching. The supervisor's time might be better spent coaching good performers to do better, rather than attempting to "make silk purses out of sow's ears."

Roy Johnson, vice-president of executive development at General Electric, has said that *on-the-job coaching* by a person's boss accounts for an important part of the person's total career development in G.E., even more so than formal training. At General Electric, where employee development is an important company activity, studies have provided this five-point guide to employee development.[1] All of these principles apply to the coaching process.

[1]Eckles, Carmichael, and Sarchet, *Essentials of Management for First-Line Supervisors* (New York: John Wiley & Sons, Inc. 1974).

1. Development is a personal matter and should be tailored to the individual—group training is okay, but personal on-job-training (OJT) is still needed.

2. Self-development is the basis for *all* development—the supervisor can only provide the climate, the opportunity, support, information, and guidance. The individual *must want to develop personally.*

3. Day-to-day experiences are the most important part of a person's development—the climate and relations with the superior appear to be most significant factor in this respect.

4. Development opportunities must be available to *all*, not just to the "bright stars." Predicting success of individuals is very risky (in one major study, almost 50 percent of the people who were assessed as "nonacceptable" performed "above average" in the first-level management job).

5. The supervisor is directly responsible for the development of the people who work under his or her direction—*this responsibility cannot be delegated.*

B.   HIGHLIGHTS OF THE AT&T JOB STUDY

Definition of the process

The AT&T first-level supervisory Mastery Model defines coaching as "a process which includes activities to help a subordinate learn to do a job correctly." This is an unusually terse definition for the Mastery Model—it is also a good deal less specific than most. This could lead a new supervisor to think that coaching is a simple process requiring little managerial skill or knowledge. Decidedly, it is not. The process, as detailed in the Mastery Model, contains *23 separate steps*; associated with these are some *25 points of knowledge* and *22 skills.*

Summary description of the process

One of the principal required skills is to determine whether or not a subordinate has the capability to improve work performance—that is, whether the subordinate will benefit from coaching. Obviously, if the subordinate lacks this capability to improve, coaching or other forms of encouragement could create false expectations in the mind of the employee. It is often more productive for the subordinate to be given a less demanding assignment better suited to his or her capabilities. This situation may call for the supervisor to employ the Career Counseling process (Process No. 13).

When it has been determined that a subordinate will benefit from coaching, because the capability is there but some skill or knowledge is lacking (or the employee does not understand fully what is required), then the supervisor needs to employ a whole array of interpersonal skills and knowledge to coach the subordinate. Among these are the skills of interviewing, listening, evaluating subordinate's performance shortcomings and coaching needs, coping with the person's sensitivities, providing one-on-one training, giving performance feedback, and reinforcing the employee's improved performance through an encouraging attitude.

It is recommended that the coaching session be documented to confirm agreements and commitments made and to ensure proper follow-up of coaching results.

C.   TASKS AND DECISION POINTS IN THE PROCESS OF COACHING A SUBORDINATE

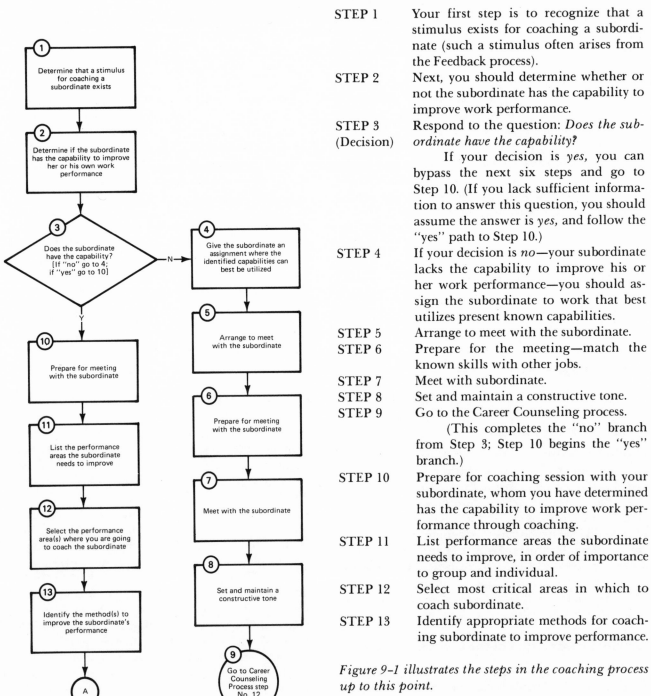

FIGURE 9-1.   Flowchart of the Coaching Process: First 13 Steps

STEP 1 — Your first step is to recognize that a stimulus exists for coaching a subordinate (such a stimulus often arises from the Feedback process).

STEP 2 — Next, you should determine whether or not the subordinate has the capability to improve work performance.

STEP 3 (Decision) — Respond to the question: *Does the subordinate have the capability?*

If your decision is *yes*, you can bypass the next six steps and go to Step 10. (If you lack sufficient information to answer this question, you should assume the answer is *yes*, and follow the "yes" path to Step 10.)

STEP 4 — If your decision is *no*—your subordinate lacks the capability to improve his or her work performance—you should assign the subordinate to work that best utilizes present known capabilities.

STEP 5 — Arrange to meet with the subordinate.

STEP 6 — Prepare for the meeting—match the known skills with other jobs.

STEP 7 — Meet with subordinate.

STEP 8 — Set and maintain a constructive tone.

STEP 9 — Go to the Career Counseling process.

(This completes the "no" branch from Step 3; Step 10 begins the "yes" branch.)

STEP 10 — Prepare for coaching session with your subordinate, whom you have determined has the capability to improve work performance through coaching.

STEP 11 — List performance areas the subordinate needs to improve, in order of importance to group and individual.

STEP 12 — Select most critical areas in which to coach subordinate.

STEP 13 — Identify appropriate methods for coaching subordinate to improve performance.

Figure 9-1 illustrates the steps in the coaching process up to this point.

STEP 14 — Select most effective method, based on subordinate's needs, cost, time available, and payoff to organization.

STEP 15 — Meet with subordinate at appropriate site for coaching.

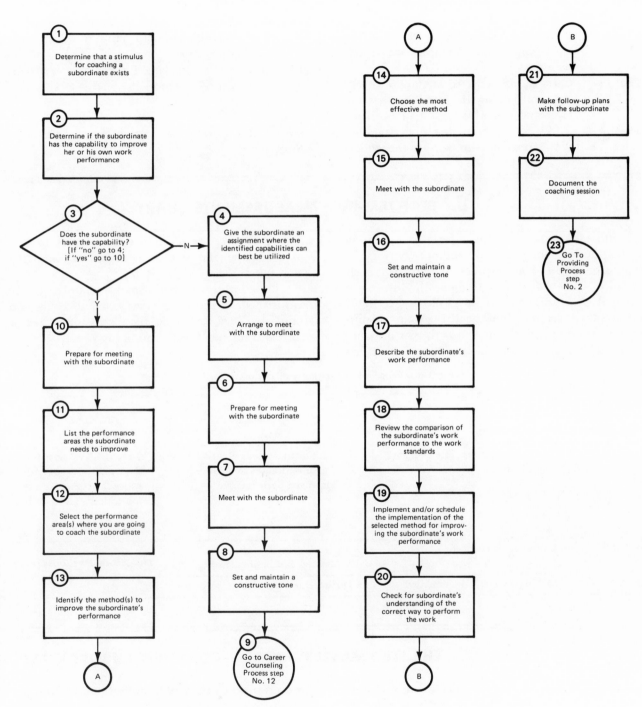

FIGURE 9-2. Coaching a Subordinate—Total Process

STEP 16   Set and maintain constructive tone.

STEP 17   Describe your subordinate's performance in terms of its effect on output requirements—and obtain subordinate's views on the performance deficiency.

STEP 18   Review the comparison of your subordinate's work performance with the work standards, with employee's participation.

STEP 19   Carry out the selected method of coaching, considering the needs, experience level, and capabilities of the subordinate.

STEP 20   Check for subordinate's understanding of the correct way to perform the work—through restatement or a demonstration of the correct procedure.

STEP 21   Make follow-up plans with your subordinate, based on critical nature of task, frequency, etc.

STEP 22   Document the coaching session in accordance with custom or standard procedure.

STEP 23   Go to Provide Performance Feedback process, Step 2.

Figure 9–2 illustrates the total process of Coaching a Subordinate.

D. PERFORMANCE MEASUREMENTS CHART

The fifth ranking duty of the supervisor, Coaching a Subordinate, involves 22 tasks and one contingency or decision point. For purposes of measuring performance, these 23 steps fall naturally into three principal *groups*. The chart that follows (see Table 9–1) lists the steps in each of the three groups, identifies the output of each group, shows the performance standards that apply to each output, and identifies the method used by second-level managers to measure the managerial performance of subordinate first-line supervisors.

These outputs, performance standards, and measurement methods were developed under the constraints recorded earlier, in the discussion of performance measurement in Planning the Work.

Table 9–1. Process 5: coaching a subordinate

Step or group of steps	Output	Performance standards	Method of measurement
Steps 1–4	Subordinates who require coaching are identified	Developmental needs identified for subordinates to achieve improved performance	The second-level boss tracks the quality and quantity of work assigned, on-the-job training given by first level, and training course attendance
Steps 5–21	Subordinate is coached	A plan for improvement is devised and implemented	The second-level boss reviews the documentation
Step 22	Coaching session is documented	Documented per local procedures	

E. THE AT&T MASTERY MODEL—COACHING SUBORDINATES

Coaching subordinates is a managerial process composed of 23 steps or tasks. The process is detailed in the following, which shows each task and contingency point together with the specific skills and knowledge required to master each.

Fundamental skills and knowledge required

In order for you to coach a subordinate effectively, it is necessary for you to know two *fundamentals of management* that apply to this managerial process for first-level supervision. These are:

| Knowledge Required | K1 | The purpose of coaching is to help the subordinate to learn the job and be self-sufficient. |
| | K2 | Data from performance feedback may be input to coaching. |

Step 1—Determine That a Stimulus for Coaching a Subordinate Exists

| Knowledge Required | K3 | The stimulus for coaching may arise from Feedback process Steps 5, 12, and 27. |
| | K4 | The stimulus for coaching may indicate more than one area in which coaching is needed. |

Step 2—Determine Whether or not the Subordinate Has the Capability to Improve Work Performance

| Skill Required | S1 | This task requires skill to determine the subordinate's capability to improve performance by weighing the information about the subordinate you have gathered from previous observations, feedback, coaching, appraisals, and/or training. It also requires skill to consider the subordinate's work history (e.g., subordinate has been coached four times on a particular job operation and still cannot perform that operation according to standards; subordinate was previously coached successfully on a more difficult task, and therefore should be coachable on a less difficult task). |

Step 3—Decision Point: Does the subordinate have the capability?

If your decision is *yes*, bypass the next six steps and go to Step 10.

| Skill Required | S2 | If you cannot answer the question posed at this point because you don't have enough data to determine it, follow the *yes* path. |

Step 4—Give the Subordinate an Assignment Where the Identified Capabilities Can Best Be Utilized

| Knowledge Required | K5 | If your decision is *no*—the subordinate does not have the capability—then you should know that this assignment is temporary because you have determined that the subordinate cannot improve the work performance. |
| | K6 | Know it is necessary to put subordinates in assignments that they can do, rather than leave them in assignments that they are incapable of doing according to output requirements. |

Step 5—Arrange to Meet with the Subordinate

Step 6—Prepare for Meeting with the Subordinate

| Knowledge Required | K7 | Know to match the identified skills of the subordinate with other jobs. |

Step 7—Meet with the Subordinate (See Meeting Process, Step 9, and Coaching Process, Step 10.)

Step 8—Set and Maintain Constructive Tone (See Informal Oral Communication Process, Step 8.)

Step 9—Go to Career Counseling Process Step 12 (This Completes the No Branch from Step 3 Above.)

Step 10—Prepare for Meeting with the Subordinate (This Begins the Yes Branch from Step 3.)

| Skills Required | S3 | You need skill to determine the time for coaching, based on: workload of yourself and subordinate availability of yourself and subordinate |

criticality of incident

the environment (e.g., give immediately if safety violation, or if a particular job cannot be continued because coaching does not take place immediately)

S4 You need skill to determine the location for coaching, based on highest payoff to the work group, subordinate, boss, organization (based on knowledge described above).

S5 You need skill to notify the subordinate in advance of the time and place for coaching activity if it will not be immediate.

S6 You need skill to prepare the content of coaching by considering such items as:

description of subordinate's performance

standards for evaluating performance

comparison of performance to standards

positive and negative impacts of subordinate's performance

the subordinate's personality (e.g., shy person, personal circumstances such as death in the family)

Knowledge Required

K8 Know to coach in private if it is apt to embarrass subordinate or is of confidential nature.

K9 Know to coach in public if work group can learn from your demonstration and you are not embarrassing the subordinate.

Step 11—List the Performance Areas the Subordinate Needs to Improve

Skill Required

S7 This task requires skill to identify, in order of criticality, the improvement areas in which to coach subordinate, based on impact on group or individual results (e.g., safety, EEO).

Step 12—Select the Performance Areas Where You Are Going to Coach the Subordinate

Skill Required

S8 This task requires skill to identify the most critical areas in which to begin coaching, based on impact on group or individual results.

Step 13—Identify the Methods to Improve the Subordinate's Performance

Knowledge Required

K10 There are various methods for coaching subordinates, such as formal training with reviews by boss, personal coaching, demonstration by self, demonstration by someone else, etc.

K11 The ability to coach demands that you know how to do the task correctly yourself, or can find out how to do it by consulting local practices, company practices, other supervisors, subject matter experts, peers, boss.

Step 14—Choose the Most Effective Method

Skill Required

S9 This task requires skill to choose the method for coaching the subordinate, based on time available, resources, cost, subordinate's needs, and pay-off to the organization.

Step 15—Meet with the Subordinate

Knowledge Required

K12 Know to meet the subordinate at the pre-arranged time and place, because if you do not, the performance deficiency may continue.

K13 Know to reschedule the meeting at a mutually convenient time and place if either party is unavailable at the last minute.

Step 16—Set and Maintain a Constructive Tone

Knowledge Required

K14 Know to use Informal Oral Process Step 8.

K15 Know to give positive feedback to subordinate for improvements made in performance areas.

| S16 | You need skill to determine whether to modify method based on input from subordinate (e.g., selected method was to teach ten steps, but subordinate expressed ignorance about only two steps). |

Step 17—Describe the Subordinate's Work Performance

| Skills Required | S10 | You need skill to review subordinate's performance in terms of how it affects output requirements. |
| | S11 | You need skill to draw out from your subordinate the reasons for the actions (e.g., lack of knowledge or skills, false assumptions about what could be omitted, oversight, laziness, etc.). |

Step 18—Review the Comparison of the Subordinate's Work Performance to the Work Standards

Knowledge Required	K16	Know to get the knowledge for this at Feedback process Step 2.
	K17	Know to discuss first the subordinate's performance results and then the acceptable levels of performance.
Skills Required	S12	You need skill to describe the behavior in terms of how it affects job performance.
	S13	You need skill to encourage subordinate's participation throughout the coaching session.

Step 19—Implement the Selected Method for Improving the Subordinate's Work Performance

Knowledge Required	K18	Know to determine the subordinate's thoughts on the rationale for the selected method.
	K19	If method selected was for formal training, schedule subordinate for training (if available).
Skills Required	S14	You need skill to tailor your demonstration and/or explanation to the subordinate's needs (e.g., new versus experienced subordinate).
	S15	You need skill to demonstrate tasks using some form of order (e.g., logical, chronological, simple to complex, general to specific, etc.).

Step 20—Check for Subordinate's Understanding of the Correct Way to Perform the Work

| Skill Required | S17 | You need skill to obtain from the subordinate either a restatement or demonstration of the correct procedure, or both, when appropriate. |

Step 21—Make Follow-up Plans with the Subordinate

Knowledge Required	K20	Know to follow up because job performance may not otherwise improve.
Skills Required	S18	You need skill to determine when the subordinate will perform this task again.
	S19	You need skill to determine criticality of the task, based on customer complaints complaints to regulatory agency safety EEO, etc.
	S20	You need skill to determine the frequency of the tasks.
	S21	You need skill to schedule follow-up observations, based on the criticality and the frequency of the task; that is, according to how long subordinate might need to practice before you expect performance standards to be met.
	S22	You need skill to express confidence in subordinate's ability to master the task.

Step 22—Document the Coaching Session

| Knowledge Required | K21 | Know to use local procedures for documenting, if they exist. |
| | K22 | If local procedures do not exist, you should know to document the following: follow-up dates |

subordinate's comments
what subordinate was coached on
what was agreed to
actions to be taken
name of person coached
date coached

K23 Coaching a subordinate may provide input to the Master Control List (see Planning Step 19) and/or a bring-up system (see Time Management).

Step 23—Go to "Provide Performance Feedback Process" Step 2

| Knowledge Required | K24 | The stimulus for coaching a subordinate may be the output of Feedback Step 26. |
| | K25 | Meeting all performance standards is one indicator that career counseling is appropriate for a subordinate. |

F. TRAINING NEEDS DIAGNOSTIC

The diagnostic test for coaching subordinates is in two sections—an *objective test* intended to test knowledge of the process, and a *role play* designed to test interpersonal and behavioral skills in applying the process.

Objective test

The objective test of five questions is designed to test four coaching skills and seven points of knowledge in coaching subordinates at the first level of supervision. The test questions and answers are found in Exhibits A and B. The specific skills and knowledge tested by the five questions are shown in Exhibit C.

Role play

The role play section of the diagnostic instrument is designed to test the subjects' behavioral and interpersonal skills in performing several duties. Included are:

informal oral communication
providing performance feedback
coaching a subordinate
written communication
controlling the work

The duty of coaching subordinates is given heavy emphasis in this exercise; 15 coaching skills and five items of knowledge are tested. (The actual role play instructions and situation background information are too voluminous to include in this book.) The specific skills and knowledge tested are:

Skills: S1, S6, S7, S8, S10, S11, S12, S13, S14, S15, S16, S17, S18, S21, and S22
Knowledges: K11, K17, K18, K20, and K22

Diagnostic test exhibit A: process 5—coaching subordinates

Coaching is the process that includes activities to help a subordinate learn to do a job correctly.

1.   In determining *when* to coach a subordinate, which of the following factors should you consider? (X-out the correct answer(s) on the answer sheet.)
    a.   relations with the union
    b.   criticality of the incident
    c.   workload of supervisor
    d.   availability of subordinate
    e.   your personal goals/objectives
    f.   AAP/EEO group results
    g.   the effect of delaying job completion

2.   Coaching is sometimes given in private and sometimes in the presence of other subordinates. Describe a situation when coaching should be given in private and when coaching should be given in public. (Write your answers on the answer sheet.)
    a.   in *public*
    b.   in *private*

3. A subordinate is having trouble with an important procedure associated with the job. This procedure is relatively complex. If not performed correctly, it will negatively impact your group's results. Assume the following methods are available for your use. What method should you select to coach the subordinate? (X-out the *correct* answer on the answer sheet.)
    a. Spend the next day with the subordinate, observing and reviewing problems.
    b. Reassign the subordinate to a less complex job.
    c. Send the subordinate to a workshop on the procedure, then follow up on the job.
    d. Gather relevant Bell System Practices and guidelines for subordinate's review.
    e. Assign subordinate to observe another subordinate perform the job.
4. You have been working with one of your subordinates. You have determined that the subordinate is not capable of doing the job assigned. What action should you take next? (X-out the *correct* answer on the answer sheet.)
    a. Instruct the subordinate again on how to perform the job.
    b. Ask your supervisor for the authority to discipline the subordinate.
    c. Assign the subordinate to a job that the subordinate can perform rather than leave in current assignment.
    d. Give feedback to the subordinate regarding your feelings about the subordinate's ability to perform the job.
    e. Document your findings and monitor the subordinate for more supporting data.
5. In which of the following situations should a subordinate be coached? (X-out the *correct* answer(s) on the answer sheet.)
    a. The subordinate has not improved performance, despite prior feedback.
    b. You are assigned to a new group.
    c. The subordinate is assigned a repetitive task.
    d. The work is new and the subordinate does not know how to do it.
    e. The subordinate asks for guidance or help.
    f. The subordinate is assigned a difficult task.
    g. The task is a particularly important task.

Diagnostic test exhibit B—answer sheet: process 5—coaching subordinates

1. a ✗ ✗ ✗ e f ✗
2. (a) WHEN THE WORK GROUP COULD LEARN FROM THE DEMONSTRATION OR IT IS NOT EMBARRASSING OR CONFIDENTIAL
    (b) WHEN IT WOULD BE APT TO EMBARRASS THE SUBORDINATE OR IT IS CONFIDENTIAL IN NATURE
3. a b ✗ d e
4. a b ✗ d e
5. ✗ b c ✗ ✗ f g

Diagnostic test exhibit C—items tested by objective test: process 5—coaching

Test question number	Items tested		Process steps
	Skills	Knowledge	
1	S3		
2	S4	K8, K9	
3	S9	K10	
4	S9	K5, K6	
5		K2, K3	

10 Creating and Maintaining a Motivative Atmosphere

PROCESS 6

A. OVERVIEW OF MOTIVATIVE ATMOSPHERE AT THE SUPERVISORY LEVEL

A motivative environment in the workplace is not necessarily one in which all employees are satisfied and happy. It is a nice "fringe benefit" if they are so, but that is not the purpose for creating and maintaining such an atmosphere. The real purpose is to encourage and induce every member of the work group to contribute his or her *best effort* to the work at all times, and to ensure that environmental conditions foster such behavior.

A motivative atmosphere is not a permissive, easy-going environment; it is rather a *demanding* one in which every member of the work group is expected to do the best work within his or her capability. This is necessary *not only* for the good of the organization—so that the group's goals will be met—but it is actually in the best interests of the individuals involved. For a first-level supervisor to insist and expect each person to do his or her best is a compliment, a mark of respect, to the individual; to ask and accept less than the person's best is demeaning.

If employees can find happiness and fulfillment in the course of applying their best efforts to their own work and contributing their full energies and intelligence to the purposes of the group, then the organization will be highly productive and rewarding to all its members.

It is vitally important that higher levels of management recognize and appreciate the value of a motivative atmosphere, and actively support their first-level supervisors in the effort. It is indeed unfortunate that many higher-level managers are convinced that their subordinate first-level supervisors are doing an adequate job of motivating their employees, even when they are not. In one large survey, eight out of ten upper managers said their supervisors were doing an adequate job of motivating and leading their employees, while only 27 percent of supervisors themselves thought so.[1] This kind of complacency by higher management can be troublesome to first-level supervisors and dangerous to the organization's morale.

[1] *Journal of Personnel Quarterly*, Fall 1970.

94

B.   HIGHLIGHTS OF THE AT&T JOB STUDY

Definition of the process

The process of creating and maintaining a motivative atmosphere in the workplace is defined in the Mastery Model in two ways. One, it is an activity that includes activities that may *help supervisors and subordinates work together*; two, it includes activities that may lead to an *environment conducive to efficient work*.

There is no contradiction or conflict between the two definitions; in fact, they reinforce one another. An environment that fosters efficient work obviously requires supervisors and subordinates to work together toward that end; and when supervisors and subordinates work together, they actually create a motivative environment in the process.

Summary description of the process

In the AT&T Mastery Model, creating and maintaining a motivative atmosphere in the workplace is treated as a *managerial process* in which the first-level supervisor plays the major role. It is a continuous, ongoing process, with no clear beginning and no end; a newly appointed supervisor is advised to start, however, by listing his or her activities that contribute to such an environment. Among these activities are:

- *Giving performance feedback* to members of the work group in a constructive reinforcing manner; subordinates have more job satisfaction knowing where they stand in regard to their performance. They are also more likely to communicate with their supervisor.
- *Coaching* subordinates who need help in mastering their jobs—knowing how and why the job must be done leads to better performance, even a measure of job enjoyment.
- *Career counseling* individuals who meet all job standards and may want more challenging work. Subordinates are more likely to produce when

they know the boss is sincerely interested in their future.

- *Communicating* freely and openly with individuals and the group. Subordinates are more receptive to rules, regulations, and changes when the boss takes time to explain why, and asks and considers their feelings.
- *Controlling progress of the work* in such a way that work is assigned according to subordinates' capabilities and subordinates know the boss's expectations, the job standards, and the impact of their output on the goals of the organization.

The supervisor is then advised to develop a list of *indicators of a motivative atmosphere* that are unique to the work group he or she supervises and to its individual members, and then to observe and compare employees' actual behavior with these indicators. Discrepancies between observed behavior and the indicators may require corrective action, depending on the nature and extent of the discrepancies.

As an example, if the good housekeeping habits of the group suddenly deteriorate, or if an individual's absenteeism becomes habitual, this behavior change should be seriously studied for its significance to the organization. The process then requires the supervisor to take steps to correct the aberrant behavior, either by counseling the individuals involved or by changing environmental conditions that may be demotivating to the group (such as lack of positive feedback, inadequate work planning, or the like).

As part of this remedial process, the supervisor is required, through interviews with individuals, to obtain from subordinates *their views* of the observed behavior change and to factor these into the corrective action.

At two points in the process, the supervisor is advised to use the Problem Solving process to resolve problems that may be causing the behavior changes observed in the group and/or its members.

C.   TASKS AND DECISION POINTS IN THE PROCESS OF CREATING AND MAINTAINING A MOTIVATIVE ATMOSPHERE

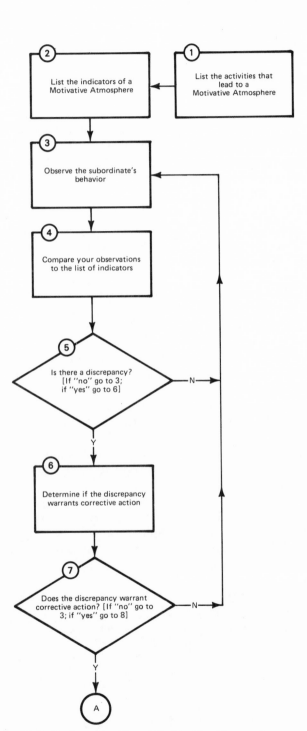

FIGURE 10-1.   Creating a Motivative Atmosphere: The First Seven Steps

STEP 1   Your first step is to list the *supervisory activities* that can help to create a motivative atmosphere in the workplace, such as coaching, career counseling, giving performance feedback, communicating, and controlling.

STEP 2   List the positive *indicators* of a motivative atmosphere that are unique to your organization and work group.

Among these are *work group indicators* like good performance measurements, low turnover, group solutions to housekeeping problems, etc. Also included are *individual indicators* like interest in work, enthusiasm, individual decisions, open about problems, etc.

STEP 3   Observe behavior of individual members of the work group.

STEP 4   Compare your observations with your list of positive indicators.

STEP 5
Decision   Respond to the question: *Is there a discrepancy between observed behavior and indicators?*

If your decision is *no*, return to Step 3 and continue observation of behavior.

STEP 6   If your answer is *yes*—there is a discrepancy—you should next determine whether the discrepancy warrants corrective action.

Keep in mind that some behavior changes are transient and superficial or not serious enough to warrant action on your part.

STEP 7
Decision   Respond to the question: *Does the discrepancy warrant corrective action by you?*

If your decision is *no*, return to Step 3 and continue observation of behavior.

If *yes*, go to Step 8.

Figure 10-1 illustrates the process of creating a motivative atmosphere through the first seven steps.

STEP 8   If your decision in Step 7 is *yes*, determine whether or not input from your subordinate is needed before taking action, such as when the causes of the discrepancy are not readily apparent.

STEP 9
Decision   Respond to the question: *Is the subordinate's input required?*

If your decision is *yes*, skip the next step and go to Step 11.

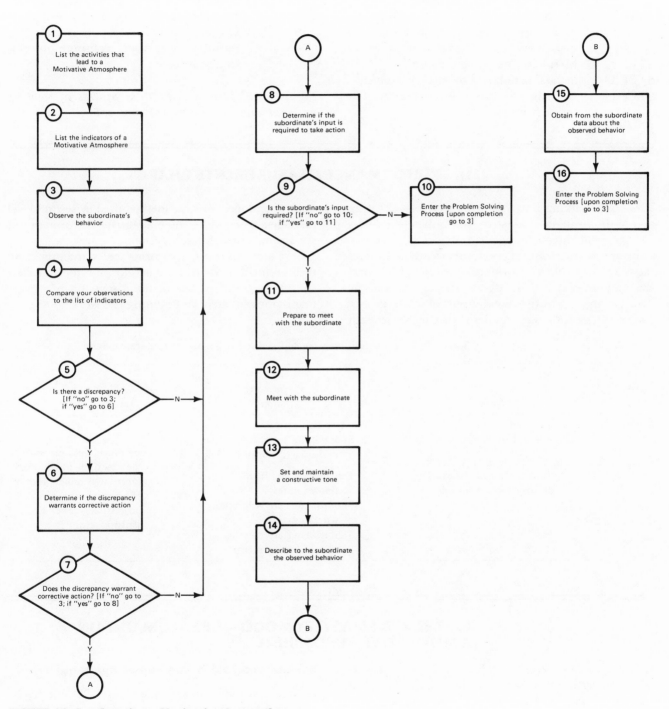

**FIGURE 10-2.   Creating a Motivative Atmosphere:
Total Managerial Process**

STEP 10   At this point, you should go to the Problem Solving process (entering at Step 2—Define Problem—and exiting at Step 10—Implement Selected Solution) to resolve the behavior discrepancy.

STEP 11   Prepare to meet with your subordinate at an appropriate time and place to discuss the suspected behavior problem.

STEP 12   Meet with your subordinate.

STEP 13   Set and maintain a constructive tone.

STEP 14   Describe to your subordinate the observed behavior.

STEP 15   Obtain your subordinate's views about the observed behavior.

STEP 16   Again turn to the Problem Solving process, either together with the subordinate or later, after additional data have been gathered. Either conclude the session or adjourn it. Upon completion, return to Step 3 and continue observation of behavior.

Figure 10-2 illustrates the total process of creating and maintaining a motivative atmosphere.

D. PERFORMANCE MEASUREMENTS CHART

The sixth ranking duty of the supervisor—Creating and Maintaining a Motivative Atmosphere—involves 13 tasks and three contingencies or decision points. For purposes of measuring performance, these 16 steps fall naturally into two principal *groups*. The chart that follows (Table 10-1) lists the steps in each of the two groups, identifies the output of each group, shows the performance standards that apply to each output, and identifies the method used by second-level managers to measure the managerial performance of subordinate first-line supervisors.

These outputs, performance standards, and measurement methods were developed under the constraints recorded earlier in the discussion of performance measurement in Planning the Work.

Table 10-1. Process 6: creating and maintaining a motivative atmosphere

Step or group of steps	Output	Performance standards	Method of measurement
Steps 1–7	Problems affecting a motivative atmosphere are identified	Attendance is good Supervisor's subordinates are enthusiastic about the job	Second-level boss measures the reactions of the work force, attendance, number of grievances, office suggestions, general attitude, etc.
Steps 8–16	Problems affecting motivative atmosphere are solved	Few complaints from subordinates Subordinates are willing to work overtime Subordinates are meeting output requirements	

E. THE AT&T MASTERY MODEL—CREATE/MAINTAIN A MOTIVATIVE ATMOSPHERE

Creating a motivative atmosphere in the workplace is not ordinarily considered a "managerial activity" in the same sense as coaching or controlling work. In the AT&T first-level supervisory job study, however, this duty is treated as an organized process of management, one consisting of 16 discrete steps or tasks.

This process is described in the following, together with the skills and knowledge associated with each task.

Fundamental skills and knowledge required

In order to conduct this managerial process effectively, it is necessary that you know this important *fundamental of management* as it relates to creating and maintaining a motivative atmosphere.

Knowledge Required   K1   A motivative atmosphere may be beneficial to *all parties involved* with the work:

- *Subordinate* benefits from increased job satisfaction; increased consideration for rewards—raises, promotions, transfers, etc.
- *Boss* benefits from improved quantity and quality of work produced by subordinates. He or she may learn better ways of doing the work from subordinates; may be perceived by higher management as a better manager because of improved group results; may have to spend less time with labor relations problems. The boss can also benefit from reduced absenteeism, a less hectic atmosphere, and fewer "fires" to put out.
- *Company* benefits from better productivity and quality; fewer absences; a larger pool of qualified, dedicated people for possible promotion to management.

Step 1—List the Activities that Lead to a Motivative Atmosphere

Knowledge Required	K2	A motivative atmosphere is the result of the first-level supervisor using other managerial processes in an effective way; that is, coaching, career counseling, giving performance feedback, communicating, and controlling according to the Mastery Models provided.

- *Giving Performance Feedback:* Subordinates will have more job satisfaction knowing where they stand in regard to their performance and will be more likely to communicate with the boss.
- *Coaching:* Subordinates are more apt to perform better and enjoy the job more when they know how and why the job must be done.
- *Career Counseling:* Subordinates are more apt to produce on the job if they know

the boss is interested in their future.

- *Communication:* Subordinates are more receptive to rules, regulations, changes, etc., when the boss takes the time to explain why, asks and considers their feelings.
- *Controlling:* Subordinates usually enjoy their jobs when they know what the boss's expectations are, what the standards are, when work is assigned according to their capabilities, when they know the impact of their outputs on the organization goals.

	K3	One of the purposes of these duties is to find out what the unique needs and desires of each individual are and to try to match them to the business needs.

Step 2—List the Indicators of a Motivative Atmosphere

Skills Required	S1	This task requires skill to identify the indicators of a motivative atmosphere that are unique to your work force, department, organization, etc.
	S2	You need skill to observe those distinctive behaviors each person displays that may indicate that the person's motivation has been affected, such as changes from: happy disposition to serious joking person to very quiet quiet person to very talkative argumentative person to passive person
Knowledge Required	K4	Some indicators of a motivative atmosphere are work group-related and some are individual-related, as shown below:

Work Group (Environment)
less hectic pace
fewer "fires" to put out
measurements (quantity, quality, absence)
more promotions
fewer grievances

higher level of friendly competition

group works out problems among themselves, such as who gets overtime, etc.

Individual
asks for more work
puts work before breaks
more interested in work
goes further on own efforts
makes own decisions
tries more on own
more willing to work overtime
generates enthusiasm (talks positively, tries to get others interested or involved)
keeps supervisor up-to-date instead of waiting to be asked
open about problems encountered instead of defensive
expresses pride in work and confidence in own ability
self-starter

	K5	Know to build and expand the list of observed indicators (behaviors) of a motivative atmosphere unique to your particular work force and that impact the work.
	K6	If you are not familiar with a subordinate's behavior (either the supervisor or the subordinate is new to the work force), it will be necessary to first observe the subordinate's behavior for some period of time before characterizing it as one type or another.

Step 3—Observe the Subordinate's Behavior

Knowledge Required	K7	Observation of these behaviors is an ongoing activity that occurs in the supervisor's daily relations with subordinates, not necessarily the formal scheduled type of observations.
Skill Required	S3	You need skill to base these observations on performance indices, personal observations, feedback from boss, peers, customers, etc.

Step 4—Compare Your Observations to the List of Indicators

Knowledge Required	K8	Behaviors can be noted mentally or in writing.
Skill Required	S4	You need skill to match indicators with observed behaviors to determine differences.

Step 5—Decision Point: Is There a Discrepancy? *If Your Decision Is* No, *Return to Step 3 and Continue Observation of Behavior.*

Step 6—Determine if the Discrepancy Warrants Corrective Action

---

Knowledge Required	K9	Some changes may be superficial and transient (e.g., isolated incident, change of clothing style, subordinate does not feel well that particular day, etc.)
	K10	Some behaviors may not warrant immediate action because the effects are not serious and the underlying causes are not identified. Therefore, more observation may be warranted.
Skill Required	S5	You need skill to determine if the difference warrants corrective action, such as in these situations:

Serious deficiencies will occur if behavior continues (increased customer complaints, potential safety problems, etc.).

Boss is going on vacation—you must deal with matter or risk situation worsening.

Subordinate is starting work that is more critical than past work.

Step 7—Decision Point: Does the Discrepancy Warrant Corrective Action? *If Your Decision Is* No, *Return to Step 3 and Continue Observation.*

Step 8—Determine if Subordinate's Input Is Required to Take Action

Knowledge Required	K11	Some indicators (hectic work group pace, lack of promotions, etc.) may not require subordinate input either to identify causes or to take action.
	K12	Some indicators and behaviors require subordinate input because the causes are not evident; for example, subordinate's absence could be caused by: health, home problem situation not within supervisor's authority—subordinate disgruntled over pay, policies, or practices ("Company doesn't care, why should I?") supervisor has not paid attention to subordinate except in negative way; absenteeism is a way of punishing boss.
	K13	It may not be appropriate to discuss a matter with a subordinate immediately; for example, if a subordinate is going on vacation, discussion should be postponed until after vacation.
Skill Required	S6	You need skill to determine whether the situation can be corrected by making use of other managerial skills, such as better planning and controlling to reduce the pace; developing subordinates so that subordinates are more promotable; verification of what happened and why it happened, etc.

Step 9—Decision Point: Is the Subordinate's Input Required? If Your Decision Is Yes, Skip the Next Step and Go to Step 11.

Step 10—Enter the Problem Solving Process (Upon Completion, Return to Step 3.)

Knowledge Required	K14	Know to enter the Problem Solving process at "Define Problem" and exit at "Implement Solution."

Step 11—Prepare to Meet with the Subordinate

Skill Required	S7	You need skill to set an appropriate time for meeting with subordinate, based on: workload of yourself and subordinate availability of yourself and subordinate criticality of incident
Knowledge Required	K15	Know to discuss this matter in private so it does not embarrass the subordinate and peers.
	K16	Know to notify subordinate in advance of time and place if discussion is not to be immediate.

Step 12—Meet with the Subordinate

Step 13—Set and Maintain a Constructive Tone

Knowledge Required	K17	You should know to use the Informal Oral Discussion process (see Process No. 9, Step 8).

Step 14—Describe to the Subordinate the Observed Behavior

Skill Required	S9	This task requires skill to describe to the subordinate what you have observed and why it concerns you.

Step 15—Obtain from the Subordinate Data about the Observed Behavior

Skill Required	S10	This task requires skill to draw out your subordinate as to why he or she behaved in the manner described.

Step 16—Enter the Problem Solving Process

Knowledge Required	K18	You should know to enter Problem Solving process at "Define Problem" and exit at "Implement Solution."

K19 In some cases, the Problem Solving process can be performed quickly, either mentally or with the subordinate within the session. In other cases, if additional research may be needed, the session should be concluded and rescheduled to a later date.

Upon completion of Step 16, return to Step 3 and continue to observe subordinates' behavior.

===

F. PERFORMANCE NEEDS DIAGNOSTIC

This is an objective test of six questions, designed to test first-level supervisors' skills and knowledge in establishing and maintaining a motivative atmosphere in the workplace. The questions and answers are found in Exhibits A and B. The three specific skills and five knowledges tested by the six questions are shown in Exhibit C.

Diagnostic test exhibit A: process 6—creating/maintaining a motivative atmosphere

This section deals with Creating/Maintaining a Motivative Atmosphere. This process includes activities that may help a supervisor and subordinate work together.

1. List *five* benefits of providing a motivative atmosphere. (Write your answers on the answer sheet.)
2. Of the six items listed below select the three that are *most effective* in producing and maintaining a motivative atmosphere. (X-out the *three* correct answers on the answer sheet.)
    a. assigning the work properly
    b. spending time with your subordinates after hours
    c. giving performance feedback to subordinates
    d. communicating with subordinates
    e. interviewing subordinates to find out their interests
    f. setting tight and demanding due dates
3. A subordinate has three weeks' vacation scheduled in the summer. The subordinate wants to take two additional weeks off without pay to go with the family to Hawaii. You checked your workload and see a major project scheduled for those two extra weeks the subordinate wants. What should you do next? (X-out the *best* answer on the answer sheet.)
    a. Explain that if you gave it to one, you would have to give it to all.
    b. Check with other supervisors to see if they have a surplus person who could be loaned to your group.
    c. Ask your other subordinates if they would be willing to shoulder the subordinate's work.
    d. Let the subordinate take the extra two weeks of vacation because such opportunities do not come very often.
    e. Explain that a major project is scheduled for those two weeks and the needs of the business require the subordinate's skills.
4. An experienced and competent employee has been making errors on simple job operations. What should you do? (X-out the correct answer on the answer sheet.)
    a. Give the subordinate more challenging assignments.
    b. Give the subordinate performance feedback.
    c. Check on the subordinate's work more frequently.
    d. Correct the work errors yourself.
    e. Have another subordinate correct the work errors.

5. Your subordinates used to get work done on time with good quality. Recently you have noticed that some jobs are not being done on time, and jobs that are done on time do not meet standards. You also hear subordinates saying such things as: "It's a pain in the neck to work around here," "Hey, boss, I'm working all the time and Lou doesn't do a thing."

     What should you do first? (Write your answer in one sentence on the answer sheet.)

6. The following is a list of statements about motivation. (On the answer sheet, place a "1" next to the letter of the statement which is a probable indicator of motivation, etc., as shown below.)

    1. Probable indicator of high motivation
    2. Not an indicator of motivation
    3. Probable indicator of low motivation

    a. makes excuses for poor quality
    b. asks for more work
    c. leaves on time
    d. tries more on own
    e. can't do a certain task
    f. makes own decisions
    g. willing to work overtime

    h. careless in work performance
    i. complains about the work
    j. expresses pride in work
    k. high error rate
    l. wants extra vacation time
    m. wants only easy assignments

Diagnostic test exhibit B—answer sheet: process 6—motivative atmosphere

1. (1) MORE JOB SATISFACTION
    (2) MORE APT TO BE CONSIDERED FOR BENEFITS—RAISES, PROMOTION, TRANSFER
    (3) IMPROVED QUANTITY AND QUALITY OF WORK PRODUCED BY SUB.
    (4) MAY LEARN BETTER WAYS TO DO THINGS FROM SUB.—LESS LABOR RELATIONS
        PROBLEMS, LESS ABSENTEEISM, ETC.
    (5) BETTER PRODUCTIVITY AND QUALITY—LESS ABSENCE
    (6) LARGER POOL OF QUALIFIED DEDICATED PEOPLE FOR POSSIBLE PROMOTION
        TO MANAGEMENT
2. X̶ b X̶ X̶ e f
3. a X̶ c d e
4. a X̶ c d e
5. USE MANAGERIAL SKILLS TO FIX THE PROBLEM/PLANNING/CONTROLLING
6. a _3_ b _1_ c _2_ d _1_ e _2_ f _1_ g _2_ h _3_ i _3_ j _1_ k _2_ l _2_ m _3_

Diagnostic test exhibit C—items tested by objective test: process 6—motivative atmosphere

Test question number	Items tested		Process steps
	Skills	Knowledge	
1		K1	
2		K2	
3		K3	
4	S5, S6	K12	
5	S6		
6		K4	

11 Time Management

PROCESS 7

A. TIME MANAGEMENT AT THE SUPERVISORY LEVEL

Hardly a week goes by without the mail bringing to my desk a brochure about a new book or a new course on the subject of time management. I find that I can save time by not reading them.

It is not that these books and courses are not useful. Many of them contain helpful ideas and tricks for controlling one's time. It's simply that, for a first-level supervisor, the whole matter of controlling time boils down to two simple management fundamentals—*concentration* and *focus.*

Concentration means to reduce the number of factors you're concerned with down to a minimum number, through application of Pareto's law of distribution, sometimes known as the 80/20 rule. This is the famous rule that says that generally about 80 percent of any result is accomplished by some 20 percent of its factors. The law says that in any multivariable situation, a "critical few" factors make most of the difference, while the "trivial many" do not have a significant effect on the total result. It is vitally important to isolate these critical factors for management attention. When these really critical tasks are done, the other things seem to come along; when they are not done, nothing else that *is* done seems to matter all that much.

Focus means to apply your maximum energy, intelligence, and effort on these critical few tasks that make the difference. When this is done, the really important work tends to be performed in a superior manner, reflecting credit on you and your organization. You are applying Pareto's law here, too—putting 80 percent of your effort on the 20 percent of the tasks that count most to overall results.

In Schoen and Durand's excellent book, *Supervision: The Management of Organizational Resources,*[1] the chapter on managing time is aptly titled "Time: The Nonrenewable Resource." The authors state that effective time management has a high payoff for the first-level supervisor in "increased productivity, improved performance, better use of abilities and talents, and the opportunity to engage in new and rewarding career and non-career pursuits." That is, indeed, a remarkably high payoff! It is hard to conceive of any other activity that can reward the first-level supervisor so well.

On the downside, the authors point out that without the ability to manage his or her own time, the supervisor will find it hard to find time to super-

[1]Englewood Cliffs, N.J.: Prentice-Hall Inc., 1979.

104

vise others. They provide these eight essentials for effective time management:

1. Know how your time was spent.
2. Set priorities.
3. Schedule time realistically.
4. Delegate effectively.
5. Lead meetings effectively.
6. Control interruptions.
7. Manage your reading load.
8. Improve your communication skills.

To this list, I would add several "time managers" that have proved useful to me personally.

- Don't let your subordinates delegate upward to you. Insist that they solve their own work problems instead of bringing them to you for solution.
- Break complex or long-term assignments into "bite-size" tasks on your To Do List, and do the job in stages. Often the highest priority elements of the assignment can be done right away, leav-

ing the less urgent parts to be done more or less at your convenience. Besides, you'll get a lot of satisfaction in seeing the job accomplished step by step, as you check off each completed task.

- It is human nature to put off or postpone tasks that are perceived to be unpleasant. When a job remains on the To Do List long past the time it should have been done, ask yourself, "What am I avoiding?" More often than not, the painful disciplinary action will then be taken; the disagreeable customer's phone call will then be returned; the hard decision will then be made—and the item can be crossed off the list.
- Setting unrealistically high goals, taking on too many commitments, or fearing failure to do a "perfect" job are negative factors that can lead to a kind of task paralysis in which managers say to themselves, "I'll wait until conditions are better," or "I need more information." Better to settle for 90 percent and get the job done than to strive for 100 percent and never complete the assignment.

B. HIGHLIGHTS OF THE AT&T JOB STUDY

Definition of the process

Time management is defined in the AT&T Mastery Model as

the scheduling of administrative responsibilities. It includes handling telephone calls, office paper flow, and work activities.

At the outset, however, the Mastery Model cautions the first-level supervisor that he or she should know "time management is not the management of time—it is a process of scheduling activities to be done during work time. . . . the continuous effective allocation of time to the work with the highest payoff."

Summary description of the process

The process identifies three aspects of time management: (1) handling incoming and outgoing phone calls, (2) managing paper flow, and (3) managing tasks by means of a daily personal work plan called a "To Do" list.

To manage each of these areas effectively requires the first-level supervisor to identify the most important

items to job performance and respond to these first. On the first two—managing phone calls and paper flow—a screening process should be set up, using a subordinate whenever possible, to cull out (and respond to) routine and nonessential matters, leaving only the time-urgent and subject-critical items for the supervisor to deal with. This not only will reduce the number of items reaching the supervisor substantially, but it will also improve the *quality* of the supervisor's responses by enabling him or her to concentrate energy and management attention on fewer items.

With respect to the personal work plan—the To Do List—the supervisor is instructed to follow a three-phase process: (1) to make a daily list of tasks, (2) to assign the highest priority to the most critical of these, and (3) to keep the list current as new tasks pop up and old ones are accomplished.

The supervisor is encouraged to *delegate* work to subordinates to the maximum feasible extent, in order to free up time for other essential work, and also contribute to subordinates' development (with due regard, of course, to possible union contract constraints and the capabilities of subordinates).

In the following section, the eleven steps in the process of managing time are described and illustrated with a flowchart of tasks and decision points.

C. TASKS AND DECISION POINTS IN THE PROCESS OF MANAGING TIME

STEP 1   Your first step is to select one of three areas of your work in which to apply the Time Management process:

STEP 2   Managing Telephone Calls: use phone as time-saving substitute for travel; set up message-taking/screening system; keep calls as brief as courtesy permits.

STEP 3   Managing Incoming Paper Flow: set up a screening system to sort, pass on, respond to, or dispose of incoming paper.

STEP 4   Managing a "To Do" System: follow Steps 5 through 11.

STEP 5   Make a "To Do" list, a plan for the day's activities.

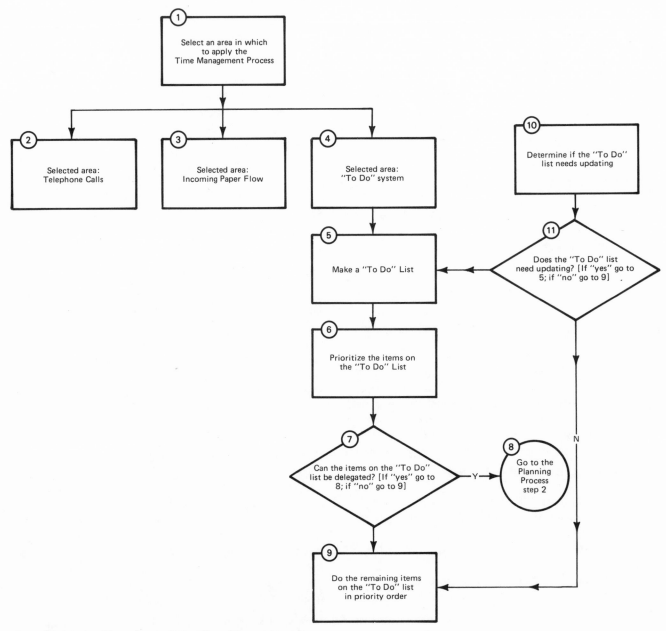

FIGURE 11-1. Flowchart of the Time Management Process

STEP 6 | Prioritize the "To Do" items in order of urgency, time required, your boss's needs, etc.

STEP 7 (Decision) | Respond to the question: *Can the items on the To Do list be delegated?*

If your decision is *No*, skip Step 8 and go to Step 9.

STEP 8 | If your decision is *Yes*—items on the To Do list can be delegated to subordinates— go to Step 2 of the Planning process and establish the *output requirements* of the work to be delegated.

STEP 9 | Do the remaining (undelegable) items on the list in priority order.

STEP 10 | Determine if the To Do list needs updating because of new assignments, roadblocks encountered, completion of tasks, cancellation of some items, changes in priorities, etc.

STEP 11 (Decision) | Respond to the question: *Does the To Do list need updating?*

If your decision is *yes*, return to Step 5 and reiterate the process.

If your decision is *no*, continue to do the tasks remaining on the To Do list.

Figure 11-1 illustrates the nine tasks and two contingencies involved in the total process.

D. PERFORMANCE MEASUREMENTS CHART

The seventh ranking duty of the supervisor— Managing Time—involves nine tasks and two contingencies or decision points. For purposes of measuring performance, these 11 steps fall naturally into four principal *groups*. The chart that follows (Table 11-1) lists the steps in each of the four groups, identifies the output of each group, shows the performance standards that apply to each output, and identifies the method used by second-level managers to measure the managerial performance of subordinate first-line supervisors.

These outputs, performance standards, and measurement methods were developed under the constraints recorded earlier, in the discussion of performance measurement in Planning the Work.

Table 11-1. Process 7: time management

Step or group of steps	*Output*	*Performance standards*	*Method of measurement*
Step 1	Deficient personal time management areas are defined	Telephone calls are handled in a timely manner	Second-level boss measures quality and quantity of first-level outputs
Step 2	Information exchanged by telephone		
Step 3	Correspondence/mail processed daily	Correspondence and Mail consistently organized	
Steps 4–11	Work completed effectively Commitments met Schedule maintained	First-level supervisor's delegates meet responsibilities effectively in the shortest amount of time Plans ahead for self and subordinates	

E. THE AT&T MASTERY MODEL—TIME MANAGEMENT

Managing your own time is a managerial process that may involve as many as 11 discrete steps. Two of these are decision points that may require you to alter the sequence of steps in the process.

The 11 steps are detailed in the following, together with the skills and knowledge you need to master each task.

Fundamental skills and knowledge required

In order for you to manage your own time effectively, it is necessary for you to know *two fundamentals* relating to time management at the first level of supervision. These are:

Knowledge Required	K1	Time management is not the management of time—it is a process of scheduling activities to be done during work time.
	K2	Time management is the continuous effective allocation of your time to the work with the highest payoff.

Step 1—Select an Area in which to Apply the Time Management Process

---

Knowledge Required	K3	The three most productive areas for time management at first level are: handling telephone calls handling paper flow using a work-to-do system
	K4	Areas selected may be worked on individually or in groups.
Skill Required	S1	You need skill to select the area in which to apply Time Management, based on the impact upon your personal job performance and the amount of time each consumes during the day.

Step 2—Selected Area: Managing Telephone Calls

Knowledge Required	K5	Know to use phone as a time-saving substitute for traveling to the other party, whether inter-building, intercity, or interstate.
	K6	Know to use steps from Informal or Formal Oral Communication when making and receiving phone calls.
	K7	Outgoing phone calls may be made efficiently, and scheduled incoming calls may be handled efficiently, by preparing an outline from which to speak. Thus, follow-up calling may be minimized.

	K8	Phone calls may generate inputs for the To Do List or Planning.
	K9	Know to use other telephone communication features (e.g., add-on, call waiting, picture-phone, etc.) to facilitate communication.
	K10	Know to perform other activities while on hold.
	K11	Know to make phone calls as brief as courtesy permits.
	K12	Know to establish a message-taking system for use while out of the workplace.
	K13	Know that having calls screened is a technique for saving time but may not always be possible.
	K14	Know to accept calls such as from boss or higher levels, customer complaints that have been screened to your level, service interruptions, and items identified as important by you.
	K15	Know to leave forwarding number when away from workplace.
	K16	Know that possible screeners (other than self) are boss, peers, subordinates.
	K17	Know to answer important phone calls when received, if possible.
	K18	Know to return calls as promised, especially important calls.
	K19	Know to return less important calls by the end of the work day, if possible.
	K20	Returning less important calls is important to maintain lines of communication and facilitate future coordination between you and caller.
	K21	Know to be available at the time promised for receiving a return call.
Skills Required	S2	You need skill to determine whether to document contents of calls.
	S3	You need skill to determine which points of phone calls to document, if documentation is appropriate.
	S4	You need skill to establish a screening system for incoming calls, based on current work load,

source and nature of call (boss, higher level, identified emergencies, etc.)

S5   You need skill to postpone certain calls, by advising that you will get back to them by a specified time.

S6   You need skill to establish a screening process with these steps:

1. The screener states office (location) and name.

2. The screener determines the topic of conversation, the name of the caller, and whether or not call must be handled immediately.

3. If call must be handled immediately, the screener routes call to appropriate party or handles the problem.

4. If call does not have to be handled immediately, the screener takes the number where the caller can be reached and arranges for call back.

Step 3—Selected Area: Managing Incoming Paper Flow

Knowledge Required	K22	Paper flow is a major means of business communication and documentation.
	K23	Responses to incoming paper flow may be either to act upon, read, or skim the paper flow, or to make these responses immediately, later, or not at all.
	K24	Know to review, or have reviewed, incoming paper flow each day.
	K25	Screening may include responding to, disposing of, or sorting incoming paper.
	K26	Some items need to be passed on to others because they were misrouted to you.
Skills Required	S7	You need skill to determine whether someone else (subordinate, peer, boss) can assist in the screening of paper flow to save time.

S8   You need skill to establish a paper flow screening process to identify importance, based on:

criteria for important items established in "Managing Telephone Calls" (see K14)

visual cues such as envelopes from usual sources of work, boss's handwriting, own name individually typed on envelope, first class mail, etc.

S9   You need skill to determine which paper flow may be responded to or disposed of by screener and which may be sorted for your attention.

S10   You need skill to prioritize paper flow as shown in "Managing Telephone Calls" (see K14, K17, K20).

Step 4—Selected Area: "To Do" System

Knowledge Required	K27	A "To Do" List is a list of tasks, a personal work plan for the day.
	K28	A "To Do" List may be written or mental (written is preferred).
	K29	A "To Do" List is subject to revision for such reasons as boss's needs, emergencies, contingencies (unavailability of needed person or resources).
	K30	A "To Do" List may be: a schedule of tasks associated with specific times of the day, such as an appointment book or a desk calendar, or a division of a day into blocks of time designated for specific kinds of activities, such as meeting 8:30–10:30, quality checks 10:30–12:00, return phone calls 4:00–5:00.

Step 5—Make a "To Do" List

Knowledge Required	K31	Making a "To Do" List *at a fixed time each day* facilitates the making of the list because it is scheduled into each day's activity.
	K32	Items for a "To Do" List come from many sources, such as:

	incoming	meetings
	paper flow	peers and co-
	telephone calls	ordinates
	boss	"bring-up" file
	Planning	personal goals
	process	Master Con-
	self-develop-	trol List
	ment	

	K33	Know to record unfilled prior commitments (from calendar or "bring-up" file).
	K34	You should know the amount of time that was used for any prior performance of a task.
	K35	Estimates of time needed for each task help to schedule items on the "To Do" List.
Skills Required	S11	You need skill to determine an appropriate fixed time each day to make a "To Do" List, such as the first thing each morning.
	S12	You need skill to record items that are useful to do (e.g., thank-you notes, reading technical journals).
	S13	You need skill to estimate time needed for an unfamiliar task by consulting such sources as boss, peers, or subordinates familiar with the task, work logs, or own judgment.

Step 6—Prioritize the Items on the "To Do" List

Knowledge Required	K36	This task requires you to know that *prioritizing* means to enter tasks on the "To Do" List based on criticality to your own performance and the best time to do them.
	K37	Know to prioritize items in terms of importance to job performance.
	K38	Know to schedule high-priority items at the best time for their performance, based on your best time for doing a given priority task (e.g., your best time for writing is after lunch), and time when resources are available.
	K39	High-priority items need not

always be done first in the day (e.g., high-priority item requiring two hours: if work starts at 8:00, with mandated meeting (established time, one hour) at 8:30, schedule the high-priority item at 9:30).

Skills Required	S14	You need skill to identify which items to do first, based on: boss's priorities own priorities commitments to other work groups deadlines human and nonhuman resources (whether available, when avail- able)
	S15	Use time estimates developed in K35 and S13 to fit other tasks into time blocks remaining after priority items are scheduled.

Step 7—Decision Point: Can the items on the "To Do" List Be Delegated?

Knowledge Required	K40	This decision requires you to know that delegable work is work that a first-level manager normally performs.
	K41	Delegated items may be either high- or low-priority items.
Skill Required	S16	You need skill to identify items for delegation based on such factors as: capabilities of subordinates to do task union contract own desire for time to work on higher priority items that can- not be delegated usefulness of performance by subordinate to his or her development

If your decision is *no*, go to Step 9.

Step 8—Go to the Planning Process.

If Your Decision Is *Yes*—Items Can Be Delegated—Go to Planning the Work Process, Step 2.

Step 9—Do the Remaining Items on the "To Do" List in Priority Order

Knowledge Required	K42	Crossing items off a "To Do" List provides a record of tasks completed and tasks remaining, and also gives a sense of accomplishment.
	K43	Completed "To Do" items may be inputs to Planning, Subordinate Development, bring-up file, Performance Feedback, Self-Development, and Problem Solving.
	K44	Completed items may need follow-up.

Step 10—Determine If the "To Do" List Needs Updating

Skill Required	S17	This task requires skill to determine whether "To Do" List needs revision during the day, based on: roadblocks encountered new inputs prioritization of new and existing inputs (see Step 6) modification of time available completion of listed items cancellation of some items reports from subordinates on status of delegated items priority of items remaining on list

Step 11—Decision Point: Does the "To Do" List Need Updating?

If your decision is *yes,* return to Step 5 and follow the process; if *no,* return to Step 9 and do the tasks remaining on the "To Do" List.

F. TRAINING NEEDS DIAGNOSTIC

This is an *objective* test of 12 questions designed to test the skills and knowledge of first-level supervisors in managing time.

The questions and answers are found in Exhibits A and B. The seven specific skills and 17 points of knowledge tested by the 12 questions are shown in Exhibit C.

Diagnostic test exhibit A: process 7—time management

Time Management is the scheduling of your administrative responsibilities. This includes handling telephone calls, office paper flow, and work activities.

1. From the list below, select the three techniques you should use to help manage your time. (X-out the *three* correct answers on the answer sheet.)
   a. Keep list of frequently called numbers.
   b. Take notes on information exchanged for all telephone calls.
   c. Maintain an appointment calendar.
   d. Keep track of things to do.
   e. Attend all meetings to keep yourself informed.
   f. Use group decision-making process.
2. You received the following note from your boss in your in-basket:

   Pat:
        I'm curious about the impact of the new data system on our 1981 budget.
                  —Your Boss

What should you do? (X-out the *best* answer on the answer sheet.)

    a.   Call your boss immediately for further instructions.

    b.   Immediately make telephone calls to staff or your peers and start gathering information.

    c.   Wait for your boss to call with further instructions.

    d.   Gather readily available information when schedule permits and call your boss to review.

3.   It is Monday. You have made a list of things to do during the week.

        You should work first on things which (X-out the correct answer on the answer sheet):

    a.   take less time to get them out of the way

    b.   are carried over from last week's list

    c.   are performed very well by you

    d.   have the biggest impact on your job

    e.   will take a lot of time

4.   You must make a telephone call to discuss several complicated matters. You have researched the different areas. What should you do to prepare for the telephone calls? (Write your answer on the answer sheet.)

5.   You are meeting in your office with a subordinate. There is no one to answer your phone. What should you do? (X-out the correct answer on the answer sheet.)

    a.   Take your telephone off hook to prevent interruptions.

    b.   Call the boss to say you will be unavailable, then ignore your telephone.

    c.   Answer your telephone and handle business; ask subordinate to leave room if call is confidential.

    d.   Answer your telephone calls and determine if you can return call to handle business.

    e.   Answer your telephone if it rings more than five times.

6.   High priority items do not always have to be worked on first thing in the morning. (X-out T for True or F for False on the answer sheet.)

7.   You have been out of the office for two days. When you return, there are 14 messages asking you to call people back. Which calls should you make *first*? (X-out the *best* answer on the answer sheet.)

    a.   whoever called you first

    b.   people returning calls you had made

    c.   names that were unfamiliar to you

    d.   long distance telephone calls

    e.   calls you think might be important

    f.   people who called you more than once

8.   You should not have anyone screen your mail because you personally are responsible for what is directed to you. (X-out T for True or F for False on the answer sheet.)

9.   Your boss is one source for identifying items you should put on a list of things to do. What are five other sources of items to put on the list of things to do? (Write your *five* answers on the answer sheet.)

10.   You have been at a three-day training class. When you return to the office, your in-basket is overflowing. What is the most efficient procedure for handling the contents of the in-basket: (X-out the correct answer on the answer sheet.)

    a.   Go through in-basket when time permits.

    b.   Read bulletins and informational materials to get caught up.

    c.   Sort items by priorities and work on highest priority items.

    d.   File each item to make room for incoming mail.

    e.   Read memos immediately and read other material as time permits.

    f.   Work through items in the order received.

11.   High priority items from your list of things to do should not be delegated to subordinates. (X-out T for True or F for False on the answer sheet.)

12.   When should work from your list of things to do be delegated to subordinates? (X-out the *three* best answers on the answer sheet.)

    a.   The work is fairly easy or repetitive.

    b.   You need time to do something else.

    c.   The delegated work may develop a subordinate's skills.

    d.   The work can be performed quickly.

    e.   Subordinates are qualified to do the work.

Diagnostic test exhibit B—answer sheet: process 7—time management

1. ╳ b ╳ ╳ e f
2. a b c ╳
3. a b c ╳ e
4. OUTLINE, REVIEW, OR ORGANIZE THE MATERIAL YOU WISH TO COVER OR PLAN WHAT YOU WANT TO SAY
5. a b c ╳ e
6. ╳ F
7. a b c d ╳ f
8. T ╳
9. (1) INCOMING MAIL   (5) CALENDARS
    (2) TELEPHONE CALLS   (6) SUBORDINATES
    (3) PEERS/COORDINATES   (7) MEETINGS
    (4) BRING-UP SYSTEM   (8) MASTER CONTROL LIST
10. a b ╳ d e f
11. T ╳
12. a ╳ ╳ d ╳

Diagnostic test exhibit C—items tested by objective test: process 7—time management

Test question number	Items tested		
	Skills	Knowledge	Process steps
1		K3	
2	S10		
3	S1, S14	K36, K37, K38, K39	
4		K7	
5	S6		
6		K39	
7		K15, K16, K17, K18, K19, K20	
8	S8	K24	
9		K32	
10	S8	K23	
11		K41	
12	S16		

12 Communication

PROCESS 8

A. OVERVIEW OF COMMUNICATION AT THE SUPERVISORY LEVEL

The first-level supervisor is perhaps the most vital link in the chain of organizational communication. It is he or she who translates the sometimes ambiguous, sometimes conflicting demands from higher levels of management into meaningful direction to his or her work group. It is the supervisor, as well, who senses the feelings and attitudes of the work group and its members and interprets them into meanings that can be conveyed upward to management for its consideration in framing policy and allocating resources.

When the first-level supervisor's communication lines to and from the work group are open and effective, then the connection between management and the operating level where the work is done will be good. When this connection is good, the chances are high that meaningful policy and intelligent directives will be converted into productive action. (It goes without saying that no supervisor can be expected to convert unintelligent top-level direction or inappropriate management policy into meaningful action.)

In other words, the company's first-level supervisors control the two-way flow of information between management and work groups. This information is crucial to the growth and profitability of the firm. The supervisor is more than a communication switchboard, of course; the truly effective supervisor applies factors of selectivity and judgment to the information flow in both directions.

Most management authorities are in close harmony on the purpose and values of communication in the business firm. Schoen and Durand[1] define communication as a transfer of meaning. Eckles, Carmichael, and Sarchet[2] define it further as the exchange and understanding of meanings, which appears to add the element of "feedback" to the process.

With regard to the importance of communication, the latter book cites research showing that first-level supervisors typically spend 74 percent of their time communicating (the percentage rises, the authors note, as the supervisor advances in the organization—81 percent of the second-level's time and 87 percent of the third-level's time is spent communicating). Schoen

---

[1]Sterling H. Schoen and Douglas E. Durand, *Supervision: The Management of Organizational Resources* (Englewood Cliffs, N.J.: Prentice-Hall, Inc., 1974).

[2]Robert W. Eckles, Ronald L. Carmichael, and Bernard R. Sarchet, *Essentials of Management for First-Line Supervisors* (New York: John Wiley & Sons, Inc., 1974).

and Durand confirm this, citing studies that show that first-level supervisors typically spend from 50 to 80 percent of their time on person-to-person communication with subordinates, with staff and service group personnel, and with other managers whose assistance and cooperation is vital to the effectiveness of the supervisor's work group.

Eckles, Carmichael, and Sarchet offer a classification of communication within the business organization into five basic types. Each of these has unique characteristics; each of them has dangers to watch for. The five types are:

1. Upward communication (beware of filters)
2. Downward communication (watch for evidence of understanding and acceptance—requires *listening*!)
3. Lateral communication (language problems)
4. Multidirectional (danger is complexities)
5. External, with the constituencies of the firm; the community, suppliers, etc. (problems involve *all* of the above)

In *Management-Minded Supervision*, Boyd[3] implies that there is another kind of communication between boss and subordinates that is neither upward nor downward as we conventionally perceive them. Boyd agrees that upward communication is essential— one of a supervisor's responsibilities is to make the boss look good and keeping him or her informed is a vital part of this. But beyond this, the supervisor has a responsibility to actively seek out and demand the information needed to perform the job, even from the boss, even from higher levels of management. In effect,

[3]Bradford B. Boyd, *Management-Minded Supervision* (New York: McGraw-Hill, 1968).

the supervisor, Boyd indicates, should "train the boss" to communicate.

This may seem rather presumptuous on the part of a first-level supervisor, to be sure, but it is essential to his or her job performance. The first requirement, of course, is for the supervisor to know what information is needed.

In most books and courses on communication, oral communication is emphasized for the great bulk of communication. Written communication normally is reserved for situations other than daily work activities; for people other than those we deal with regularly; and for occasions requiring a permanent record.

In this connection, it is customary to find in many offices little paper pads headed "AVO—Avoid Verbal Orders." Worse advice would be hard to find for the first-level supervisor! Verbal (oral) orders are usually the best kind; written orders are often the worst.

Oral communication is favored because, according to Schoen and Durand:

1. It is personal and the message can be tailored to the individual.
2. It can bring immediate feedback.
3. The recipient can respond at once.
4. You can test whether the message was really received and understood.
5. It is a rapid, natural, and easy way to communicate.

All communication experts stress the art and skill of *listening*, and every supervisor should learn to listen well, especially when interviewing.

Most experts caution against the use of written memos intended to protect oneself against criticism— the infamous CYA (Cover Your Ass) memos used by bureaucratic managers everywhere.

B.   HIGHLIGHTS OF THE AT&T JOB STUDY

Definition of the process

The communication process is defined in the first-level Mastery Model as "the exchange of opinions, ideas, facts, and/or feelings." The process includes "activities such as face-to-face contact, writing letters or memos, formal meetings, and telephone conversations."

Summary description of the process

The communication process as detailed in the Mastery Model is quite simple; it is intended to guide the first-level supervisor to the *communication method* that best suits the particular work situation, the nature of the information to be exchanged, and the type of recipients for whom the information is intended.

The supervisor is given three options: (1) *person-to-person oral communication* suited to informal, unstructured situations such as daily contact with members of the supervisor's own work group; (2) *formal oral communication* suited to structured situations involving two or more persons, for which some preparation is necessary—that is, meetings; and (3) *written communication and documentation* usually used for upward communication or for occasions requiring a written record (or when immediate feedback is not important).

When the supervisor selects the method he or she feels is most suitable to the occasion, the supervisor is directed to the process model that prescribes the specific tasks and decision points involved in that particular communication method. These are:

- Informal oral communication—Process No. 9
- Formal oral communication (Meetings)—Process No. 14
- Written communication and documentation—Process No. 11

C.   TASKS AND DECISION POINTS IN THE PROCESS OF COMMUNICATION

STEP 1   Your primary task is to determine that a stimulus exists for communication; that is, a genuine need has arisen that requires you to exchange information with others.

STEP 2   Your next task is to determine the most appropriate *method* to use in communicating; that is, the best way to get your message across. Most often, your method is *oral communication*, but there are occasions when *written communication* is better suited to your purpose.

STEP 3   If your selected communication method is *oral*, you should skip the next step and go to Step 5.

STEP 4   If your selected method is written communication, you should go to Process No. 11—Written Communication—for guidance.

STEP 5   If you have selected oral communication,
(Decision)   respond to the question: Is the oral communication to be *formal* (a meeting involving two or more people that normally requires advance preparation), or *informal* (a less structured form of communication, often person-to-person)?

STEP 6   If your decision is that the appropriate communication method is *informal*, go to Process No. 9—Informal Oral Communication—for guidance.

STEP 7   If your decision is that the appropriate communication method is *formal*, go to Process No. 14—Meetings (Formal Oral Communication).

Figure 12–1 illustrates the flow of steps in the process of communication. Flowcharts of the three specific methods of communication referred to will be found in the sections in which they are described.

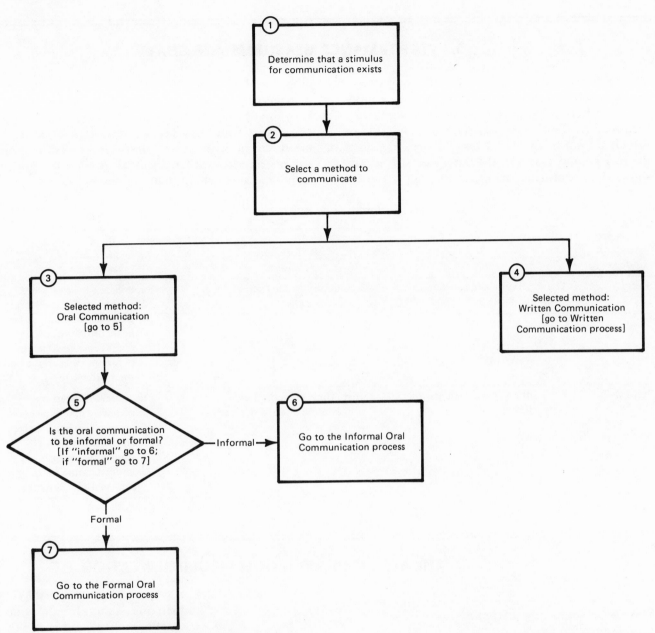

FIGURE 12-1. Process 8: Communication

D. PERFORMANCE MEASUREMENTS CHART

The eighth ranking duty of the supervisor—Communication—involves six tasks and one contingency or decision point. For purposes of measuring performance, these seven steps fall naturally into two principal *groups*. Table 12–1 lists the steps in each of the two groups, identifies the output of each group, shows the performance standards that apply to each output, and identifies the method used by second-level managers to measure the managerial performance of subordinate first-line supervisors.

These outputs, performance standards, and measurement methods were developed under the constraints recorded earlier, in the discussion of performance measurement in Planning the Work.

Table 12–1. Performance measurement

Step or group of steps	*Output*	*Performance standards*	*Method of measurement*
Step 1	The supervisor knows when to communicate	Communication is exchanged when necessary	Supervisor's boss measures output by feedback from other departments. Boss hears problems, plans, etc., from the supervisor before hearing about them from others.
Steps 2–7	The method of communication is selected	Most efficient method of communication is selected	Boss observes meetings, reviews written notes, memos, letters. Boss checks supervisor's subordinates for understanding of information they reveal.

E. THE AT&T MASTERY MODEL—COMMUNICATION

Step 1—Determine that a Stimulus for Communication Exists

Knowledge Required

K1   Communication is the exchange (two-way) of information, ideas, concepts, thoughts, and/or feelings.

K2   The three principal methods of communication are Informal Oral, Formal Oral (Meeting), and Written Communication.

K3   The sequence of steps for a communication may be partially or totally overridden in situations in which time is short (e.g., a situation of imminent danger).

K4   The necessity for a particular communication should be reviewed periodically so that unnecessary communication may be avoided.

K5   The stimulus for a communication may come from other managerial processes, such as Performance Feedback, Subordinate Development, Controlling the Job, the boss, other supervisors, dangers to safety, etc.

K6   The stimulus for a communication may contain the topic(s) and purpose(s) for the communication.

K7 The stimulus for a communication may identify the recipient(s), the method, variety (e.g., discussion), or the time for the communication.

Step 2—Select a Method to Communicate

Skill Required

S1 You need skill to determine the appropriate methods (if not specified by authority), based on factors such as:
time
place
immediacy
number of recipients
most effective and efficient way to attain purpose of the communication
topic
amount of content to be communicated

Knowledge Required

K8 Use of a particular communication method may be prescribed by authority (e.g., boss says *write* a letter, company Accident Prevention Plan requires a monthly safety *meeting*, local practice says give performance feedback by *oral communication*).

K9 The method may be prescribed by a situation (e.g., you need to *talk* with subordinate whose performance is slipping; to assist subordinate in learning difficult process, you need to *write* out steps to help subordinate recall them; great quantity of discussion material needs to be covered with 30 people, so a *meeting* is required).

K10 Selecting a particular method to attain the purpose of a communication implies knowledge of each method in terms of its pluses and minuses, characteristics, and steps.

K11 The steps of a method do not change because the receiver is a boss, subordinate, peer, or customer.

K12 Informal Oral Communication is the exchange or transmission of information, ideas, concepts, thoughts, and/or feelings through speech, usually in an unstructured situation with little or no preparation; that is, no agenda is required and no minutes are kept (see Informal Oral Communication—Process No. 9).

K13 Formal Oral Communication (Meetings) involves the exchange or transmission of information, ideas, concepts, thoughts, and/or feelings through speech in a structured situation with some preparation; that is, agenda is followed, minutes are recorded, handouts may be distributed, visual aids may be used (see Meetings—Process No. 14).

K14 The stimulus for an oral communication may determine whether to use Discussion, Interview, or Negotiation skills.

K15 An oral communication may involve:
1. Discussion—used to exchange knowledge and opinions
2. Interviewing—used to obtain information and opinions
3. Negotiation—used to obtain own ends and resolve differences

K16 Written Communication is the exchange or transmission of information, thoughts, ideas, concepts, and/or feelings through the written word (see Written Communication—Process No. 11).

Step 3—Selected Method: Oral Communication (Go to Step 5.)

Step 4—Selected Method: Written Communication (*Go to Written Communication—Process No. 11.*)

Step 6—Go to the Informal Oral Communication Process. (See Process No. 9.)

Step 5—Decision Point: Is the Oral Communication to Be Informal or Formal? *If Your Decision Is Formal, Go to Step 7.*

Step 7—Go to the Formal Oral Communication Process. (See Process No. 14.)

F.   TRAINING NEEDS DIAGNOSTIC

This is an objective test of two questions designed to test the skills and knowledge of first-level supervisors in communicating with others. The questions and answers are found in Exhibits A and B. The specific skill and the five points of knowledge tested by the questions are shown in Exhibit C.

Diagnostic test exhibit A: process 8—communication

This section deals with the Communication process. Communication is the exchange of ideas, opinions, facts, feelings, etc. The Communication process includes such activities as face-to-face contact, writing letters and memos, formal meetings, and telephone conversations.

1.   Listed below are situations you may encounter as a supervisor. What is the *most appropriate* method for communicating in each situation? (Write your answer on the answer sheet.)
    a.   providing feedback to a subordinate on a task that was observed as being below standard
    b.   conveying an important message to a member of departmental peers
    c.   communicating with a coordinate in a different city to clarify or interpret information needed by the coordinate to complete a portion of a job
    d.   providing your boss with information that concerns your subordinate's developmental plan
    e.   providing information on an anticipated methods change
    f.   obtaining assistance from multiple sources to solve an important problem that affects several groups

2.   For each situation below, select the *most appropriate* type of oral communication. (Write the letter corresponding to your answers on the answer sheet in the blanks provided. Answers may be selected more than once.)

Situation
1.   "Let us work out when you may take a week of vacation, Pat."
2.   "Let's get together to talk about the new computer, Ed."
3.   "John, collect data on Harry's performance with business customers."
4.   "Let's go over where we are as a result of today's meeting."
5.   "Al, would you please represent our position at Bob's Workman Compensation Hearing?"

Type of Oral Communication
a.   Interview: to obtain information or opinions
b.   Negotiate: to reach own goal or to resolve differences
c.   Discuss: to exchange knowledge and opinions

Diagnostic test exhibit B—answer sheet: process 8—communication

1.   (a) FACE-TO-FACE
     (b) LETTER/CONFERENCE CALL
     (c) TELEPHONE
     (d) WRITTEN
     (e) WRITTEN
     (f) MEETING
2.   1. <u>B</u>   2. <u>C</u>   3. <u>A</u>   4. <u>C</u>   5. <u>B</u>

Diagnostic test exhibit C—items tested by objective test: process 8—communication

Test question number	Items tested		
	Skills	Knowledge	Process steps
1	S1	K8, K9, K16[*]	
2		K15	

[*]Plus Knowledge K2 from Meetings process.

13 Informal Oral Communication

PROCESS 9

A. OVERVIEW OF INFORMAL ORAL COMMUNICATION AT THE SUPERVISORY LEVEL

In the course of carrying out your primary duties as a first-level supervisor, you are required to communicate frequently with other people in the workplace. Most often, of course, you will be communicating with members of your own work group, your subordinates. It is probable that 90 percent of this communication will be through speech, by far the most common kind of human communication and probably the most effective for conveying ideas, opinion, facts, and feelings. In the AT&T Mastery Model, this is called Oral Communication and is further refined into *Informal* and *Formal* types.

Informal Oral Communication is the ordinary unstructured and unrehearsed kind used in our everyday contacts with people. Most often it is with individuals. Formal Oral Communication involves structure and preparation and can involve sizable numbers of people—in other words, meetings.

The first-level supervisor's world in particular is a highly verbal one. Oral communication is favored as a general communication method by supervisors everywhere, and for several good reasons. Among these are:

- It is in what the computer mavens call "real time"—that is, it can be received immediately and the recipient can respond at once (quick feedback).
- The message can be adapted to individual receivers.
- The "sender" can close the feedback loop by responding immediately to concerns (or lack of comprehension) by the receiving person(s).

Reliance on speech alone as a means of communicating, however, can be dangerous to a supervisor's job performance.

Barriers to understanding

The dangers are many. There are barriers to understanding in every person-to-person discussion. One obvious one is the transient nature of the spoken word. Another is that words may have different meanings to the speaker and the listener. (It has been said, for example, that when two accountants sit down to a discussion, the first ten minutes should be spent defining the terms they use.) A third barrier is the "listening barrier"—a speaker may talk at a rate of 125 words per minute, while a listener can function at a rate three to five times faster; consequently, the listener's mind tends to wander away from the speaker's subject.

The most dangerous barrier to understanding, however, is that the self-interests of sender and receiver may be far apart. As a consequence, the recipient's self-interests may "filter out" or distort the real meaning because it collides with his or her needs and desires, attitudes, or perceptions.

Reinforcement is needed

Supervisors all too often fail to consider this factor; they assume because the message was transmitted, it was received as intended—a most dangerous assumption for a supervisor to make, because real understanding and genuine acceptance are rarely achieved on the basis of a single oral communication. What is required is reinforcement through repetition, demonstration, illustration, example, questioning, feedback from the hearer, and proof of understanding and acceptance of the message.

"But first of all," the old farmer said, as he picked up the two-by-four to speak to his mule, "you gotta get his attention."

B.   HIGHLIGHTS OF THE AT&T JOB STUDY

Definition of the process

In the AT&T Mastery Model of first-level performance, communication through speech is given the rather more precise designation, Informal Oral Communication. It is defined as a process of communication that occurs in an unstructured situation and requires little or no preparation. This is less a definition than a *distinction* from formal oral communication (meetings), which does require advance preparation and calls for some structure during the communication.

It would seem, at first glance, that person-to-person oral communication is the simplest of all managerial duties; one that comes naturally to supervisors; and one for which little or no training is required. On the contrary, the Mastery Model describes Informal Oral Communication as a complex managerial process consisting of as many as two dozen separate steps—19 tasks and 5 critical decision points.

Summary description of the process

Despite the qualifier "informal," the process does require a measure of advance preparation. The process starts by determining who the participants are (this is not always obvious), based on the purpose and nature of the communication and the stimulus that initiated the need for the communication process to take place.

The supervisor is then required to set an appropriate *time* for communicating, to establish an appropriate *place* for it to take place, and to notify all participants in an appropriate manner.

The actual process of communicating orally calls upon the supervisor's interpersonal skills to set a constructive atmosphere (tone) for the session, to guide the process, to listen to others, and to ensure that understanding and acceptance have been achieved as a result. The process employs three distinct types or methods of communicating orally: interviewing, discussing, and negotiating. Depending on the situation and the nature of the information to be communicated, one or more of these may be used. Each of these requires unique skills and knowledge on the part of the supervisor, of course, because each of these methods has a distinctly different purpose; thus:

- *Interviewing* is the method used *to obtain information* from other persons for use by the supervisor in making a decision. Questioning is used extensively.

- *Discussing* is the method used *to exchange information* and opinion relevant to an issue, in order to clarify unclear points and to ensure that others' views are considered in formulating a position on the issue. This is a "talking out" process.

● *Negotiating* is the method used *to gain agreement* on a contentious matter on which the parties have decidedly different desires. Normally, the supervisor decides in advance what it is he or she wants and then attempts to guide the negotiation toward that goal. A good negotiation usually requires compromise and/or concessions from both parties.

Irrespective of the method the supervisor uses, it is necessary that he or she determine whether or not the purpose of the informal oral communication has been achieved, and to follow-up and document the process if required. The most important aspect of follow-up is for the supervisor to make good on any commitments made during the process.

In what follows, the steps in the Oral Communication Process are described and illustrated with flowcharts.

C.   TASKS AND DECISION POINTS IN THE INFORMAL ORAL COMMUNICATION PROCESS

The total process involves some 24 separate steps—19 tasks and five decision points. The first eight steps are described below and illustrated by the flowchart in Figure 13-1.

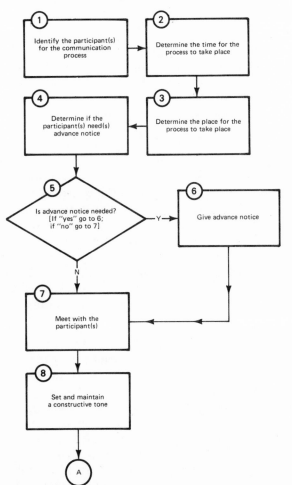

FIGURE 13-1.   **The First Eight Steps in the Informal Oral Communication Process**

STEP 1	The first task is to identify the participants for the communication process—specifically, who is to be involved in the transfer of information.
STEP 2	Determine the most appropriate *time* for the communication to take place, depending on availability of participants, urgency of the situation, etc.
STEP 3	Determine the most appropriate location for the communication to take place, based on convenience for participants, need for privacy, etc.
STEP 4	Determine whether the participants need advance notice.
STEP 5 (Decision)	Respond to the question: *Is advance notice warranted?* If your decision is *no*, proceed directly to Step 7.
STEP 6	If your decision is *yes*, give *advance notice* of the time and location for communication to take place.
STEP 7	Meet with the participants, provided the time and location have been agreed to.
STEP 8	Set and maintain a constructive tone, an atmosphere conducive to free, open, and productive discussion by all participants, so that the purpose of communication will be achieved.

STEP 9   Select the appropriate method for communicating—interviewing, discussing, or negotiating.

STEP 10   Select method: *Interviewing*—obtaining all relevant information from others, clarifying it as needed.

STEP 11   Select method: *Discussing*—exchanging information and views with others.

STEP 12   Select method: *Negotiating*—reaching agreement on issues about which there is apparent lack of agreement among participants.

STEP 13   Having selected and used the appropriate method, determine whether the purpose of the informal oral communication has been achieved by recalling or restating those purposes and asking yourself and others whether they were actually accomplished.

STEP 14
(Decision)   Respond to the question: *Was the purpose achieved?*

      If your decision is *yes*, skip the next two steps and go directly to Step 17.

STEP 15   If your decision is *no*—the purpose was not achieved—go to the Problem Solving process.

STEP 16
(Decision)   Now respond to the question: *Is the problem solved* (so that the purpose of the communication is achieved)?

      If your decision is *no*—the problem is not solved—return to the Problem Solving process (and redefine the problem).

STEP 17   Determine if follow-up is required.

STEP 18
(Decision)   Respond to the question: *Is follow-up needed?*

      If your decision is *no*, skip Step 19, go to Step 20, and end the informal oral communication.

STEP 19   If your decision is *yes*—follow-up is needed—then follow-up on the informal communication process (especially by making good on any commitments you have made during the process).

Figure 13-2 illustrates Steps 9 through 19 of the process.

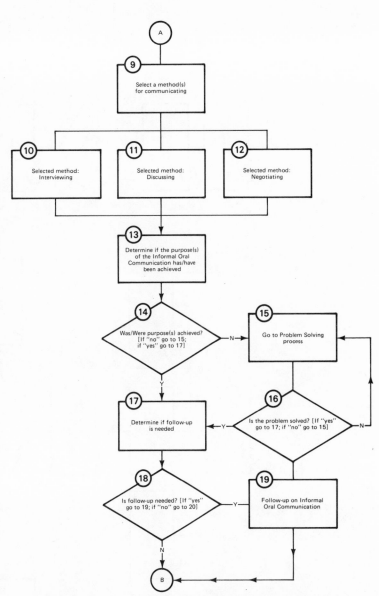

FIGURE 13-2. Flowchart showing Steps 9 through 19

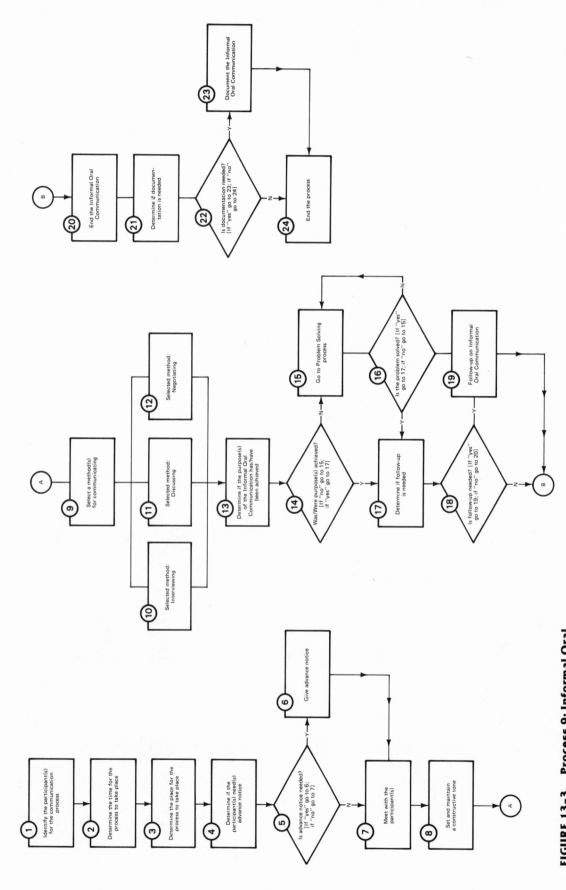

FIGURE 13–3. Process 9: Informal Oral Communication

STEP 20   End the informal oral communication.
STEP 21   Determine whether or not documenta-
          tion is needed.
STEP 22   Respond to the question: *Is documen-*
(Decision)   *tation needed?* If your decision is *no*,
          skip Step 23; go to Step 24 and end
          the process.

STEP 23   If your decision is *yes*, document
          the communication in accordance with
          custom, local practice, or possible
          future need.
STEP 24   End the process.

The chart in Figure 13–3 depicts the total process of Informal Oral Communication.

D.   PERFORMANCE MEASUREMENTS CHART

The ninth ranking duty of the supervisor—Informal Oral Communication—involves 19 tasks and five contingencies or decision points. For purposes of measuring performance, these 24 steps fall naturally into four principal *groups*. The chart that follows (Table 13–1) lists the steps in each of the four groups, identifies the output of each group, shows the performance standards that apply to each output, and identifies the method used by second-level managers to measure the managerial performance of subordinate first-line supervisors. These outputs, performance standards, and measurement methods were developed under the constraints recorded earlier, in the discussion of performance measurement in Planning the Work.

Table 13–1.   Process 9: Informal oral communication

Step or group of steps	Output	Performance standards	Method of measurement
Steps 1–7	The time, place, and participants for the exchange of information are determined	The communication produces the desired results	The second-level boss measures the outputs by feedback from participants, observations, and by review of documentation
Steps 8–16	The information is exchanged		
Steps 17–20	Follow-up action is planned		
Steps 21–24	Exchange of information is documented, if necessary		

E.   THE AT&T MASTERY MODEL—INFORMAL ORAL COMMUNICATIONS

Informal oral communication is a complex managerial process that may involve as many as 24 steps or tasks. Midway through the process, you are required to decide which of three given methods is most appropriate to the situation: interviewing, discussing, or negotiating.

At five points in the process, you are required to make decisions that affect your subsequent path through the remaining steps. The 24 steps are described in detail in the following, together with the skills and knowledge required for mastery of each task.

Step 1—Identify the Participants for the Communication Process

---

Skill Required	S1	This task requires skill to determine participants, based on: mandate that communication take place purposes of communication contents and topics of communication stimulus (e.g., boss says talk to all EEO/AA potential promotables)
Knowledge Required	K1	Know that participants may be subordinates, peers, boss, customers, community members, etc.
	K2	Based on determination of contents, new inputs from stimulus, inputs from boss, and your own determination that the proposed Informal Oral Communication applies to more or fewer persons than originally determined, you may have to change participants.

Step 2—Determine the Time for the Process to Take Place

Skill Required	S2	This requires skill to schedule the time for Informal Oral Communication, based on: stimulus (example: boss says "Ask Ed today when he wants to take a vacation.") time best suited for the communication (example: may be better to talk with subordinate at time other than subordinate's end of shift) own available time availability of peer, customer, subordinate
Knowledge Required	K3	You may have to change scheduled time whenever any of the above factors change.
	K4	The best time to communicate may be the moment when the

need to communicate is first noted.

	K5	There may be circumstances when face-to-face communication cannot occur, so another communication method (letter, telephone) must be used.

Step 3—Determine the Place for the Process to Take Place

Skill Required	S3	This task requires skill to select the place, based on: place required by the stimulus place convenient for self place convenient for participants suitability for achievement of the purpose, and suitability for delivery of the content (e.g., quiet, private place for private matters such as illness, family matters) inputs from boss
Knowledge Required	K6	You may have to change the selected place whenever any of the factors noted in Step 2 change.

Step 4—Determine if the Participants Need Advance Notice

Knowledge Required	K7	Know whether both parties are available now if communication is to take place now.
	K8	Know to notify participants of time and place if both parties are not available.

Step 5—Decision Point: Is Advance Notice Warranted? If Your Decision Is No, Go to Step 7.

Step 6—Give Advance Notice

Step 7—Meet with the Participants

Knowledge Required	K9	If either party cannot come to the selected place at the scheduled

time, reschedule the communication at a *mutually convenient* time and place.

Step 8—Set and Maintain a Constructive Tone

Skills Required	S4	This task requires skill to set the appropriate constructive tone, based on such factors as: purpose and contents of the communication personalities of self and other participant whether participant is in a non-traditional job; that is, treat the person as an individual and not as a stereotype
	S5	This task requires skill to use nonverbal communication methods (e.g., sitting or standing quietly, eye contact with participant, displaying interest with face).
	S6	You need skill to guide informal oral communication to its purpose, by conveying: interest in the other's ideas respect for the other and the other's ideas encouragement of communication and the other's growth in self-esteem lack of threat to the other
	S7	You need skill to listen to the other (the average person is a poor listener!)
	S8	You need skill to determine when and whether to give/obtain concurrence, response, input, or acknowledgement from the participant, based on the complexity of the oral communication's contents and purpose (e.g., it may *not be* necessary to check whether a subordinate understands when to go on coffee break, but it *may be* necessary to check whether a subordinate knows how to run a repair truck).
Knowledge Required	K10	Setting and maintaining a constructive tone means creating an atmosphere that facilitates the achievement of the purpose of the communication. This is achieved through verbal, nonverbal, and environmental means (e.g., quiet, private place for personal matters such as subordinate's illness).
	K11	You should know to state the purpose and expected outcomes of the informal oral communication early.
	K12	Verbal concurrence may not be necessary as long as a participant does what is required.

Step 9—Select a Method for Communicating

Step 10—Select Method: Interviewing

Skill Required	S9	If selected method is interviewing, you need skill to: obtain all relevant information from others clarify information as needed

---

Step 11—Select Method: Discussing

Knowledge Required	K13	Know to obtain the other's views, opinions, etc.
	K14	Know to let the other speak.
	K15	Know to listen to the other.
	K16	Know to use Skill S4 to set a constructive tone for the discussion.

Step 12—Select Method: Negotiating

Knowledge Required	K17	Negotiation is a means of solving a problem or making a decision by reaching agreement on issues.
Skills Required	S10	You need skill to state opposing views (yours and the other's).
	S11	You need skill to exchange information according to discussion model (Step 11).
	S12	You need skill to identify areas of agreement.
	S13	You need skill to continue discussion on areas where agreement does not exist.

S14   You need skill to determine if the negotiation is wandering or at an impasse. If so, restate views and note the areas of agreement achieved so far as an aid to clarifying what has been achieved and what remains to be achieved.

S15   You need skill to select alternate means to achieve an agreement if the first negotiation means has not worked, such as:
compromise own position
suggest the other party compromises position
list the positive consequences of agreement (e.g., the boss wants to try something that requires a subordinate to take on more responsibility. The subordinate may resist until realizing that it may be beneficial to the subordinate or work group.)
bring out negative consequences of not making an agreement

S16   You need skill to determine if a pause in negotiation would be helpful to allow participants to "cool off" or identify other potential solutions. If so, set follow-up time or date.

S17   You need skill to determine when minimal acceptable level of agreement has been met.

Step 13—Determine if the Purpose of the Informal Oral Communication Has Been Achieved

---

Skill Required   S18   This requires skill to determine whether purposes were achieved by recalling or restating those purposes and asking self and/ or others whether they were achieved, as follows:
If the purpose was discussion, were information and opinions exchanged?
If the purpose was interview, were your questions answered?
If the purpose was negotiation, were your objectives attained?

Step 14—Decision Point: Was Purpose Achieved?

If your decision is *yes,* skip the next two steps and go directly to Step 17.

Step 15—Go to the Problem Solving Process

Knowledge Required   K18   If your decision is *no*—purpose was not achieved—then you should know to enter Problem Solving process at "Define Problem" and exit at "Implement Solution."

Step 16—Decision Point: Is the Problem Solved?

Knowledge Required   K19   This decision requires you to know that the outcome of Step 16 may not be the achievement of the purpose originally defined in Step 15; that is, the outcome may be to defer discussion of an unresolved matter to a later time.

If your answer is *no*—the problem is not solved— return to the Problem Solving Process.

Step 17—Determine if Follow-up Is Needed

Skill Required   S19   This task requires skill to determine the need for follow-up, based on whether a need exists to resume the Informal Oral Communication later, or a commitment was made to other (example: "I'll try to arrange a transfer").

Step 18—Decision Point: Is Follow-up Needed?

If your decision is *no,* skip Step 19 and go to Step 20.

Step 19—Follow-up on Informal Oral Communication

Knowledge Required	K20	You should know to follow-up and make good on your commitments in an Informal Oral Communication (example: give training dates to subordinate, as requested by subordinate).

Step 20—End the Informal Oral Communication

Step 21—Determine if Documentation Is Needed

Skill Required	S20	This task requires skill to determine whether documentation is needed, based on: your needs (record comments by boss on career opportunities in the company for a person with your particular set of skills) whether others request documentation (write down vacation dates of subordinates for boss) future usefulness of document (don't document conversation

about who left lights burning or personal car)

Step 22—Decision Point: Is Documentation Needed?

If your decision is *no*, go to Step 24.

Step 23—Document the Informal Oral Communication

Skill Required	S21	This task requires skill to prepare documentation, based on: local practice (example: material that may be an input to disciplinary action) future use of document (example: a discussion with the boss on your own career plans might need to be documented to aid in future course planning)

Step 24—End the Process

F. TRAINING NEEDS DIAGNOSTIC

The diagnostic test for informal oral communication is in two sections: an *objective test* intended to test knowledge of the process, and a *role play* designed to test interpersonal and behavioral skills in applying the process.

Objective test

This is an objective test of three questions designed to test first-level supervisors' skills and knowledge in using the informal oral communication skills of interviewing, discussion, and negotiation. The questions and answers are found in Exhibits A and B. The seven specific skills and two points of knowledge tested by the questions are shown in Exhibit C.

Role play

The role play section of the diagnostic instrument is designed to test the subjects' behavioral and interpersonal skills in performing several duties. Included are:

informal oral communication
providing performance feedback
coaching a subordinate
written communication, and
controlling the work

The duty of informal oral communication is given heavy emphasis in this exercise; 12 oral communication skills and five items of knowledge are tested. (The actual role play instructions and situation background information are too voluminous to include in this book.) The specific skills and knowledge tested are:

Skills: S5, S6, S7, S8, S9, S10, S11, S12, S13, S14, S15, and S18.
Knowledges: K11, K13, K14, K15, and K16.

Diagnostic test exhibit A: process 9—informal oral communication

This section deals with Informal Oral Communication. Informal Oral Communication occurs in an unstructured situation and requires little or no preparation.

1. It is February 15. Your boss has asked you to determine vacation preferences by tomorrow. You do not have to make up a schedule at this time, but just find out when people want to take vacation. Next week you will make up the schedule based on the workload and seniority. You have eight subordinates. You know that most of them already know when they want to take vacation because they have been asking about the schedule. One subordinate has been with the company only three weeks and is not eligible for vacation. Three subordinates claim their ethnic group has been discriminated against in past vacation assignments. Six subordinates will be in the office this morning. The other two will not be in until this afternoon. Last year you lost one of your vacation weeks because you did not take vacation and can only carry over one week.

    What actions should you take before meeting tomorrow with your boss to discuss vacation preferences? (Write your answer on the answer sheet.)

2. Setting and maintaining a constructive tone means creating and sustaining an atmosphere that helps to achieve the communication's purpose.

    Below are eleven statements. What four statements would *most* help to set or maintain a constructive tone while communicating? (X-out the *four* constructive-tone statements on the answer sheet.)
    a. "That's really off the point."
    b. "I appreciate your suggestion on work assignments."
    c. "You're wrong about the contract."
    d. "I know we're talking about how to prevent computer reruns, but what do you think about Mike's promotion?"
    e. "Let me see if I understood you."
    f. "Don't you think we can work out whose responsibility it is?"
    g. "There's no way I can let you go to the auditing class next month."
    h. "That's what I think about it so far. I'd like to hear what you think about it."
    i. "How's the little lady making out as a pole climber?"
    j. "I don't have time to talk to you any longer."
    k. "Why is your work group so noisy? Don't you know how to control them?"

3. It is September 12. You need to find out whether Pat, a subordinate, can go to an important training class during the week of October 4. You make a mental note to talk to Pat after lunch before Pat returns to the field. After lunch you talk with Pat for a few minutes. Expressing great interest in the class, Pat points out a schedule conflict with an assignment received earlier. (Write your answers on the answer sheet.)
    a. What should you say next?
    b. What should you do after the conversation is over?
    c. Has your purpose for the conversation been met? (Explain your answer.)

Diagnostic test exhibit B—answer sheet: process 9—informal oral communication

1. ASK BOSS IF YOU NEED TO KNOW YOUR OWN VACATION PREFERENCES
    CONTACT EIGHT SUBORDINATES TO DETERMINE THEIR PREFERENCES
    CONTACT SIX IN OFFICE, TWO ELSEWHERE
2. a ̶b̶ c d ̶e̶ ̶f̶ g ̶h̶ i j k
3. (a) YOU'LL PROMISE TO F/U TO TRY TO RESOLVE SCHEDULE CONFLICT
    (b) FOLLOW-UP ON "A"
    (c) NO, DID NOT FIND OUT IF PAT CAN GO TO TRAINING

Diagnostic text exhibit C—items tested by objective test: process 9—informal oral communication

| Test question number | Items tested | | Process steps |
	Skills	Knowledge	
1	S1, S2, S3	K1	
2	S6, S7	K10	
3	S18, S19		

14 Self-Development

PROCESS 10

A. THE FIRST-LEVEL SUPERVISOR'S NEED FOR SELF DEVELOPMENT

All development is self-development. A person's supervisor—and the company—can provide the climate, the opportunities, support, information, and guidance, but in the last analysis, it is the person alone who must develop his or her own capabilities, skills, and knowledge. The first requirement is that the individual must earnestly *want to improve*.

The benefits of self-development to the individual are many, of course, but the foremost of these are personal growth and fulfillment and enhanced job satisfaction.

Basic to improved job performance in almost any managerial capacity are such things as ability to reason, to solve problems, and to think clearly. Effective speaking is essential; ability to express oneself in writing becomes more valuable the higher one goes in the organization.

Reading is an essential part of any self-development program, as is observation of successful people. An inquisitive mind is a valuable asset to any manager wanting to develop; being born with one helps, but the quality can be developed through exercise.

B. HIGHLIGHTS OF THE AT&T JOB STUDY

Definition of the process

The Mastery Model defines self-development as "the process used by supervisors to identify their own requirements for producing better results on the current job and implementing plans to meet these requirements."

Summary description of the process

The process of self-development begins with a personal "inventory" of your own capabilities (based on your review of documents such as position descriptions and performance appraisals, as well as discussion with your boss), and a comparison of these capabilities with the requirements for producing better results on the job (which you also produce).

Next, you should prepare, based on this comparison, a list of needed improvement areas and rank this list in order of importance to job performance. Then you should develop a "self-development" plan or program of training, such as outside courses of study, development assignments, etc. Needless to say, your self-development plan must consider the cost of the self-development activities, the time they may take, and the effect on current work activity.

An essential part of the process is to always maintain your current job performance in the face of changes in the job caused by technological change or reorganization; these may require you to initiate further self-development activities.

C. TASKS AND DECISION POINTS IN THE PROCESS OF SELF-DEVELOPMENT

STEP 1 Determine the job requirements for you yourself to produce results on your current job; confirm these requirements with your boss.

STEP 2 Assess yourself against the job requirements. (In a new job, this should be done as soon as possible after you are familiar with the job content.)

STEP 3 (Decision) Respond to the question: *Do you meet the job requirements?*

STEP 4 If your answer is *yes,* you should, of course, take whatever action is necessary to *maintain your current job performance,* keeping in mind that changes in the business (new technology, reorganization, etc.) may create new demands on you for self-development.

STEP 5 If your decision is *no*—you do not meet the job requirements—then your next task is to list performance areas in which improvement is needed.

STEP 6 Prioritize these improvement areas in terms of their criticality to job performance, extent of your deficiencies, etc.

STEP 7 Next you should select a method to improve your performance, such as through training, tuition plan courses, or developmental assignments, keeping in mind the cost, the time required away from your job, the needs of your boss, etc.

STEP 8 Make a performance development plan.

STEP 9 Implement your performance development plan. (After you have completed your planned self-development activities, you should return to Step 2 and reassess yourself and your newly acquired skills against the job requirements.)

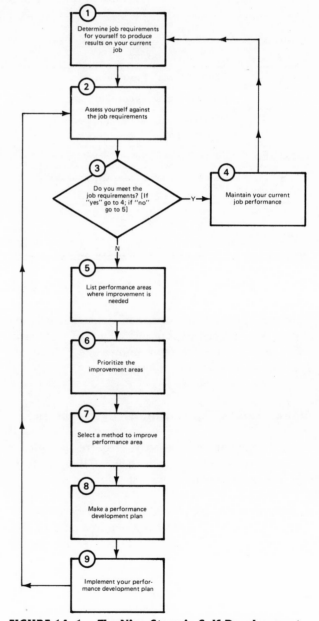

FIGURE 14-1. The Nine Steps in Self-Development

D. PERFORMANCE MEASUREMENTS CHART

The tenth ranking duty of the supervisor—Self-Development—involves eight tasks and one contingency or decision point. For purposes of measuring performance, these nine steps fall naturally into five principal *groups*. The chart that follows (Table 14–1) lists the steps in each of the five groups, identifies the output of each group, shows the performance standards that apply to each output, and identifies the method used by second-level managers to measure the managerial performance of subordinate first-line supervisors.

These outputs, performance standards, and measurement methods were developed under the constraints recorded earlier, in the discussion of performance measurement in Planning the Work.

Table 14–1. Process 10: self-development

Step or group of steps	Output	Performance standards	Method of measurement
Step 1	Requirements of job identified		
Step 2	Job deficiencies identified		
Steps 5, 6	Deficient areas documented and prioritized	First-level supervisor has basic knowledge to perform the job	The second-level boss measures by observing the first-level's ability to perform the job
Steps 7, 8	Plan developed for self-development		
Step 9	Plan implemented and acquired skills assessed		

E. THE AT&T MASTERY MODEL—SELF-DEVELOPMENT

Self-development is a managerial process consisting of nine well-defined steps or tasks. Each of these tasks calls on certain skills and knowledge. These are described in detail in the following.

Fundamental skills and knowledge required

Self-development, to be effective, requires knowledge of *five fundamentals of management* that apply to first-level supervision. These are:

Knowledge Required

K1   Self-development consists of:
identifying requirements for producing better results on the current job.
assessing your own capabilities compared with the job requirements.
developing and implementing plans to meet the job requirements.

K2   Self-development is necessary to maintain current job effectiveness; that is, technical competence.

K3   Self-development is a *shared responsibility* of you yourself and your boss.

K4   Know that you must actively participate in self-development plans to *increase your current job effectiveness.*

K5   Know that if your self-development is not facilitated by the boss, then you must play a more active role by initiating contacts with the boss.

Step 1—Determine Your Job Requirements to Produce Results on Your Current Job

Skill Required	S1	You need skill to develop a list of your job or position requirements and confirm the list with your boss.
Knowledge Required	K6	Inputs of information needed to determine your own requirements for *producing better results* come from such sources as: feedback on your job performance your boss performance appraisals job/position descriptions material from training curriculums
	K7	The list of job requirements may have to be revised at times, such as: change of boss change of job requirements feedback (ongoing or formal) change of job description

Step 2—Assess Yourself against the Job Requirements

Skill Required	S2	You need skill to match your self-assessment against the list of job requirements from Step 1.
Knowledge Required	K8	This should be done in a new job as soon as possible after you are familiar with the job content.
	K9	Know to obtain information needed to assess yourself against job requirements from such sources as: appraisal/feedback from boss pretests in technical courses feedback from peers/subordinates own self-assessment own experience

Step 3—Decision Point: Do You Meet the Job Requirements?

If your decision is *no*, skip Step 4 and go directly to Step 5.

Step 4—Maintain Your Current Job Performance

Knowledge Required	K10	Self-development needs may arise from changes in the business such as technological changes or reorganization.

Step 5—List Performance Areas Where Improvement Is Needed

Skill Required	S3	You need skill to identify and list improvement areas based on input from Step 2.

Step 6—Prioritize the Improvement Areas

Skill Required	S4	You need skill to prioritize improvement areas according to: criticality to job performance how deficient a critical area is compared to satisfactory performance how important it is to perform according to standards; that is, knowledge of preparing appraisals is more critical than knowing letter formats sometimes not knowing one step in a very critical process is less important than not having knowledge about a whole process
Knowledge Required	K11	Know to check local procedures for assistance in prioritizing improvement areas (example: safety is to take precedence over improved letter writing).

Step 7—Select a Method to Improve Performance

Knowledge Required	K12	Know to work on the improvement area given the highest priority first.
Skills Required	S5	You need skill to identify all available methods to improve performance, such as: training job aids

developmental assignments
tuition plan courses
boss
peers

| S6 | You need skill to select method, using criteria such as:
the boss
organization mandates
most efficient method according to training time needed
cost of developmental activities
personal preferences for activities |

Step 8—Make a Performance Development Plan

Knowledge Required	K13	A self-development plan may impact Planning the Work and Managing Time.
	K14	Some development plans require documentation according to local practices or procedures.
Skill Required	S7	You need skill to set time frames for specific activities and schedule training.

Step 9—Implement Your Performance Development Plan

| Skill Required | S8 | It takes skill to determine the worth and applicability of self-development activities, based on meeting those requirements, cost to meet them, and the time it takes to improve the deficiency. |
| Knowledge Required | K15 | Know to provide feedback regarding the worth and applicability of self-development activities for improving deficient areas to interested persons, such as:
your boss
your peers
your subordinates
the training-development organization |
| | K16 | Know to reassess the job performance skills acquired through self-development activities, as in Step 2. |

F. TRAINING NEEDS DIAGNOSTIC

This is an objective test of three questions designed to test first-level supervisors' skills and knowledge in self-development. The questions and answers are found in Exhibits A and B. The four specific skills and eight points of knowledge tested by the questions are shown on Exhibit C.

Diagnostic test exhibit A: process 10—self-development

This section deals with Self-Development. In this process, you identify your own requirements for producing better results on the current job and implement plans to meet those requirements.

1. What is the *most important* payoff (result) to the company when you increase your technical and managerial competency? (X-out the correct answer on the answer sheet.)
    a.   self-satisfaction
    b.   better relationships with subordinates
    c.   continued job effectiveness
    d.   better rate of return
    e.   larger pool of promotable managers
2. You have been the supervisor of a work group for six months. You want to develop your technical and managerial competency. What four steps should you take *before* implementing a self-development plan? (Write the *four* steps on the answer sheet.)
3. You have participated in a self-development activity. What are the two *most important* follow-up actions to take? (X-out the *two* correct answers on the answer sheet.)

a. Provide feedback regarding worth and applicability of the developmental activity to your boss.
b. Notify the personnel organization to update your personnel records.
c. Determine what self-development activity to do next, based on the activity just completed.
d. Document a plan to use the outputs of the developmental activity with your work force.
e. Assess transfer of acquired skills to your job performance areas.

Diagnostic test exhibit B—answer sheet: process 10—self-development

1. a b ⌧ d e
2. (1) FIND OUT JOB REQUIREMENTS/OBJECTIVES/GOALS/ETC.
   (2) CONFIRM JOB REQUIREMENTS WITH THE BOSS
   (3) IDENTIFY DEFICIENCIES
   (4) RANK ORDER DEFICIENCIES
3. ⌧ b c d ⌧

Diagnostic test exhibit C—items tested by objective test: process 10—self-development

Test question number	Items tested		Process steps
	Skills	Knowledge	
1		K2	
2	S1, S4, S5	K1, K3, K4, K5, K6	
3	S7	K15, K16	

15 Written Communication and Documentation

PROCESS 11

A. OVERVIEW OF WRITTEN COMMUNICATION AT THE SUPERVISORY LEVEL

At the first level of supervision, communicating with others through the medium of writing is used less frequently than the other two methods, informal oral communication and meetings. It is, nonetheless, an extremely important communication means, and the managerial skills and knowledge it requires must be acquired by the new supervisor. These skills and knowledge are not easy ones to master, but they are essential to superior job performance.

In recent years, a lot of attention has been given to the "failure" of our educational system to provide its graduates with basic writing skills. So many students entering college are lacking in these skills that colleges and universities have been forced to give them remedial high-school-level courses in writing before permitting these students to move on to college-level work.

Even worse, some colleges and universities are turning out graduates who have not mastered the skill of writing clear, concise, grammatically correct sentences and paragraphs. When these people enter management, they often continue to turn out reports, letters, and memos that are confusing, ambiguous, and at times meaningless. As a consequence, the recipients of these muddled messages frequently do not know what to do, or may follow the incorrect course of action.

Lawyers are allegedly the most notorious offenders against clear, understandable writing, but this may be the nature of the profession. Accountants deal mostly with numbers, so they may be forgiven. But engineers, scientists, and marketing majors are expected to be able to write clear, coherent, and cogent reports that will stimulate effective action by subordinates, while providing reassurance to superiors that things are under control in the laboratory, the shop, and the marketplace.

Most appalling of all is to find MBAs and PhDs unable to express themselves clearly and succinctly in writing after 18 or 20 years of schooling. A recent story in the *Wall Street Journal* reported that several large corporations have been forced to set up in-house courses on writing for their managers, even high-level executives.

Writing is not easy, nor is it the most comfortable of disciplines for an action-oriented supervisor who prefers to deal with people face-to-face. Yet to perform the job well, the first-level supervisor must

140

write clear, understandable letters and memos, and meaningful reports. And if the first-level supervisor aspires to higher-management rank, clear writing is absolutely vital to success. (Note the modifier *clear* writing. What is required is not "good writing" in the same sense as a best-selling novel or nonfiction book, but simply clear and forceful organization and expression of ideas. Anyone can learn how, and the payoff for the study and practice it takes can be high in terms of career advancement.)

B. HIGHLIGHTS OF THE AT&T JOB STUDY

Definition of the process

The AT&T Mastery Model defines this first-level duty as a managerial process that includes activities such as writing letters, reports, and memos, completing forms, and maintaining local documentation.

The Mastery Model requires the supervisor to know several fundamentals of management as they apply to written communication and documentation at the first level. Principal among these is the need to know on what occasions written communication should be used; among these are:

- when a permanent record is needed for future reference,
- when a large number of people must be reached in a short period of time,
- there is a need to clarify points and gain agreement on an issue,
- to provide a common topic for discussion,
- when oral communication is not feasible, and
- when this method is mandated by policy, standard practice, such as for documenting employee appraisals, grievances, safety bulletins, etc.

Summary description of the process

The process begins with a determination of when the communication is needed (due date), and what ideas it must convey to the readers (its purpose). The supervisor is then advised to pull together all pertinent data on the subject to be covered from various sources, organize it, and select the most relevant information to be included. If the topic is complex or requires a lengthy exposition, an outline should be prepared. Next, an appropriate format for the communication should be selected.

Now the written communication itself can be produced. This step of the process is one of the most demanding tasks in the entire Mastery Model; it calls for *ten* high-level skills and *nine* specific items of knowledge (more than any other single task in any process). Here is where the supervisor's writing skill comes into play. If the subject is at all complex, draft versions should be prepared and rewritten (few people, even professional writers, can produce a final version of a written piece without rewriting). Finally, the written communication or documentation should be produced in a form best suited to the need for duplication and distribution.

C. TASKS AND DECISION POINTS IN THE PROCESS

STEP 1   Determine when the written communication or documentation is due. Schedule the task if drafts, higher-level reviews, reproduction, and distribution are required.

STEP 2   List the general ideas you want to communicate.

STEP 3 Decision   Respond to the question: *Is additional information necessary before you produce the written communication?*

If your decision is *no*, skip the next three steps and go directly to Step 7.

STEP 4   If your decision is *yes*, then your next task is to determine the sources of the information you need, such as company practices, your associates, your boss, etc.

STEP 5   Collect the information you think you will need.

STEP 6   Analyze the information; that is, sort it out in terms of what is useful to your

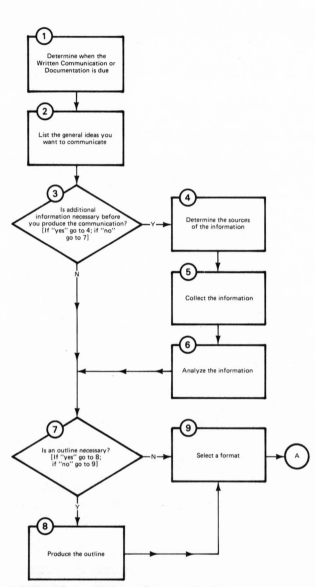

FIGURE 15-1. Written Communication: The First Nine Steps

purpose and what is not useful.

STEP 7   Ask yourself: *Is an outline necessary?*
Decision   If your decision is *no,* skip Step 8 and go to Step 9.

STEP 8   If your decision is *yes*—the subject is important enough or complex enough that an outline is needed—then your next task is to produce the outline.

STEP 9   Select a format for your written communication that is appropriate both for the subject to be covered and for the audience that must be reached (remember that the formats for certain kinds of written communication and documentation are mandated).

Figure 15-1 depicts the flow of tasks and decisions in the process up to this point—Steps 1 through 9.

STEP 10   Having collected all necessary information, prepared an outline (if needed), and selected a format, you can now proceed to produce the written communication or documentation, following the task schedule prepared in Step 1.

STEP 11   Determine whether the written communication or documentation is ready for release; that is, whether it is complete, appropriate for the purpose, free of serious errors, and meets your own job requirements.

STEP 12   Respond to the question: *Is it ready*
Decision   *for release?*
                 If your decision is *yes,* skip Step 13 and release the communication as specified in Step 14.

STEP 13   If your decision is *no*—the communication is not ready in all respects for release—then your task is to *revise it* as necessary to make it ready.

STEP 14   Release the written communication or documentation in accordance with custom or standard practice.

Figure 15-2 illustrates the complete process of written communication and/or documentation at the first-level of supervision.

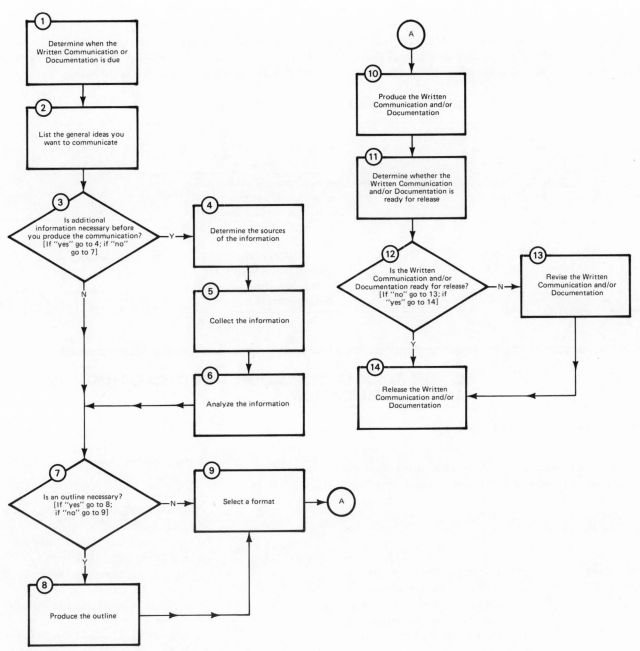

FIGURE 15-2.   Flowchart of the Total Process

D. PERFORMANCE MEASUREMENTS CHART

The eleventh ranking duty of the supervisor—Written Communication and Documentation—involves 11 tasks and three contingencies or decision points. The chart that follows (Table 15-1) identifies the output of the 14 steps, shows the performance standards that apply to this output, and identifies the method used by second-level managers to measure the managerial performance of subordinate first-line supervisors.

These outputs, performance standards, and measurement methods were developed under the constraints recorded earlier, in the discussion of performance measurement in Planning the Work.

Table 15-1. Process 11: written communication

Step or group of steps	Output	Performance standards	Method of measurement
Steps 1–14	Written communication/documentation is produced	Communication/documentation is completed on time Communication/documentation is concise, direct, and of proper length. Grammar is correct. All necessary information is supplied. Style is matched to purpose and receivers	Second-level boss reviews the written communication/ documentation

E. THE AT&T MASTERY MODEL—WRITTEN COMMUNICATION AND DOCUMENTATION

Fundamental skills and knowledge

In order to communicate with other people effectively in writing, it is necessary for you to know *four fundamentals of management* that apply to written communication and documentation at the first-level of supervision. These are:

Knowledge Required	K1	The stimulus (activating event or person) for written communication may determine both its purpose and the topics to be covered.
	K2	The stimulus may also determine such things as: the receivers of the communication the due date how often the communication is needed
	K3	Written communication/documentation is sometimes the man-

dated method for such situations as:
documenting employee appraisals
formal grievances
salary change recommendations
safety bulletins
correspondence with customers
documenting feedback

K4 Written communication is used to:
provide permanent records for reference
provide a common topic for discussion
reach a large number of people in a short period of time
force the communicator to be more concise and accurate
clarify points and gain agreement
communicate when oral communication is not possible

Step 1—Determine When the Written Communication or Documentation Is Due

Skills Required	S1	When scheduling a writing task so that due dates are met, you need skill to consider such things as: time needed to do a rough and a final draft time needed to proofread and correct time needed to have it signed by higher levels, if required
	S2	If the stimulus does not specify a due date, you need skill to set your own due date, considering such things as: your work load your "To Do" List the urgency of the matter your Master Control List (The sooner you write what has to be written, the less chance that you will forget about it.)
Knowledge Required	K5	The stimulus may specify when the written communication is due.

Step 2—List the General Ideas You Want to Communicate

Skill Required	S3	You need skill to determine what ideas you want to communicate by analyzing: the stimulus similar communication and documentation handbooks or practices
Knowledge Required	K6	In some cases, only a mental list is needed, such as when you write a brief memo.

Step 3—Decision Point: Is Additional Information Necessary before You Produce the Communication?

Skill Required	S4	You need skill to determine if you have enough information to achieve the purpose of what you are writing. For example: when writing to a customer about a

complaint, a simple statement of your company's practice may be enough. In other cases, a skeleton outline or your opinion may suffice (e.g., the boss asks for a few suggestions). In sensitive cases such as EEO/AAP, Total Performance Reviews, union grievances, etc., a detailed and completely accurate report may be necessary.

If your decision is *no*, the next three steps can be bypassed; go to Step 7.

Step 4—Determine Sources of the Information

Knowledge Required	K7	The purpose of the communication, the addressee, or similar communications may indicate sources of information.
	K8	Sources of information can be found in many places, such as, for example: company practices local practices federal regulations your boss job incumbents your peers outside resources
	K9	Most subjects that first-level supervisors write about have sources of information that are well documented; for example: company practices on how to handle a trouble can serve as basis for a write-up local practices may specify how to write up a Total Performance Review departmental practices often specify how to format and report monthly results
	K10	When you cannot find any sources of information or do not know where to look for them, you should go back to the stimulus (such as your boss or person who requested the written communication) and ask where the sources of information are.

Step 5—Collect the Information

Skills Required	S5	You need skill to prioritize sources of information, based on their usefulness, completeness, availability, and cost to use.
	S6	You need skill to determine whether the communication can be cancelled if you cannot get the information you need.

Step 6—Analyze the Information

Skill Required	S7	In order to decide which information to include in your writing, you need skill to: look for data that will support your key points look for data that will explain how or why to do something look for points that may convince the reader that your viewpoint is correct look for points in the information that may challenge, contradict, or invalidate the points you are trying to make look for key points in the data confirming or exemplifying what you are trying to get across. (If, for example, you are writing a memo on how to drive safely in ice and snow, you may find key points in a Triple A (AAA) pamphlet on winter driving which confirm your other information on safe winter driving.)

Step 7—Decision Point: Is an Outline Necessary?

Knowledge Required	K11	You may not need an outline if the matter is simple and/or brief (example: a note to your boss about a 2 p.m. meeting).
Skill Required	S8	You need skill to prepare an outline if your subject: is complex or lengthy must be sequential or logical (example: your answer to a

customer complaint requires citations from regulatory agency rulings at appropriate points in your narrative).

Step 8—Produce an Outline

Skills Required	S9	You need skill to list all key points and arrange your key points in an order that supports your purpose or demonstrates your point.
	S10	You need skill to associate supporting data with the key points they support.
Knowledge Required	K12	Know to save all information until you have completed your writing. (You may decide later to include information not used at this stage.)

Step 9—Select a Format

Knowledge Required	K13	Some formats are mandated, such as performance appraisals, correspondence formats, service breakdown reports, vouchers, etc.
Skill Required	S11	You need skill to select an appropriate format when no format is mandated, based on: the addressee your purpose whether the written communication is formal or informal whether a complete sentence or a telegraphic style is appropriate

Step 10—Produce the Written Communication and/or Documentation

Knowledge Required	K14	Know to include supporting data or backup data as additional information to help you achieve your purpose.
	K15	Some final written communication and documentation may be produced without drafts (memos, notes, etc.)
	K16	Some written material may require one or more drafts and

revisions to achieve its purpose, such as a letter for higher level signature.

K17 Know to produce written communication and documentation according to mandated or selected format.

K18 Using an outline (if determined in Step 8) will assist in producing a written communication or documentation that (a) includes all selected information, (b) covers all key points, and (c) reads in a logical and coherent manner.

K19 You should know local procedures and practices on retaining and filing copies.

K20 Some written communication and documentation do *not* require follow-up; for example, FYIs, bulletin board items.

K21 Some written communication and documentation do require follow-up; for example, suspensions, written reprimands.

K22 Know to put dates for follow-up in the bring-up file.

Skills Required

S12 You are expected to have sufficient skills in grammar, syntax, vocabulary, and spelling to achieve the purpose of your writing.

S13 You need skill to determine whether other departments' support is needed to produce documents for release, such as graphics, word processing, administrative support, and reproduction.

S14 If follow-up is necessary, you need skill to determine the follow-up method, based on local practice (telephone, letter, etc.).

S15 You need skill to determine which documents are to be retained in personal files, based on likelihood of future usefulness as reference items.

S16 You need skill to determine what supporting documentation to use *as attachments,* based on quality of supporting documentation, type of supporting documenta-

tion (chart, matrix, graph, illustration). (Keep in mind the necessity not to overburden the text with too much supporting information.)

S17 You need skill to determine what supporting documentation to place *in the text* of the written communication or documentation, based on purpose of documentation, needs of addressee, space available in text.

S18 You need skill to determine the need for follow-up, based on whether a reply and/or action was requested.

S19 You need skill to construct the written communication or documentation using good grammar, correct spelling, appropriate vocabulary, and clear sentence structure.

Step 11—Determine Whether the Written Communication and/or Documentation Is Ready for Release

---

Skill Required

S20 You need skill to determine whether errors or deficiencies exist, based on the stimulus and your own job requirements with respect to the following:
purpose of the communication
selected format
tone
typographical errors
grammar
sentence structure
paragraphing
persons who will initial or sign
titles
file numbers
distribution list
address
routing order for addresses

Knowledge Required

K23 Some written communication and documentation need not be completely error-free with respect to mechanical production, such as a note to a subordinate.

Step 12—Decision Point: Is the Written Communication and/or Documentation Ready for Release?

If your decision is *yes,* skip Step 13 and go to Step 14.

Step 13—Revise the Written Communication and/or Documentation

| Skill Required | S21 | You need skill to correct and revise any deficiencies and errors identified in Step 11. |

Step 14—Release the Written Communication and/or Documentation

| Skill Required | S22 | You need skill to determine the need for reproduction (copies), and method of release, based on local practices, with respect to type of envelope, type of delivery service to use (company, U.S. Mail, UPS, etc.). |

F. TRAINING NEEDS DIAGNOSTIC

The diagnostic test for written communication and documentation is in two sections—an *objective test* intended to test knowledge of the process, and a *role play* designed to test interpersonal and behavioral skills in applying the process.

Objective test

The objective test of five questions is designed to test four skills and six points of knowledge at the first level of supervision. The test questions and answers are found in Exhibits A and B. The specific skills and knowledge tested by the five questions are shown in Exhibit C.

Role play

The role play section of the diagnostic instrument is designed to test the subjects' behavioral and interpersonal skills in performing several duties. Included are:

informal oral communication
providing performance feedback
coaching a subordinate
written communication
controlling the work

This exercise covers the duty of written communication and documentation in order to test four specific skills and two items of knowledge as follows:

Skills: S11, S16, S17, and S19.
Knowledges: K14 and K17.

Generally, this exercise tests the supervisor's ability to first select an appropriate format for the written communication where no standard format is prescribed; to follow administrative procedures; and then to produce a written communication that is complete, comprehensive, and clearly written.

Diagnostic test exhibit A: process 11—written communication

This section deals with the process of Written Communications. This process includes activities such as writing letters, reports, or memos.

1.   A supervisor wrote a letter for the boss's signature. The six steps shown below were carried out. However, the supervisor omitted an important step.
   I.   What additional step was omitted? (Write your answer on the answer sheet.)
   II. After what step shown below should it be performed? (X-out the step on your answer sheet.)
      a.   wrote the first draft   d.   had letter typed
      b.   reviewed with boss   e.   submitted letter to boss
      c.   wrote final draft   f.   boss signed
2.   In producing reports, letters, and memos, it is important to know local administrative procedures. In what three areas from the list below is procedural knowledge most important? (X-out your *three* answers on the answer sheet.)

    a.   format

    b.   intercompany mail systems

    c.   signatory procedures

    d.   high-speed reproduction systems

    e.   addressee information

    f.   type of paper

3.   What are the *five* requirements of effective written communication? (X-out the *five* answers on the answer sheet.)

    a.   double-spaced

    b.   conciseness

    c.   clear or understandable

    d.   technical terms

    e.   organized thoughts

    f.   appropriate choice of words

    g.   formal tone

    h.   appropriate grammar

    i.   complete sentences

    j.   typed

4.   Seven key steps in writing a formal report are listed below. Put them in the order in which they should be carried out. (Place the letter next to the number that corresponds to the order they should be performed on the answer sheet.)

    a.   analyze the information

    b.   outline the material

    c.   collect the information

    d.   write the report

    e.   identify the sources of information

    f.   list what you want to communicate

    g.   determine when the report is due

5.   Nine of the ten statements shown below fit logically into the outline on the answer sheet. Place the statements where they properly belong in the outline. (You can use the blank outline below to work out your answers. *Remember* to put your final answers on the answer sheet. Place the letter of the proper statement for each space on the answer sheet.)

    a.   the shape is complementary to the design of the decor

    b.   business customers rarely buy Snoopy phones

    c.   the colors are attractive

    d.   distracting

    e.   residential customers often buy Snoopy phones

    f.   equipment attractively designed

    g.   tempting to steal

    h.   unnecessary expense

    i.   equipment competitively priced

    j.   customer selection of design line phone

Outline

I.   _____

    A.   _____

          1.   _____

          2.   _____

    B.   _____

II.   _____

    A.   _____

    B.   _____

    C.   _____

Diagnostic test exhibit B—answer sheet: process 11—written communication

1. I. PROOFREAD
    II. a b c ⨉ e f
2. ⨉ b ⨉ d ⨉ f
3. a ⨉ ⨉ d ⨉ ⨉ g ⨉ i j
4. 1st <u>G</u> 2nd <u>F</u> 3rd <u>E</u> 4th <u>C</u> 5th <u>A</u> 6th <u>B</u> 7th <u>D</u>
5. I. <u>E</u>
        A. <u>F</u>
            1. <u>C*</u>
            2. <u>A*</u>
        B. <u>I</u>
    II. <u>B</u>
        A. <u>D*</u>
        B. <u>G*</u>
        C. <u>H*</u>   *ANY ORDER

Diagnostic test exhibit C—items tested by objective test: process 11—written communication and/or documentation

Test question number	Items tested		
	Skills	Knowledge	Process steps
1	S20		
2		K3, K9, K13, K17	
3	S12	K18	
4			1, 2, 4, 5, 6, 8, 10
5	S7, S9, S10		

16 Knowledgeable Representative of the Company

PROCESS 12

A. OVERVIEW—THE FIRST-LEVEL SUPERVISOR'S RELATIONS WITH OUTSIDERS

Many business managers fail to recognize that the business firm and its environment are a unit, inseparable. The industry the company is a part of, the markets it serves, the competitors it meets in the marketplace, the regulatory agencies whose rules and regulations constrain its activities, the financial institutions that provide capital, and, of course, the community of which it is an integral part—all interact with the organization, all directly affect its activities, and all are affected in turn by the actions of the company.

When a person becomes a member of company management, even at the lowest level, he or she becomes a representative of the firm, both within its walls and outside in the larger community. Among the several hats worn by the first-line supervisor is that of public relations person. The supervisor represents the firm wherever he or she goes—in social groups, at professional gatherings, and in community affairs.

Perhaps no organization recognizes this more than the Bell System. First and foremost AT&T is a service organization, and just about every man, woman, and child in the nation is a customer. Bell people, over one million of them, live and work in every city, town, and hamlet of the United States.

AT&T management actively encourages its people to get involved with community activities and to participate in public service clubs like Rotary, Jaycees, and Chambers of Commerce. Bell System managers serve regularly as small town mayors, council members, and school board heads. Bell people everywhere head up volunteer fire departments, scout troops, and community chest drives.

AT&T actively courts all of its constituencies, including its many shareholders. In *The Biggest Company on Earth*,[1] Kleinfield describes AT&T's Shareholder-Management Visit program, in which management employees of a Bell System operating company pay personal calls on shareowners living in their neighborhoods, on their own time, to hear what may be on their minds and to answer questions about the company. (Not all companies are that enlightened, to be sure. The *Wall Street Journal* recently quoted a corporate executive with a quite different view, in these words, "If a shareholder doesn't like the way my company is being run, he can always sell his stock".)

[1]Sonny Kleinfield, *The Biggest Company on Earth* (New York: Holt, Rinehart and Winston, 1981).

Kleinfield describes one such visit on which he accompanied a middle manager from New Jersey Bell. The manager is quoted as saying, if there is criticism on one issue or another, "We talk about it some, chew it over, and sometimes they realize they didn't understand the issue that well. I don't feel my role is to convince them of anything, only to make the Bell System's position entirely clear. If I find any degree of negativism, I try to explore it. Some of them are tickled silly just to have someone paying a call on them."

A firm doesn't have to be the biggest company on earth to benefit from good relations with its constituencies—shareowners, suppliers, customers, lenders, employees, and its neighbors in the community. And every manager should become an emissary to those with whom he or she comes in contact, because he or she benefits as well as the firm itself.

B. HIGHLIGHTS OF THE AT&T JOB STUDY

Definition of the process

The Mastery Model states, "Managers within the Bell System are perceived as representatives of the System by customers, neighbors, civic groups, and subordinates. This process involves representing and sharing knowledge of the Bell System when appropriate."

Summary description of the process

This duty of the first-level supervisor is relatively simple; it is nevertheless a structured managerial process just as are the other 13 duties. In its simplest terms, representing the firm in a knowledgeable manner requires the supervisor to present the best face of the company to its publics—customers, suppliers, community leaders, political bodies, shareholders, even neighbors and friends. These individuals and groups expect members of management to be knowledgeable about the company and to speak for it on occasion, whether formal or informal.

When a supervisor lacks the knowledge needed to represent the company in an exemplary manner, he or she is required by the process to first seek out the source of such knowledge, next to take action to acquire the information required, and then to represent the company as called for by the occasion.

The next section describes this first-level supervisory duty in terms of the six steps—five tasks and one decision point—that make up the process. Included in this discussion is a flowchart of the process.

C. TASKS AND DECISION POINTS IN THE PROCESS OF REPRESENTING THE FIRM

STEP 1 The first step is to recognize that an occasion exists (a stimulus) that requires you to function as a representative of the firm. This could be an invitation to address a community group or social organization, a letter of complaint from a person who lives in your neighborhood, or a request to visit a local shareholder under the company Shareholder Visit Program.

STEP 2 Next you should determine what level of knowledge about the company is required in order to carry out this duty in a competent and effective manner.

STEP 3 (Decision) At this point you should respond to the question: *Do I possess the required level of knowledge called for by the occasion?*

STEP 4 If your answer is *no*—you do *not* have the required level of knowledge—then your next task is to identify the sources of knowledge you need.

STEP 5 Next you should do whatever is necessary to acquire the level of knowledge required by the occasion.

STEP 6 Finally, you should take action to meet with the particular group or individual involved and represent the company in a knowledgeable manner.

Figure 16–1 depicts the flow of tasks and contingency points in the process for first-level supervisors.

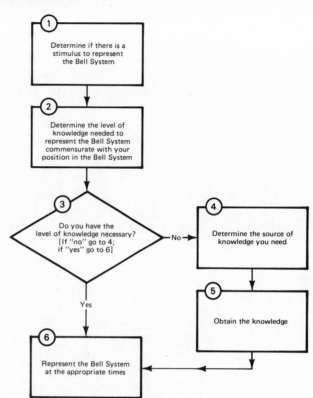

FIGURE 16–1   Flowchart of Process 12— Knowledgeable Representative of the Company

D. PERFORMANCE MEASUREMENTS CHART

This duty involves six steps—five tasks and one decision point. For purposes of measuring performance of the supervisor, all of these steps fall into a single group. Shown below are the output of this group of tasks, the performance standard that applies, and the method used by second-level managers to measure performance of subordinates in this managerial process.

- Output—The first-level supervisor represents the company to customers, neighbors, political groups, the community, etc.

- Performance Standard—The first-level supervisor correctly answers questions regarding company matters.

- Method of Measurement—The first-level supervisor's performance is measured by superior through a) observation, b) feedback from customers, community leaders, etc., and c) ability of first level to perform without requesting guidance from the second level.

E. THE AT&T MASTERY MODEL—KNOWLEDGEABLE REPRESENTATIVE OF THE COMPANY

Representing the firm to its many and varied constituencies is a *management process* consisting of six specific steps or tasks. These steps are described below, together with the skills and knowledge that the first-level supervisor should possess in order to master the process.

Fundamental skills and knowledge required

In order for you to function effectively as a knowledgeable representative of the company, it is necessary for you to know *two fundamentals of management.*

Knowledge Required

K1   As a member of management within the _____ Company, you are perceived as a representative of the firm by customers, neighbors, political groups, relatives, friends, civic organizations, and subordinates. Your level of knowledge of the company should be commensurate with your position.

K2   There are other reasons to be a knowledgeable representative of the company. Among these are:
You may view the firm in a more positive way.
By knowing how your individual job contributes to the whole, it can make your contribution and those of your subordinates more meaningful.
You may accept more responsibility for the organization.
It can increase your confidence in your job performance.

Step 1—Determine If There Is An Occasion, a Need, or a Stimulus to Represent the Company

Your first task is to be aware that occasions arise in which you will be called upon to act as a representative of the firm, and to respond to these occasions.

Step 2—Determine Your Required Level of Knowledge

Knowledge   K3   Individuals and groups are likely
Required   to ask questions in such areas as:
history of the company
equal employment opportunity
products and services
government regulation and legislation
organization and reorganization
pricing
relationship of divisions and subsidiary companies to the parent corporation
competition

Step 3—Decision Point: Do You Have the Level of Knowledge You Need?

If your decision is *yes,* bypass Steps 4 and 5 and go directly to Step 6.

Step 4—Determine the Sources of the Knowledge You Need

Step 5—Obtain the Knowledge

Step 6—Represent the Company on the Appropriate Occasions

F. TRAINING NEEDS DIAGNOSTIC

This is an objective test of six questions (highly specific to the Bell System) designed to test first-level supervisors' knowledge of company activities that are likely to be questioned by outsiders. These relate to "Knowledge K3" on the Mastery Model. Questions and answers are found in Exhibits A and B.

Diagnostic test exhibit A: process 12—knowledgeable representation of the Bell System

As a manager within the Bell System, you are perceived as a representative of the Bell System by customers, neighbors, civic groups and your subordinates.

1. Match the Bell System organization on the left with the service it provides from the right hand column. (X-out the correct letter on the answer sheet.)

    Organizations
       I. AT&T General Departments
      II. Western Electric
     III. Long Lines
     IV. Bell Telephone Laboratories

    Services
    a. manufacture and supply of equipment
    b. operation of interstate network services
    c. provision of central staff services
    d. research and development
    e. provision of local telephone service
    f. technical design and planning for local Company's plant needs

2. The AAP/EEO Consent Decree ended in January, 1979. (X-out T for True or F for False on the answer sheet.)
3. The Bell System has recently reorganized its departments. Formerly, there were Commercial Departments (the Business Offices), Plant Installation Departments, and Plant Repair Departments. What are the *two* departments or segments that now incorporate those former groups? (Write the two answers on the answer sheet.)
4. As a result of the reorganization, what segment or department now includes the organization called Operator Services or Traffic? (Write the answer on the answer sheet.)
5. It is legal for customers to buy telephones and install them in their homes, if they notify the Telephone Company that they have done so. (X-out T for True or F for False on the answer sheet.)
6. Who regulates long distance interstate rates? (Write your answer on the answer sheet.)

Diagnostic test exhibit B—answer sheet: process 12—representative of company

1.   I. a b ☒ d e f
      II. ☒ b c d e f
     III. a ☒ c d e f
     IV. a b c ☒ e f
2. ☒ F
3. BUSINESS
    RESIDENCE
4. NETWORK
5. ☒ F
6. F.C.C.

Diagnostic test exhibit C—items tested by objective test: process 12—knowledgeable representative of company

Test question number	Items tested		Process steps
	Skills	Knowledge	
1		K3	
2		K3	
3		K3	
4		K3	
5		K3	
6		K3	

17 Career Counseling Subordinates

PROCESS 13

A. OVERVIEW OF CAREER COUNSELING AT THE SUPERVISORY LEVEL

Surveys of first-level supervisors' morale and attitudes toward their companies and their jobs consistently find that supervisors are concerned with their inability to do an adequate job of motivating, developing, and counseling the people who report to them. In a recent survey conducted in conjunction with the supervisory job studies, for instance, nearly half the supervisors surveyed (45.5 percent) indicated that they had insufficient time for these activities. Additionally, nearly 40 percent felt that higher management gave this aspect of the supervisor's job low priority.

Yet these same supervisors, when asked to rate the importance to their own job performance of 39 environmental factors, gave a high rating to their *own* opportunities for career advancement and professional growth. So it seems that while many first-level supervisors appreciate the value of personal development and earnestly want to do more for their own subordinates, they feel frustrated by lack of time and management support for the effort.

If this is true, then it is an encouraging sign, for in the past it was the exception rather than the rule for first-level supervisors to be sensitive to the personal needs and aspirations of individual members of their work groups. Awareness by supervisors that the people reporting to them can benefit from development and career counseling, and that the supervisors themselves can gain from it, is a mighty first step toward the really productive organization. The typical new first-level supervisor, unfortunately, has little comprehension of what career counseling is and how to do it. Who should be counseled? When is counseling required?

Few supervisors, in my experience, even consider this to be part of their job, believing that such activities are the responsibility of the personnel staff. They feel, with some justification, that finding new and better jobs for their best people is acting against their own self-interest, which is, after all, to get the work out. Supervisors feel that promoting their best performers out of the jobs they are doing well, possibly out of the work group to which they are valued contributors, is to lose a valuable resource.

What these short-sighted supervisors fail to realize, of course, is that they may lose these superior performers to another company, very likely a competitor, if they fail to guide these subordinates into more rewarding jobs within the organization. In short, if the supervisor doesn't provide career counseling, someone else will.

B. HIGHLIGHTS OF THE AT&T JOB STUDY

Definition of career counseling

Career counseling is defined in the first-level Mastery Model as a process of:

> . . . helping subordinates achieve realistic personal job goals. It includes planning activities to help place subordinates in appropriate jobs.

Summary description of the process

Whenever a subordinate's performance meets all performance standards of the job, and he or she has indicated a desire for more challenging work, that individual is a prime candidate for career counseling from the supervisor.

Assuming the subordinate's desire for challenge is sincere, the supervisor should first attempt to provide more challenging assignment related to the subordinate's present job. If the subordinate is not satisfied by this, then the supervisor should attempt to determine the subordinate's qualifications for a new job.

If the subordinate is interested in moving to a new job, but appears *not* to be qualified for it, the supervisor should plan, together with the subordinate, activities such as training to help him or her qualify for the new job. (Note: *Qualification* for a job is a sensitive area, and a supervisor is cautioned not to make judgments about subordinates' lack of qualifications for specific work without consulting personnel specialists.)

The supervisor has a responsibility to help the subordinate succeed in the new assignment or job; he or she should never knowingly choose an assignment or a job in which the subordinate has a high risk of failure. At all times, too, the subordinate should be given the opportunity to express his or her own desires for assignment or type of work; when this matches a company need, both the company and the individual gain (and the supervisor is entitled to credit for developing an individual).

C. TASKS AND DECISION POINTS IN THE PROCESS

STEP 1	Determine if a stimulus exists for career counseling a subordinate. (One such stimulus, of course, is when a subordinate's performance meets *all* performance standards of his or her job).
STEP 2	If a stimulus exists, the next task is to arrange to meet with your subordinate for the purpose of career counseling. (For guidance on this step, you can refer to Steps 6 and 7 of Process Number 14—Meetings.)
STEP 3	Prepare for the career counseling meeting by matching the identified skills of your subordinate with other jobs.
STEP 4	Meet with your subordinate.
STEP 5	Set and maintain a constructive tone for the session (as prescribed in Step 8 of Process No. 9—Informal Oral Communication).
STEP 6	Determine whether or not your subordinate wants a more challenging assign-

ment on the present job, using your *interviewing* skills (see Process No. 9 for guidance on this task).

STEP 7 Decision	Based on this interview, respond to the question: *Does your subordinate want a more challenging assignment?*
	If your decision is *no*, skip the next four steps, which deal with this part of career counseling, and go directly to Step 12.
STEP 8	Determine areas in which to offer more challenging assignments, such as rotation, training others, delegation of authority, etc., keeping in mind your subordinate's capabilities, personal aspirations, and job maturity.
STEP 9	Assign the work, being sure to (1) set objectives for results together with your subordinate, (2) record the assignment, and (3) establish necessary controls (see Process No. 1—Planning the Work, and

STEP 10   Process No. 2—Controlling the Work).
          Document the career counseling session and its results in accordance with standard practice (or need for follow-up).

STEP 11   Provide feedback on performance to your subordinate, in accordance with Process No. 4, starting with Step 2.

Figure 17-1 depicts the flow of tasks and decisions in the Career Counseling Process up to this point.

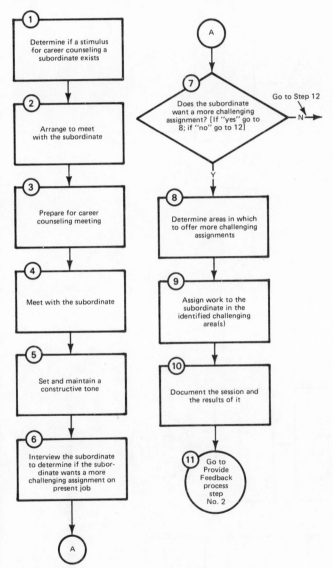

FIGURE 17-1. Career Counseling: The First Eleven Steps

STEP 12   If your decision in Step 7 was *no*—your
Decision   subordinate does not want a more challenging assignment on the present job—then you should respond to the question: *Is your subordinate interested in a new job?*

          If your decision is *yes*, skip Step 13 and go to Step 14.

STEP 13   If your decision is *no*—your subordinate is not interested in a new job—then document this fact for the Total Performance Review and inform your subordinate of your action.

STEP 14   If your decision in Step 12 was *yes*, then your next task is to determine the requirements of the new job.

STEP 15   Determine your subordinate's qualifications with respect to these requirements. (This may have already been done in Step 6 earlier, or in the Coaching Process.)

STEP 16   Based on comparison of the last two
Decision   items, respond to the question: *Is the subordinate qualified for the new job?*

          If your decision is *no*, skip Step 17 and go to Step 18. (Caution: This determination may be a Personnel Department responsibility, not yours to make.)

STEP 17   Follow company procedures to place the subordinate in the new job.

STEP 18   If the decision in Step 16 was *no*—the subordinate is not qualified for the new job—then your task is to plan activities that will qualify him or her, such as training.

STEP 19   Implement the planned activities to qualify the subordinate.

STEP 20   Document the results of the career counseling, and establish a baseline to determine when the subordinate has met the qualifications for the new job.

Figure 17-2 (next page) illustrates the total process of Career Counseling subordinates.

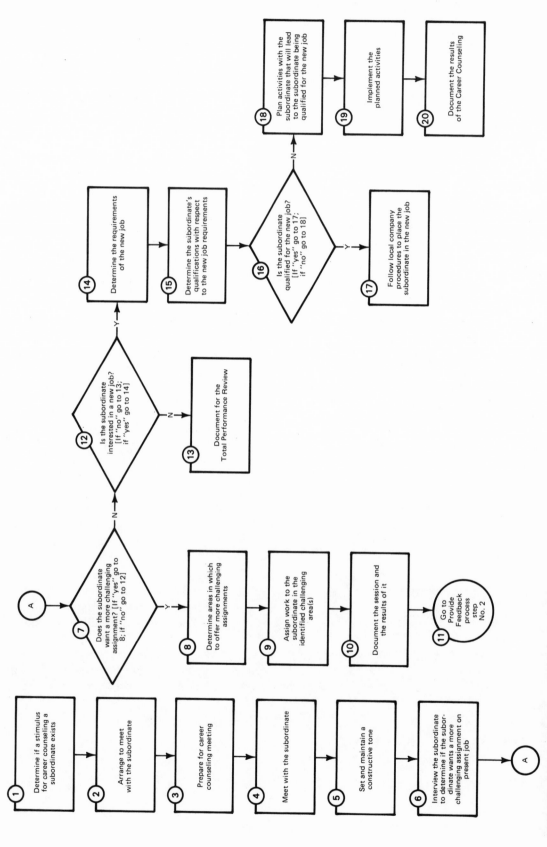

FIGURE 17–2. Total Process of Career Counseling

D. PERFORMANCE MEASUREMENTS CHART

The thirteenth ranking duty of the supervisor—Career Counseling a Subordinate—involves 17 tasks and three contingencies or decision points. For purposes of measuring performance, these 20 steps fall naturally into five principal *groups*. The chart that follows (Table 17-1) lists the steps in each of the five groups, identifies the output of each group, shows the performance standards that apply to each output, and identifies the method used by second-level managers to measure the managerial performance of subordinate first-line supervisors.

These outputs, performance standards, and measurement methods were developed under the constraints recorded earlier, in the discussion of performance measurement in Planning the Work.

Table 17-1. Career counseling a subordinate

Step or group of steps	*Output*	*Performance standards*	*Method of measurement*
Steps 1-5	Subordinate selected for career counseling Career counseling meeting conducted	Developmental needs for subordinates are identified	
Steps 6-11	Subordinate given more challenging assignments	Programs initiated to develop technical and managerial skills	The second-level boss reviews the career counseling documentation
Steps 12-17 (less Step 13)	Steps are taken to place the subordinate in a new job	First-level supervisor actively seeks job opportunities for subordinates	
Steps 18, 19	Plans are made and implemented to qualify the subordinate for a new job	First-level supervisor devises a written plan and follows up on the plan	
Step 13 and Step 20	Career counseling meeting is documented	Meetings are documented	

E. THE AT&T MASTERY MODEL—CAREER COUNSELING A SUBORDINATE

Career counseling a subordinate is a managerial process that may involve as many as 20 steps. Each of these tasks and contingency points is described in the following, together with the associated skills and knowledge needed to master each one.

Fundamental skills and knowledge required

In order to counsel a subordinate to achieve realistic personal job goals in an effective way, it is necessary for you to know this fundamental of management related to career counseling.

| Knowledge Required | K1 | Career counseling is helping subordinates establish realistic personal job goals and planning activities to achieve the goals. |

Step 1—Determine that a Stimulus for Career Counseling a Subordinate Exists

| Knowledge Required | K2 | One indicator that career counseling is appropriate for a subordinate is when that subordinate's |

performance meets all performance standards.

K3   The stimuli for career counseling are Feedback Steps 5 and 27, or local practices and assessment information.

Step 2—Arrange to Meet with the Subordinate

See *Meetings* process Steps 6 and 7 for guidance.

Step 3—Prepare for Career Counseling Meeting

| Knowledge Required | K4 | Know to determine new jobs for subordinate based on matching identified skills of subordinate with other jobs. |

Step 4—Meet with Subordinate

Step 5—Set and Maintain Constructive Tone

See Step 8 of the Informal Oral Communication process.

Step 6—Interview the Subordinate to Determine If Subordinate Wants a More Challenging Assignment on Present Job

| Knowledge Required | K5 | Some subordinates who meet standards may not want a more challenging assignment or have new job interests. |

Step 7—Decision Point: Does the Subordinate Want a More Challenging Assignment?

If the answer is *no*, skip the next four steps and go directly to Step 12.

Step 8—Determine Areas in Which to Offer More Challenging Assignments

| Knowledge Required | K6 | Know to ask for subordinate's inputs about more challenging assignments. |

K7   Union contracts and local procedures may prohibit the assignment of some tasks.

K8   Know to offer assignments that support company EEO/AA goals (for example, offer an assignment in a nontraditional area such as assigning a female clerk to assist in selecting tools for placement on equipment trucks).

K9   Know not to intentionally choose an area in which the subordinate cannot succeed.

K10   You should know the challenging assignments available, such as:

give a subordinate part of your own work
special assignments
more difficult jobs
oral presentations
rotate jobs
participate in cross-training
be in charge
train others

Step 9—Assign Work to Subordinate in Challenging Area

Skill Required	S1	This task requires skill to set objectives for the new assignment with subordinate (see Controlling the Work).
Knowledge Required	K11	Know to log assignment and objectives on Master Control List per the Planning Process.
	K12	Know to use all steps in the "Controlling the Work" process.

Step 10—Document the Session and Its Results

See Coaching process, Step 22.

Step 11—Go to Provide Performance Feedback Process, Step 2

Step 12—Decision Point: Is the subordinate interested in a new job?

If the answer is *yes*, skip Step 13 and go to Step 14.

Knowledge Required	K13	If subordinate says yes, determine what new jobs the subordinate is interested in.
	K14	Know to suggest and discuss the new jobs determined in Step 3 (or in Coaching Step 6).

Step 13—Document for the Total Performance Review

Knowledge Required	K15	If subordinate does not meet work standards, document and take appropriate actions per local practice.
	K16	You should know to inform subordinate of documentation.

Step 14—Determine the Requirements of the New Job

Skill Required	S2	You need skill to determine the requirements of the new job suggested by the subordinate, if requirements are not already determined.
Knowledge Required	K17	The information to make the above determination can be found in personnel department, job briefs, position descriptions, etc.

Step 15—Determine Subordinate's Qualifications with Respect to the New Job Requirements

Knowledge Required	K18	You should know to perform this step if it has not been performed in Step 3 (or in Coaching Step 6).

Step 16—Decision Point: Is the subordinate qualified for the new job?

Knowledge Required	K19	You should know whether this determination can be made locally by you or should be made by the Personnel Department.
	K20	If this determination should be made by the Personnel Department, know to wait for its deter-

mination before resuming the process.

If your decision is *no*, go to Step 18.

Step 17—Follow Local Company Procedures to Place the Subordinate in the New Job

Knowledge Required	K21	You should know where to check for job availability: Personnel Department, peers, etc.
	K22	Know, if the job is not available at this time, to find out from above resources when to follow-up.
	K23	Know where to find procedures to get subordinate new job: Personnel Department, boss, peers, etc.

Step 18—Plan Activities to Help Subordinate Qualify for the New Job

Knowledge Required	K24	Know that the planned activities cannot interfere with the subordinate's ability to meet current output requirements.
	K25	Planned activities might include: company courses on own time (Tuition Aid), other assignments in current job that might prepare the subordinate for the new job, etc.
	K26	Know to include the subordinate's ideas in the planning process to increase the likelihood of the subordinate's becoming qualified.
	K27	Know to establish checkpoints with the subordinate with respect to attaining desired qualifications (see Planning process).
	K28	Know to document plan on the Master Control List, or in accordance with local practices.

Step 19—Implement the Planned Activities

Knowledge Required	K29	Results of implementing the plan may provide input to the

Feedback process.

K30 In order to implement the activities, it may be necessary to communicate with other departments, boss, union, peers, etc.

Knowledge Required

K31 Know to document results of career counseling feedback, and to establish a baseline to determine when the subordinate has met the qualifications for a new job.

K32 Know to document the results of career counseling on the Master Control List or in accordance with local procedure.

Step 20—Document the Results of the Career Counseling

F. TRAINING NEEDS DIAGNOSTIC

This is an objective test of eight questions designed to test the knowledge of first-level supervisors in career counseling subordinates. The questions and answers are found in Exhibits A and B. The 17 specific points of knowledge tested by the questions are shown on Exhibit C.

Diagnostic test exhibit A: process 13—career counseling

Career Counseling is helping subordinates achieve realistic personal job goals. This includes planning activities to help place subordinates in appropriate jobs.

1. Five of your subordinates are described below. Which two would you select first to counsel on possible jobs? (X-out the *two* correct answers on the answer sheet.)
    a. Subordinate is meeting all job requirements and is content with current assignment.
    b. Subordinate has been on job two months and expresses interest in a different assignment.
    c. Subordinate has been trained and is not capable of performing current assignment.
    d. Subordinate has been performing job in a satisfactory manner for two years and is interested in a new assignment.
    e. Subordinate has been on job two months and does not know how to perform certain procedures.
2. It is not necessary to consider Bell System EEO/AAP goals when you give special assignments to subordinates *within your group.* (X-out T for True or F for False on the answer sheet.)
3. You should consider union contracts and local job descriptions when you give special assignments to your subordinates. (X-out T for True or F for False on the answer sheet.)
4. You are working to get a subordinate promoted. The company has imposed a freeze on all promotions and moves. You cannot locate a new job for that subordinate. What action should you take next? (X-out the *best* answer on the answer sheet.)
    a. Leave subordinate on current assignment and monitor the subordinate's satisfaction with it.
    b. Encourage subordinate to look for more challenges off the job.
    c. Delegate special assignments and parts of your work to the subordinate.
    d. Refer problem to your boss.
    e. Contact the people responsible for nonmanagement personnel moves.
5. A subordinate, who is ready for movement, expresses interest in a particular new job. You do not know the requirements of that job. Which two sources, of those listed below, should you consult first? (X-out the *two* best answers on the answer sheet.)
    a. your boss
    b. your subordinate
    c. personnel department
    d. your peers
    e. job briefs/descriptions
    f. appraisal documentation

6. A subordinate wants a transfer to a new job. The subordinate is not fully qualified for the job desired. You plan to help the subordinate develop the necessary skills.
   a. When would these developmental activities take precedence over the subordinate's current job requirements? (Write your answer on the answer sheet.)
   b. In addition to Bell System training courses, what are two other activities that could help the subordinate develop the necessary skills? (Write your answer on the answer sheet.)
7. Give one reason why you should include your subordinate's input in developing a plan for improving the subordinate's skills. (Write your answer on the answer sheet.)
8. You and one of your subordinates have agreed upon a developmental plan. The plan includes sending the subordinate to a training class. You have scheduled the training, the subordinate has been notified, and you have arranged for coverage. What are the two additional things you must do? (Write the *two* answers on the answer sheet.)

Diagnostic test exhibit B—answer sheet: process 13—career counseling

1. a b ☒ ☒ e
2. T ☒
3. ☒ F
4. a b ☒ d e
5. a b ☒ d ☒ f
6. (a) NEVER
   (b) NON-BELL SYSTEM COURSES, (TUITION AID) OTHER ASSIGNMENTS IN CURRENT JOB
7. INCREASED INVOLVEMENT, BETTER COMMITMENT TO FOLLOW THE PLAN
8. (a) DOCUMENT THE DEVELOPMENT PLAN
   (b) SCHEDULE OR PLAN TO MONITOR OR FOLLOW-UP

Diagnostic test exhibit C—items tested by objective test: process 13—career counseling

Test question number	Items tested		
	Skills	Knowledge	Process steps
1		K2, K5[*]	
2		K8	
3		K7	
4		K10	
5		K17	
6		K23, K24, K25	
7		K24, K26	
8		K27, K28, K31, K32	

[*]Also tests knowledge K56 of Feedback process, and knowledge K25 of Coaching.

18 Meetings

PROCESS 14

A. OVERVIEW OF MEETINGS AS A COMMUNICATIONS MEANS AT THE SUPERVISORY LEVEL

Discussions on productivity invariably label the business meeting as an impediment to productivity improvement. Robert Sibson's book, *Increasing Employee Productivity*, for instance, dismisses meetings as "self-imposed unproductive practices." He observes that each meeting frequently generates yet more unproductive work, such as the next meeting and preparation time spent in advance.

Sibson has a point, even though he comes down rather too heavily with it. Many meetings *are* unproductive. Too many are held for social purposes. Some, in fact, are wasteful and counterproductive. But so, on occasion, are other forms of human communication—memos and telephone discussions, even face-to-face conversation. Nevertheless, meetings are one of the *principal means of communication* in a contemporary organization of any size, and one of the most effective if properly conducted.

The value of meetings

Meetings can be the most effective mechanism for promoting group spirit, a sense of organizational "one-ness," and unity of purpose and direction among the disparate functions and individuals in a large organization. The elements of any organization, whether functional or program-oriented, tend to drift away from the central objectives and purposes of the organization as an entity. If permitted to proceed on their own for any length of time, they may drift so far off course that bringing them back can be difficult and disruptive. Properly managed, meetings can provide a means to revitalize, refocus, and redirect the energies, resources, and capabilities of the total organization toward its overall objectives.

Making meetings productive

Good management is what differentiates the productive meeting from the wasteful one. Good management of meetings begins, as does good management of any activity, with a statement of purpose. It is probable that lack of stated purpose is responsible for more waste of management time in meetings than all other causes combined. Sloma, in *No-Nonsense Management*, states, ". . . one hears classifications of meetings: to inform, to make a decision, to formalize assignments. There is, in fact, only one purpose to every meeting—to enhance the prospects of achieving the firm's goals and objectives.'' An organization that adopts this purpose as a principle, and couples this with action to make the firm's goals known and accepted, will assure that every meeting is a productive one. The other kind will never be held in the first instance.

Few organizations, however, seem to recognize the need for a statement of purpose for meetings, much less a policy governing their scheduling and conduct. It almost seems that the topic is considered too trivial to acknowledge with a policy statement. A written company procedure to guide the conduct of meetings is virtually unknown; yet countless hours of management time will be wasted in meetings if managers do not observe certain basics in regard to *scheduling, advance notification, agenda development and issuance, attendance, recording of action assignments, standards for audiovisual presentations, pre-meeting preparation, and post-meeting actions.*

It is positively shameful that so many important meetings are held without benefit of a discussion agenda. Even when an agenda is prepared, it is often issued insufficiently in advance of the meeting to allow participants to prepare themselves for the discussion. And how few meetings really stick to the agenda when one is available! What may be worse, from a productivity viewpoint, are the meetings held to present proposals or study findings without participants having had an opportunity to review the presentation beforehand. Surely a manager who has studied a proposal thoroughly before the meeting can make more thoughtful marginal comments, ask more penetrating questions, and contribute more meaningful insights to the discussion.

Actually, it has been proven useful to go a step further and require each meeting participant, after reading the presentation material, to submit a list of questions to the meeting leader or principal speaker in advance. Given the benefit of this input, the leader can give a more considered response—or incorporate the most important observations into his or her presentation. There may be no better way to keep the meeting focused on the major issues, keep the meeting brief, and produce more meaningful output.

Need for advance preparation

Advance preparation can be even more important for the manager who may be less articulate, less assertive,

and less comfortable in the extemporaneous setting of an unstructured meeting. All good managers are not equally eloquent, and it is important that the input of those less so be considered. Too often, the most articulate manager is permitted to dominate the meeting, even when she or he may have little of substance to import.

Output of the meetings

Output, of course, is what productivity is all about, yet many meetings, sad to say, produce no output. Incredibly, a group of ten, twenty, or more highly-paid managers can spend hours in a meeting and nothing will be recorded in the form of action assignments to implement decisions arrived at. Lacking documentation directing that certain actions be taken, there is a high probability that *no* action will be taken. The meeting ends, the participants go their separate ways, and they are caught up in the daily demands of their respective jobs. Recollections of what was decided in the meeting fade, and within a few days no two managers will agree completely on what was decided.

It is vitally important, therefore, that someone be delegated to record notes of assignments made in every meeting—not minutes of "who said what," but specific actions to be taken by specific individuals; not a legal record of proceedings, as in a directors meeting, but a document designed to force people to act.

It is rare that a meeting resolves a problem completely. Even if a solution is arrived at, action on someone's part will be required to implement the solution. A decision made is of no value, no matter how high up in the organization it is made, until the decision is made effective through a commitment to action and work assignments to individuals.

The solution to every problem frequently carries the seeds of new problems. To the extent that these can be anticipated, the discussion in the meetings should attempt to identify consequences of solutions proposed and decisions reached. The record of the meetings should reflect these, and should record the tasks of defining and refining these potential problems, so that action can be taken to prevent them or to mitigate their impact.

Action assignments in writing

Misunderstandings will occur despite sincere efforts on the part of all participants to express themselves clearly and on the part of others to understand. Often there will be unarticulated disagreement with conclusions reached and decisions made. Frequently, these misunderstandings and disagreements surface only later, after commitments have been made and irrevocable action taken. Action assignments in writing serve to document conclusions reached and commitments made in the meeting, so that all participants will know without question what is required of them afterward.

Meeting minutes are not generally considered to be "control reports," yet they can be one of the most vital reports in terms of controlling the direction of the enterprise. What is required is a reorientation from a sterile, passive historical record to a dynamic, future-oriented record of actions to be taken, by whom, and when. The traditional meeting minutes are too often written as a history of the event, to be filed in the archives for future reference should a question arise as to what transpired. Their purpose is protective and defensive, rather than constructive and productive.

B.   HIGHLIGHTS OF THE AT&T JOB STUDY

Definition of the process

In the first-level supervisory job study, the fourteenth duty, *meetings*, is given the designation "Formal Oral Communication," and is defined as a managerial process that

. . . includes one-on-one encounters and meetings with more than one person. It requires some *preparation* beforehand and some *structure* during the communication.

The distinction between this process and the *Informal Oral Communication* process is clear. Informal Oral Communication usually occurs in an unstructured situation and requires little or no preparation.

The job study notes that most meetings conducted (led) by first-level supervisors normally are participated in only by their subordinates. Even so, the Mastery Model requires the supervisor to follow a well-structured *managerial process* of tasks and decision points.

Summary description of the process

These steps cover *advance preparation*, the *conduct of the meeting*, and *post-meeting follow-on*. The process begins with the making of several lists—a list of points to be covered, a list of things to do, and a list of things to get—all based on the purpose and the nature of the planned meeting. The process then requires the supervisor to select an appropriate time and place for the meeting, to notify participants in advance, and to do and get all the things on the prioritized lists.

The conduct of the meeting itself is structured in order to make it more productive. The process prescribes how to open the session, how to ensure that all agenda points are covered, how to ensure that the meeting has accomplished its purpose, how to ensure the understanding and agreement of participants, how to ensure that the meeting results are recorded and documented—even how to bring the meeting to a graceful close.

Finally, the Mastery Model describes what a first-level supervisor should do when attending a meeting held by someone else. Such meetings can be critically important to a supervisor and the work group, especially when held by higher-level management for communicating top management policy, changes in corporate direction, and other vital information that must be translated into action at the operating levels of the firm.

C. TASKS AND DECISION POINTS IN THE PROCESS

STEP 1   The first step is to determine whether you are conducting the meeting or are attending a meeting conducted by someone else. (This is usually obvious, but not always—it is a matter of who controls the agenda.)

STEP 2   *If leading the meeting,* list points to be covered, based on the purpose of the meeting.

STEP 3   Prepare for the meeting by first determining which of these four basic types of meetings it is to be:

Informational/Discussion: to share or acquire new information

Problem Solving: to gain input from many persons to assist in the solution of a problem

Venting: to clear air—make people feel better

Demonstration/Instructional: to share new procedures/teach a skill

and then by listing *things to do* and *things to get* in advance of the meeting.

STEP 4   Prioritize things to do and things to get, based on when they are needed, how difficult they are to do or to get, your own workload, etc.

STEP 5   Identify the participants (usually subordinates for meetings led by first-level supervisors).

STEP 6   Select a time and a place for the meeting, considering the factors of workloads, travel time, convenience of participants, etc.

STEP 7   Notify the participants (sufficiently in advance) about time, place, purpose, pre-meeting requirements, etc.

Figure 18–1 illustrates the process up to this point, Steps 1 through 7.

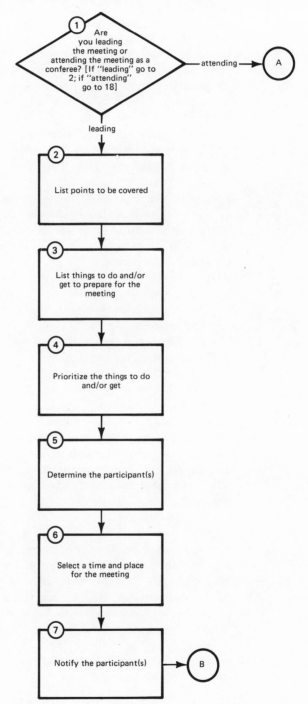

FIGURE 18-1. Meetings: The First Seven Steps

STEP 8   Do and get the things listed in Step 4. (If one or more of these are unavailable, determine the effect on your planned meeting.)

STEP 9   Meet with the participants, and make sure a note-taker is assigned.

STEP 10   Open the meeting by reviewing the purpose and objectives of the meeting, introducing participants when required, announcing procedural items such as facilities, breaks, etc.

STEP 11   Cover the points on your agenda in a way that is appropriate to the particular type of meeting (see Step 3 for meeting types).

STEP 12   Determine whether or not the purposes of the meeting have been achieved, by questioning, testing, or observing reactions of participants to ensure understanding of key points.

STEP 13 Respond to the question: Were the purposes achieved?
(Decision)
          If your decision is *yes*, skip the next step and go to Step 15.

STEP 14   If your decision was *no*—the purposes of the meeting were not achieved—you should turn to the Problem Solving Process (No. 3) for help, starting with Define the Problem and ending with Implement Solution.

STEP 15   Summarize conclusions and/or commitments made (and verify understanding and agreement by the participants of what has happened and what is to be done).

STEP 16   Close the meeting with an expression of appreciation to participants. Meeting minutes should be distributed, if appropriate, as soon as possible afterward.

STEP 17   Your final task, if conducting the meeting, is to document the meeting, if appropriate, in accordance with standard practice or custom.

Figure 18-2 graphically depicts the next 10 steps in the process of conducting a meeting.

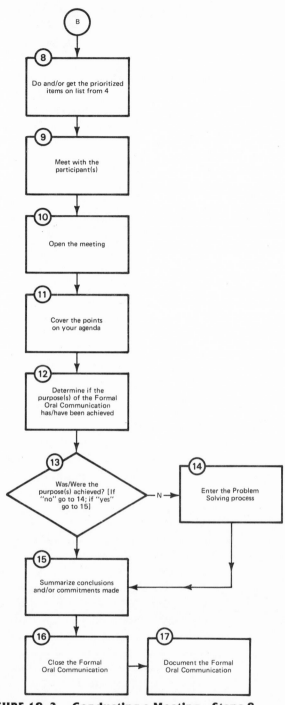

FIGURE 18-2. Conducting a Meeting—Steps 8 through 17

This flowchart illustrates the steps in the total process of conducting and participating in meetings. Steps 18, 19, and 20 apply when participating in a meeting *conducted by someone else (see next page for detailed description of these three steps).*

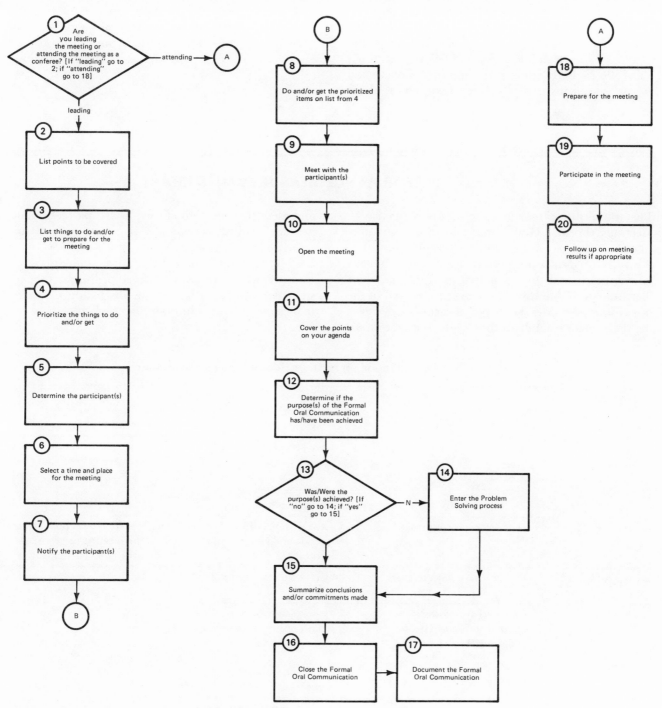

FIGURE 18-3. Flowchart of the Meeting Process

If attending a meeting conducted by another person, these steps apply:

STEP 18   Prepare for the meeting, using information provided to you about the purpose, agenda, advance reading required, participants, etc. (If information is lacking, you should seek it out before attending.)

STEP 19   Participate in the meeting actively and constructively, and take notes about items important to your job, your boss, future reference, etc.

STEP 20   Follow up on meeting results by sharing relevant information with subordinates, peers, your boss; and by following through on any commitments made by you. (These could be input to your "To Do" List as well as to future planning.)

D. PERFORMANCE MEASUREMENTS CHART

The fourteenth principal duty of the supervisor—Meetings (Formal Oral Communication)—involves 18 tasks and two contingencies or decision points. For purposes of measuring performance, these 20 steps fall naturally into five principal *groups*. The chart that follows (Table 18-1) lists the steps in each of the five groups, identifies the output of each group, shows the performance standards that apply to each output,

and identifies the method used by second-level managers to measure the managerial performance of subordinate first-line supervisors.

These outputs, performance standards, and measurement methods were developed under the constraints recorded earlier, in the discussion of performance measurement in Planning the Work.

Table 18-1. Process 14: meetings (formal oral communication)

Step or group of steps	Output	Performance standards	Method of measurement
Steps 1–8	Content of the meeting and all logistics are planned in advance and the agenda is prepared	Proper participants are selected Objective of the meeting is defined	The second-level boss reviews the agenda and plans
Steps 9, 10, 11	The meeting is conducted	First-level supervisor followed agenda and kept meeting on track	The second-level boss attends the meeting or gets feedback from participants
Steps 12–17	The meeting's objectives are met	Objectives of the meeting are met	
Steps 18, 19	First-level supervisor is prepared to participate in the meeting	First-level supervisor's contributions to the meeting are meaningful First-level supervisor is cooperative	The second-level boss observes, receives feedback, or reviews the minutes
Step 20	Follow-up action is taken	First-level supervisor follows-up on commitments First-level supervisor keeps boss informed	

E. THE AT&T MASTERY MODEL —MEETINGS (FORMAL ORAL COMMUNICATION)

Conducting meetings is a managerial process that can involve some 20 steps. The process begins with a question: Are you leading the meeting, or are you attending a meeting led by another person? If your answer is the former, you will be involved in as many as 17 tasks; if the latter, you are required to do only three of the tasks.

The entire process is described in detail in the following. Each of the 20 steps is described along with the skills and knowledge required to master each task and the process itself.

Fundamental skills and knowledge required

In order for you to conduct meetings productively, you should know *four fundamentals of management* that apply to this managerial process at the first level of supervision. These are:

Knowledge Required

K1 A meeting is a formal oral communication that involves two or more people as well as some preparation. Examples: Total performance review—two persons; Safety meeting—more than two persons.

K2 The purposes and topics for a meeting are determined by the stimulus (the person or event that initiates the meeting).

K3 The stimulus may determine who attends the meeting.

K4 You should also know *not to* hold too many meetings.

Step 1—Are You Leading the Meeting or Attending the Meeting as a Conferee?

If leading, go to Step 2 on next page; if attending, go to Step 18 on page 177.

LEADING THE MEETING

Step 2—List Points to Be Covered

Skills Required	S1	This task requires skill to determine the purpose of the meeting.
	S2	You need skill to identify the points to cover, based on the purpose of meeting (for example, a total performance review requires performance data, standards, comparison of performance to standards, and plans to maintain and improve performance).
	S3	You need skill to review old meetings, refer to company practices, consult your boss, peers, subordinates, and/or local practices to help determine points to be covered.
Knowledge Required	K5	You should know to document the points to be covered.

Step 3—Prepare for the Meeting

Skills Required	S4	You need skill to determine the type of meeting, based on the following categories:
		Information/Discussion: to share or acquire new information
		Problem Solving: to gain input from many persons to assist in the solution of a problem
		Venting: to clear air—make people feel better
		Demonstration/Instructional: to share new procedures/teach a skill
	S5	You need skill to prepare a list of things to do or get, based on points to be covered—such as agenda, handouts, pre-meeting memos, audio-visuals, note-takers, special speakers, etc.

Step 4—Prioritize the Things to Do and/or Get

Skill Required	S6	This task requires skill to put items needed for meeting in rank order of importance, based on:
		when needed
		time available to prepare
		how difficult given item is to do or get
		how long it would take to do given item
		own workload
		availability of resources at critical times (example: someone in town for just two days)
		what must be done before you can notify attendees

Step 5—Identify the Participants

Skills Required	S7	You need skill to identify attendees, based on who needs to be involved, or based on points to be covered in meeting as determined in Step 2.
	S8	You need skill to use records of past similar meetings to identify possible attendees.
Knowledge Required	K6	Know that the stimulus may determine who attends.
	K7	Attendees from outside your own work group may assist in problem solving.
	K8	Most meetings led by first-level supervisors involve only their own subordinates.

Step 6—Select a Time and Place for the Meeting

Skills Required	S9	You need skill to establish *the time* for the meeting, based on schedules, workload, travel time, etc.
	S10	You need skill to establish *the place* for the meeting, based on convenience for the participants (consider travel time), subject of meeting, requirements for special types of equipment, number of participants, etc.
Knowledge Required	K9	The stimulus for the meeting may determine time and/or place.

K10   If time and/or place cannot be arranged, know to use a method of communication other than a meeting.

K11   A time and place convenient to participants may make participants more apt to attend, more receptive, and more productive, so that they may better contribute to achieving meeting's purpose.

Step 7—Notify the Participants

Skills Required   S11   You need skill to determine the factors of which attendees must be notified, such as time, place, topics to be covered, pre-meeting work, speakers.

S12   You need skill to select the appropriate means of notification (face-to-face, telephone, writing), based on the amount of time between notice of meeting and holding of meeting.

S13   You need skill to determine if attendees are required to take some action prior to the meeting.

Knowledge Required   K12   Some high-priority items from your meeting list may need to be seen to before attendees can be notified.

K13   Advance notice will enable participants to better prepare for meeting.

Step 8—Do and/or Get Prioritized Items on List from Step 4

Skill Required   S14   This task requires skill to determine the criticality of any item that is unavailable. Must the meeting be cancelled, or can the meeting be held without the item? For example, if guest speaker cannot make it to the regular weekly staff meetings, you might still hold the staff meeting. If, however, a guest speaker cannot attend a meeting that is centered on the informa-

tion from the guest speaker, you would cancel the meeting.

Knowledge Required   K14   Meetings may be changed in content, postponed, or cancelled because one or more of the items on the list developed in Step 3 cannot be done or obtained.

K15   Know to meet at the established time and place.

K16   Know to arrive before the attendees, to take care of such "housekeeping" items as setting up visual aids, arranging for coffee breaks, etc.

Step 9—Meet with the Participants

Skill Required   S15   You need skill to review with participants the topics or business to be covered and length of time to cover the items.

Knowledge Required   K17   If a note-taker has not been assigned, nominate a person for that role now.

Step 10—Open the Meeting

Knowledge Required   K18   Know to solicit new agenda items at the start of the meeting.

K19   Reviewing the purpose and objectives of the meeting at the beginning encourages participants to work towards the goals of the meeting.

K20   Know to inform participants about housekeeping items (breaks, facilities, lunch, time frames, etc.).

Skill Required   S16   You should decide whether to introduce participants (based on number of participants and participants' previous acquaintance with each other).

Step 11—Cover the Points on Your Agenda

Knowledge Required   K21   Know to lead the meeting using, as appropriate, interviewing skills, discussion skills, and negotiating skills.

K22 The method by which agenda items are covered may differ, based on the type of meeting (see next point).

K23 A meeting may be a combination of the following types:
- *Informational Meetings*—Discuss techniques, listen to responses, share information, present new ideas, persuade participants, test participants for understanding of new information.
- *Demonstration/Instructional Meetings*—Illustrate equipment usage/operation, etc.; use demonstration equipment (exhibits or facsimiles); allow time for practice; apply motor skills if dexterity is required; use role play drills; have an application step; test participants; evaluate their skill.
- *Venting (Complaint Session)*—Establish role of participants; facilitate, do not allow anyone to dominate; control session so that feelings do not get out of control; remain nonjudgmental, probe participants for reasons behind problems; make commitments to solve problems when possible; be honest, sincere, subjective, open in expressed feelings because of personal views.
- *Problem Solving/Decision Making*—Brainstorm ideas, select PS model; as meeting leader, do not dominate session or judge ideas as they are generated; encourage creativity; listen to all input; evaluate ideas according to model; be objective, give every idea a fair review; select solution; make decision, gain group's concurrence; develop backup solution, if necessary; plan follow-up on solution.

Step 12—Determine If the Purposes of the Meeting Have Been Achieved

Skills Required	S17	You need skill to determine critical points that must be understood.
	S18	You need skill to determine, by reactions of participants, if purpose has been achieved (excessive questions, facial expressions, etc.).
	S19	You need skill to determine which participants understand what critical points.
	S20	You need skill to determine which participants do *not* understand what critical points.
	S21	You need skill to select a means to determine understanding (pencil and paper test, simulations, surveys, using technical equipment, role playing, questioning by leader, participants' self-evaluation, etc.).
Knowledge Required	K24	Not every point needs to be understood by every participant.

Step 13—Decision Point: Were the Purposes Achieved?

If your decision is *yes,* skip the next step and go to Step 15.

Step 14—Enter the Problem Solving Process

| Knowledge Required | K25 | If your decision is *no*—the purposes of the meeting were not achieved—you should know to enter Problem Solving process at "Define the Problem" and exit at "Implement Method." |
| | K26 | Know that the problem as originally stated may not be resolved. However, a kind of resolution may be reached so that the meeting may end (for example, the original problem may be restated as a different problem, which is then solved; or the meeting may be postponed so resolution may be attempted later). |

Step 15—Summarize Conclusions and Commitments Made

Knowledge Required	K27	Know to summarize orally conclusions and/or commitments to further action made in the meeting.
	K28	Know to make a preliminary summary of the meeting in writing.
	K29	Know to verify summary with participants. (You may want to ask one or more participants to summarize the meeting. This approach could serve as a final check for understanding and/or agreement about what has happened and what is to be done.)
Skill Required	S22	You need skill to determine whether or not another meeting is needed.

Step 16—Close the Meeting

Knowledge Required	K30	Know to express appreciation to all participants for their contributions to the meeting.
	K31	You should know if meeting minutes are appropriate, and who requires copy of minutes.
	K32	Valuable information may be received from peers, friends, boss, subordinates, etc., by asking their opinion on how meeting went after other participants have left.
	K33	Information about the way you were perceived and the techniques you used, may help you in planning and conducting future meetings.

Step 17—Document the Meeting

Skill Required	S23	You need skill to determine if documentation is necessary (for example, you should document what happened in formal appraisal session, grievance session, meeting with vendor, etc.).
Knowledge Required	K34	Know to retain documentation as required by local practices and procedures.

ATTENDING THE MEETING

These steps apply if you are simply participating in a meeting led by someone else.

Step 18—Prepare for the Meeting

Skills Required	S24	If you cannot attend, you should determine whether a substitute is appropriate.
	S25	You need skill to determine what materials to bring to meeting, based on purpose, length, own degree of participation, information received on agenda, etc.
	S26	You need skill to determine if reading or other preparation is needed before attending meeting.
	S27	You need skill to determine your own commitment to action, based on your workload, boss's objectives, degree of participation in future meetings, responsibilities as defined by boss, departmental responsibility, payoff, personal goals, etc.

Step 19—Participate in the Meeting

Knowledge Required	K35	Your role as a participant may be accomplished by contributing ideas, participating in discussion, demonstrating a skill, etc.
	K36	You should know when to take notes (to document agreements, technical points, employee problems, union problems, points to review with boss, etc.).
	K37	You should be *on time* for meeting.

Step 20—Follow-up on Meeting Results (If Appropriate)

Skill Required	S28	You need skill to determine when to review the content of meeting with peers, boss, or subordinates, based on their need to know about new procedures and policies.

Knowledge   K38   You should know to get minutes
Required   of meeting, if appropriate.
            K39   Know to follow-up on commit-
                  ments made at meeting. Know

that these commitments may be
inputs for a "To Do" List and
may be included in plans for
future work.

F.   TRAINING NEEDS DIAGNOSTIC

This is an objective test of 12 questions designed to test first-level supervisors' skills and knowledge of communicating through the medium of meetings.

The questions and answers are found in Exhibits A and B. The 11 specific skills and 11 points of knowledge tested by the questions are shown in Exhibit C.

Diagnostic test exhibit A: process 14—meetings (formal oral communication)

This section deals with Formal Oral Communication. The activities in this process include meetings with one or more persons. A Formal Oral Communication requires some preparation and may be structured.

1.   Your boss recently received a report from the Corporate Training Center detailing a problem. It seems that managers are cancelling requests for training after the cancellation deadline. Last quarter you requested six seats for your group and only sent two trainees. This affects the efficiency of the training organization. It also affects your budget because tuition money is not refunded after the deadline. The other three first-level supervisors reporting to your boss have also been cancelling seats. Therefore, your boss has asked you to run a meeting on this problem. He has set a new objective for next quarter: 90 percent of all allocated training seats must be filled.
     a.   What should your objective be for this meeting?
     b.   Who should you invite to attend this meeting?
     (Write your answers on the answer sheet.)
2.   After running a meeting, it is helpful to ask a few of the participants how the meeting went. (X-out T for True or F for False on the answer sheet.)
3.   You are closing a problem-solving meeting. Which three activities listed below would be most appropriate to do? (X-out the *three* correct answers on the answer sheet.)
     a.   Thank participants for their contributions.
     b.   Read the minutes.
     c.   Restate the meeting objectives.
     d.   Determine whether another meeting is needed.
     e.   Summarize conclusions or commitments.
     f.   Review each participant's contributions.
4.   Which of the following is the *first* consideration in selecting a meeting site? (X-out the correct answer on the answer sheet.)
     a.   ventilation and lighting in the room
     b.   accessibility to the participants
     c.   the size of the room
     d.   proximity to your work location
     e.   privacy
     f.   telephone in the room
5.   There are various ways to notify participants of a meeting. For each situation listed below on the left, select the one method from the right-hand list that should be used to notify participants of the meeting. (Write the number of your answer on the answer sheet.)

Situation
   a. The meeting is one month from now.
   b. The meeting will include 25 people.
   c. The meeting is with coordinates from other locations and the meeting is tomorrow afternoon.
   d. You will be working with the participants during the next two days.
   e. There is a pre-meeting package for participants.
   f. The meeting is with one of your subordinates.

Method
   1. by telephone
   2. in writing
   3. face to face

6. What four items should always be included in a letter inviting participants to a meeting? (Write your *four* answers on the answer sheet.)

7. When opening a meeting, it is appropriate to solicit related agenda items. (X-out T for True or F for False on the answer sheet.)

8. Shown below are activities that may be important in opening a meeting. What is the *most important* activity to perform? (X-out the correct answer on the answer sheet.)
   a. introduce participants
   b. define your role
   c. state the meeting's objective
   d. review lunch, break, lavatory, and message arrangements
   e. select person to take notes

9. A meeting you are running on an office problem has been in progress for 20 minutes. Only one of two people besides you has contributed ideas. The group has not yet defined a solution to the problem.
   What two approaches would lead to more participation? (Write your *two* answers on the answer sheet.)

10. You are running a meeting. One subordinate expresses a viewpoint different from those of other subordinates. What action should you take? (X-out the correct answer on the answer sheet.)
   a. Agree with the subordinate to encourage more discussion.
   b. State your own opinion.
   c. Acknowledge the subordinate's opinion.
   d. Ask the subordinate to express that viewpoint later.
   e. Restate the viewpoints of the other subordinates.

11. When you cannot attend a meeting, you should always send a substitute for yourself. (X-out T for True or F for False on the answer sheet.)

12. In order to keep the communication channels open, you should always review with your boss the contents of meetings you attend. (X-out T for True or F for False on the answer sheet.)

Diagnostic test exhibit B—answer sheet: process 14—meetings

1. (a) (GIVE CREDIT FOR ANSWER THAT WILL INSURE THAT 90 PERCENT OF SEATS WILL BE FILLED.) FOR EXAMPLE, DEVELOP AN ACTION THAT WILL GUARANTEE THAT 90 PERCENT OF SEATS WILL BE FILLED
   (b) THE OTHER THREE FIRST-LEVEL SUPERVISORS
2. ☒ F
3. ☒ b c ☒ ☒ f
4. a ☒ c d e f
5. (a) _2_ (b) _2_ (c) _1_ (d) _3_ (e) _2_ (f) _3_
6. (1) DATE
   (2) TIME
   (3) PLACE
   (4) MEETINGS OBJECTIVES OR PURPOSE

7. ☒ F
8. a b ☒ d e
9. (1) SUMMARIZE THE PROGRESS SO FAR
    (2) DIRECT A QUESTION TO THE OTHER MEETING PARTICIPANTS
    (3) RESTATE THE OBJECTIVE
10. a b ☒ d e
11. T ☒
12. T ☒

Diagnostic test exhibit C—items tested by objective test: process 14—meetings

Test question number	Items tested		Process steps
	Skills	Knowledge	
1	S1, S2, S7, S8	K2, K6	
2		K32, K33	
3	S22	K27, K30	
4	S9, S10	K11	
5	S12		
6	S11		
7		K18	
8		K19	
9		K21	
10		K21	
11	S24		
12	S28		

19 Enabling Knowledge of Guiding Policies, Administrative Procedures, and Standard Practices

During development of the Skill/Knowledge Mastery Model, it became evident to the Job Study Task Force that mastery of many tasks depended highly on knowledge of the policies, procedures, and standard practices that guide and govern the activities of work groups and their first-level supervisors. These can be either company-wide or local in scope.

"Local" procedures and practices are locally developed methods for performing job functions. Some of these are developed in the absence of a company-wide procedure covering the situation; some are developed because they fill a need unique to the local area, division, district, or work location; others are developed because they fill a particular local need better than an existing company-wide procedure or standard practice.

Local procedures and practices are guides to many tasks, such as:

● Logging results
● Attendance practices
● Union/management relations
● Performance reviews

As an example, a form designed by a district manager to record ongoing performance feedback would be considered a local procedure.

Most of the 14 generic managerial processes used by the first-level supervisor have one or more tasks that need the guidance of policies, procedures, and standard practices. For a first-line supervisor to carry out these managerial duties effectively, he or she must have adequate knowledge of these governing documents. Such knowledge, in fact, is an essential prerequisite to training in these processes.

As an example, the process "Providing Performance Feedback" is particularly dependent on local procedures. Seven of the 28 steps in the process require knowledge of certain governing local practices. Local policies, procedures, and standard practices should be followed, for example, when *documenting points covered in the discussion* with the subordinate, when *writing a performance appraisal*, when *making plans to improve subordinate's performance,* and when *discussing the consequences of the subordinate's performance.* In addition, the supervisor is advised to always follow the union contract and/or local procedures when *giving unfavorable feedback* to a subordinate.

NEED FOR TRAINING IN THIS AREA

Clearly, knowledge of company-wide or local administrative practices is essential to mastery of the first-level supervisory job. This knowledge, in fact, is an integral part of the Mastery Model, as a foundation for applying managerial skills to tasks. Without such knowledge, it is believed that first-level supervisors will tend to use the 14 processes out of context with procedures and practices. This can result in actions that, while technically correct, are inappropriate in terms of company needs, objectives, and relations with others.

Accordingly, one of the major recommendations made by the Study Group is that newly appointed first-level supervisors should be provided with knowledge of local policies, administrative procedures, and standard practices as soon as possible after appointment. In AT&T, this is considered to be the responsibility of the training organizations of the local operating companies.

Additionally, it was recommended that second-level supervisors—the bosses of the target population—should be made aware of the importance of providing this knowledge to their newly appointed subordinates quickly. The task of ensuring that this is done in an effective manner is also considered to be a responsibility of the local operating company training organizations.

SPECIFIC DUTIES, TASKS, SKILLS AND KNOWLEDGE AFFECTED

The table which follows lists the first-level duties and tasks that are deemed to be dependent on knowledge of local policies, administrative procedures, and standard practices. The tables are organized by managerial process in the same order in which they appear in the Mastery Model. The column at the far right shows the specific skill or knowledge that is concerned with local procedures and standard practices; these skills and knowledges are keyed by number to the Mastery Model of each process.

Tasks and decisions requiring knowledge of guiding policies, procedures, and practices

First-level managerial process	Process step number	Task/decision	Mastery model knowledge/skill
1. *Planning the work*	4	Examine information about this type of work	K10
	16	Identify planning checkpoints	S9
	17	Determine if there are local procedures for logging checkpoints	K29
	19	Construct master control list	S11
	20	Record the checkpoints	S12
2. *Controlling the work*	9	Evaluate completed work	K30
	15	Document findings/results	S13
3. *Problem solving*	3	Does standard operating procedure exist to solve the problem?	K4
	4	Is the SOP appropriate to use at this time?	S5
	5	Identify sources of information about the problem	S6
	12	Determine if documentation needed	S14
	15	Document and/or inform	K17

First-level managerial process	Process step number	Task/decision	Mastery model knowledge/skill
4. *Providing performance feedback*		Fundamental Knowledge for Process	K4
	1	Determine that stimulus exists for giving feedback to a subordinate	S2
	13	Discuss consequences of the subordinate's performance	S14
	17	Document points covered with subordinate	K30
	21	Write a performance appraisal	K39
	26	Gain agreement on levels of performance for the next performance review period	K48
	27	Make final plans for maintaining and/or improving performance results	K55
	28	Close the total performance review	K58
5. *Coaching subordinates*	13	Identify the methods to improve the subordinate's performance	K11
	22	Document the coaching session	K21
6. *Create/maintain a motivative atmosphere*	8	Determine if subordinate's input is required to take action	K12
7. *Time management*	7	Can the items on the "To Do" List be delegated?	S16
8. *Communication*	2	Select a method to communicate	K8
9. *Informal oral communication*	23	Document the informal oral communication	S21
10. *Self-development*	7	Select a method to improve performance	S6
	8	Make a performance development plan	K14
11. *Written communication/ documentation*		Written communication is sometimes the mandated method	K3
	3	Is additional information necessary before you produce the communication?	S4
	4	Determine sources of information	K8, K9
	9	Select a format	K13
	10	Produce the written communication	K19
	14	Release the written communication	S22
13. *Career counseling a subordinate*	1	Determine that a stimulus exists for career counseling a subordinate	K3
	13	Document for the total performance review	K15
	17	Follow local company procedures to place subordinate in new job	K23
	18	Plan action to help subordinate qualify for new job	K28
	20	Document results of career counseling session	K32
14. *Meetings*	2	List points to be covered	S3
	17	Document the meeting	S23
	17	Document the meeting	K34

20 The Second-Level Manager

THE SECOND STEP UP THE MANAGEMENT LADDER

Many observers of the management scene have noted that the change from *member of a work group* to *member of management* represents a difficult, sometimes traumatic, transition for many people. Not everyone can accomplish the conversion without an adverse impact on relations with other members of the work group.

A subsequent elevation to the second level, however, tends to be a far less wrenching experience for the typical supervisor. Normally the manager will have had several years on the first level in which to develop and hone his or her managerial skills and knowledge. True, the new second-level manager is more remote than ever from the technical aspects of the work in which he or she was once expert in a "hands-on" manner. True, the supervisor must develop new skills and knowledge in order to cope

with a new set of demands from higher management. And it is true as well that the new second-level supervisor must now "manage people who manage people," with all that this implies to relations with others.

Fortunately, the generic managerial skills and knowledge acquired and refined during the time worked as a first-level supervisor are usually the type that carry the manager through the difficult early period in the new job. What is more, the general *duties* of the second-level job are similar in many respects. What is new and different to the typical newly appointed second level is a higher degree of identification with overall corporate goals, more intensive involvement in the setting of these goals, a compelling need to delegate more effectively, greater decision-making autonomy, and the increased accountability for results that accompanies authority.

ROLE OF THE SECOND-LEVEL MANAGER

The derivation of the principal duties of a manager at the second level of the organization was discussed in Chapter 4. The final listing, in order of importance, of the 14 second-level duties was given there; it is repeated here for ready reference.

1. Planning the Job
2. Controlling the Job
3. Providing Performance Feedback
4. Managing Time
5. Decision Making/Problem Solving
6. Maintaining Upward Communication
7. Maintaining Downward Communication
8. Maintaining Peer/Coordinate Communication
9. Creating a Motivative Atmosphere
10. Developing Subordinates

11. Self-Development
12. Providing Written Communications
13. Involvement with Meetings
14. Community Relations

The three significant differences between this list and the 14 principal duties of a first-level supervisor are: the combining of decision making with problem solving; the breakout of communications into three types—upward, downward, and peer/coordinate; and the inclusion of "developing subordinates" on the list. (This is not to imply that these are the only differences between the jobs of first- and second-level supervisors; on the contrary, there are substantial differences in tasks, subtasks, skills, and knowledge required.)

NEW DEMANDS ON LONG-RANGE SKILLS

For the second-level manager, the nature of *planning* becomes somewhat longer range; the manager must develop a new time horizon. Instead of days or weeks, the manager must think and plan in terms of months and quarters in the future. The problems faced at this level tend to be more "people-centered," of course, and less directly related to the actual work in process at the moment.

Delegation is much more critical to job performance at the second level. What is being delegated are not simply tasks but a share of the manager's authority. In so doing, it should be emphasized, the manager loses none of the authority granted as part of the job, nor does he or she transfer responsibility or accountability to the subordinate. Actually, by delegating authority, the second level gains by the giving—the gain is more competent, self-assured sub-

ordinates. Also gained is the capability to reach out for new, added authority and thereby enhance one's personal value to the organization.

So it goes through the list of second-level managerial duties. The newly appointed supervisor now deals almost exclusively with other members of management, so upward communications, and communications and coordination with other departments occupy a major share of time and energy. The meetings attended are more often ones in which the manager plays the leading role. Thus the skills of oral communication, negotiating, and leading discussion become more essential to effective job performance. The new second-level supervisor may also play a larger role in company/community relations because of higher company rank.

HIGHLIGHTS OF THE SECOND-LEVEL MASTERY MODEL

The Mastery Model of the second-level supervisor's job was constructed in several stages. The first stage was identification and validation of the principal *managerial duties* of the job, and the ranking of these duties in order of importance to job performance.

The second stage was to identify the major *managerial task* components of the 14 principal duties. The number of major tasks per duty varies from one to five; there is a total of 34 tasks in all.

The third stage was to break out the managerial

subtasks of which each major task is composed. The number of subtasks in each principal duty ranges from two to two dozen, with a total of 98.

The fourth stage was to identify the specific *skills* and *knowledge* associated with each duty, task, and subtask. For each principal duty, the number of skills and knowledge ranges from a low of six for Duty No. 8—Communication with peers and associates—to a high of 62 for Controlling the Work.

In the full Mastery Model, there are 137 items of knowledge and 164 skills associated with the duties, tasks, and subtasks. Thus the model, in condensed summary form, is made up of

- 14 principal managerial duties,
- 34 major managerial tasks,
- 98 managerial subtasks,
- 137 items of managerial knowledge, and
- 164 managerial skills.

The table that follows (Table 20-1) illustrates the enormous complexity of the second-level supervisory job in numerical fashion. This table is, in effect, a symbolic model of the model.

Therefore, the second-level job in its entirety is composed of 433 separate and distinct managerial elements—to which must be added the 14 principal duties themselves—to make a grand total of 447 elements in the managerial repertoire of a second-level master performer. To this must be added some two dozen enabling cluster skills of negotiating, leading discussion, and interviewing. Obviously, this does not include the many specialty and technical skills and knowledge the supervisor needs to call on in the performance of the job. A schematic diagram of the Mastery Model might look like Figure 20-1. Obviously, this diagram is highly simplified, even oversimplified, because it fails to show the differences in complexity and learning difficulty of each task, subtask, skill, and knowledge. (It also does not show the deficiencies in skill and knowledge that were exposed by the Diagnostic Test of the target population.)

The task force classified the individual skills and knowledge into three categories, in terms of learning difficulty, as follows:

1. A simple knowledge or skill to be included in a preview step in training; any knowledge statement indicating the consequences of performance.
2. A step in a procedure; an activity that has the potential to be supported by a performance aid; an activity supported by cluster skills.
3. Complex discriminations and generalizations; activities requiring in-depth analysis; activities with multiple stimuli; sequences of behavior.

Table 20-1. Second-level duties, tasks, subtasks, skills and knowledge

Duties	Major tasks	Subtasks	Knowledge	Skills	Total items
1. Planning	3	19	24	13	59
2. Controlling	5	24	20	42	91
3. Performance Feedback	2	3	7	7	19
4. Managing Time	4	8	19	16	47
5. Decision Making	2	6	3	11	22
6. Upward Communication	1	2	5	5	13
7. Downward Communication	1	2	4	3	10
8. Peer Communication	1	2	3	3	9
9. Motivative Atmosphere	1	3	6	5	15
10. Developing Subordinates	5	12	21	25	63
11. Self-Development	2	5	8	7	22
12. Written Communication	1	3	5	8	17
13. Meetings	3	9	11	13	36
14. Community Relations	3	—	1	6	10
TOTAL	34	98	137	164	433

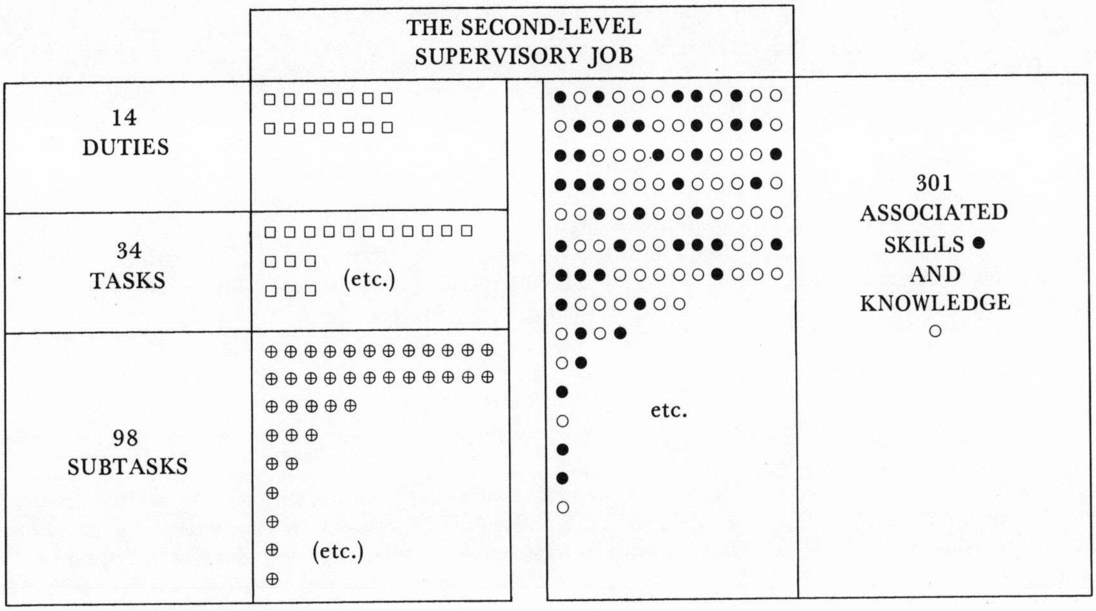

FIGURE 20-1. Mastery Model

ENABLING CLUSTER SKILLS

During development of the Mastery Model of second-level performance it became evident to Youngblood's study group that certain skills were common to mastery of many duties. Three of these in particular were identified as *enabling* skills:

1. Skill in leading discussions
2. Skill in interviewing
3. Skill in negotiating

These three skills transcend the boundaries of the 14 managerial duties and are considered *enabling cluster skills*. The major duties they affect, and the ways in which they should be used, are shown in the following listings. Because of their importance to mastery of second-level supervisory performance, these enabling cluster skills are an integral part of the Mastery Model.

Enabling cluster duty no. 1—leading discussion

Major duty	Use of discussion skills
1. Planning the Work	Start discussion with positive comments to encourage participation of subordinate.
2. Controlling the Work	Use nonthreatening approach to ensure a continuing dialogue between your subordinate and yourself.
3. Performance Feedback	Express appreciation, confidence, and approval of subordinate's work performance.
4. Managing Time	Keep your own comments on track by following an orderly sequence.
5. Decision Making/Problem Solving	Guide discussion to keep subordinate on track.
6. Upward Communication	Obtain information and suggestions from subordinate before giving own.
7. Downward Communication	Encourage subordinate to participate throughout the discussion.
8. Peer Communication	Acknowledge subordinate's comments as useful to the discussion.
9. Motivative Atmosphere	Paraphrase subordinate's comments to communicate own interpretation of subordinate's viewpoints.
10. Developing Subordinates	Check for mutual understanding between yourself and subordinate.
11. Self-Development	Summarize key points of discussion outcome.

Enabling cluster duty no. 2—interviewing skills

Major duty	Use of interviewing skills
1. Planning the Work	Involve subordinate by creating a comfortable atmosphere.
2. Controlling the Work	Use appropriate questioning technique to acquire the desired information from subordinates.
3. Performance Feedback	Use listening skills that enable you and subordinate to achieve mutual understanding.
4. Managing Time	Clarify or obtain clarification of information as appropriate.
5. Decision Making/Problem Solving	Check for mutual understanding of exchanged information.
6. Upward Communication	Acquire all relevant information from subordinate.

Enabling cluster duty no. 3—negotiating skills

Major duty	Use of negotiating skills
1. Planning the Work	Create an atmosphere that enables your subordinates to maintain their self-esteem.
2. Controlling the Work	Obtain clarification of opposing views between yourself and your subordinate.
3. Performance Feedback	Determine areas of agreement between yourself and your subordinate.
4. Managing Time	Determine areas of disagreement between yourself and your subordinate.
5. Decision Making/Problem Solving	Determine reasons for your subordinate's position.
6. Upward Communication	Determine most effective means to achieve mutual agreement.
7. Downward Communication	Compromise your own position when appropriate.

The second-level Skill/Knowledge Mastery Model may be described and discussed more fully in a subsequent volume, along with the Diagnostic Test instrument developed and administered to the second-level target population. The study process followed by Youngblood's team, and the techniques used to gather data, analyze it, develop and test the Mastery Model will also be presented in detail in that volume. That book will also describe the Diagnostic Test methodology in detail. For those readers who may be interested in the job study procedure, however, the next chapter provides a brief discussion of the process.

III The Job Study Process and AT&T Generic Management Training

21 The Job Study Process

As one might expect of an organization as mature and populous as the Bell System, most activities that affect large numbers of people or are repetitive in nature, are guided and governed by formal policies, administrative procedures, and standard practices in writing. *Training* is one such activity. The principal guiding document in this instance is a highly refined procedure called the AT&T Training Development Standards (TDS). This procedure represents the cumu-lative experience of many years of training development in the Bell System, and serves as the "bible" for studying jobs and developing training programs throughout the company. (This procedure is, of course, proprietary to AT&T. In order to put the Job Studies and the Mastery Model that form the basis for this book into proper perspective, however, Charles Sherrard has given me permission to describe the process briefly.)

THE BELL SYSTEM JOB STUDY PROCEDURE—TRAINING DEVELOPMENT STANDARDS

Seven distinct phases make up the TDS process. *Phase 1* is a Preproject Study, the purpose of which is to review training requests that originate throughout the Bell System of operating companies to determine whether training is really necessary, or whether another approach might be more appropriate to the perceived problem or alleged performance deficiency. The principal outputs of Phase 1 are:

- Deficiency analysis summaries
- Recommendations for further action

Phase 2 of the Training Development Standards is the definitive and detailed job study upon which this book is based, and out of which the Skill/Knowledge Mastery Model evolved. The purpose of Phase 2 is to define the valid training needs of the target population and to recommend the kind of training or other remedial action that is appropriate to the deficiencies disclosed in Phase 1, based on intensive data collection and analysis of job performance. Outputs of Phase 2 are:

- Detailed procedures for tasks with deficiencies
- Skills and knowledge required to perform
- Entry level skills and knowledge
- Recommendations for training or alternative remedies

- Training objectives
- Criterion test
- Job performance test
- Training design document, including specifications for carrying out the training

Phase 3 of the TDS—Training Design—produces a "blueprint" for training, either to modify an existing program or to build a new one from the ground up. The Phase 2 Job Study content forms the foundation for the training design. In this phase, the instructional content identified in the job study is organized into groupings called "clusters"; these are further detailed into instructional steps for which specific instructional activities are described.

These preliminary instructional steps are then modified to form lessons, and the preliminary clusters are modified to form "units" or modules, thereby focussing on the training presentation. Outputs of Phase 3 are:

The next three phases of the TDS are: *Phase 4*, Development of training materials and developmental testing of same; *Phase 5*, Field testing and modification; and *Phase 6*, Training introduction, with adaptation to local circumstances as required.

The final *Phase 7*, Follow-up evaluation, involves an appraisal of how well the needs turned up by the Preproject Study have been met, and whether or not the training content is well matched with the current job. This review also looks at the results of nontraining recommendations made in Phase 2, whether the training is being administered as intended, and whether the training is being delivered to the right people.

THE PHASE 2 JOB STUDY

The presentation is Part II, the main body of this book, is based on the Phase 2 Job Study report, which presents and discusses the Skill/Knowledge Mastery Model, the Diagnostic Test, and data collection and analysis process.

The Training Development Standards provides a structured algorithm, or decision tree, designed to guide the study group through a complex chain of tasks and decision points. The chart that follows (Figure 21-1) illustrates a small portion of the algorithm for TDS Phase 2. The bold line traces the path taken by the Job Study Task Force in conducting the study. Both job studies of supervision followed a similar path through the algorithm, with a few more steps in the case of the second-level study because of its pioneering nature.

192

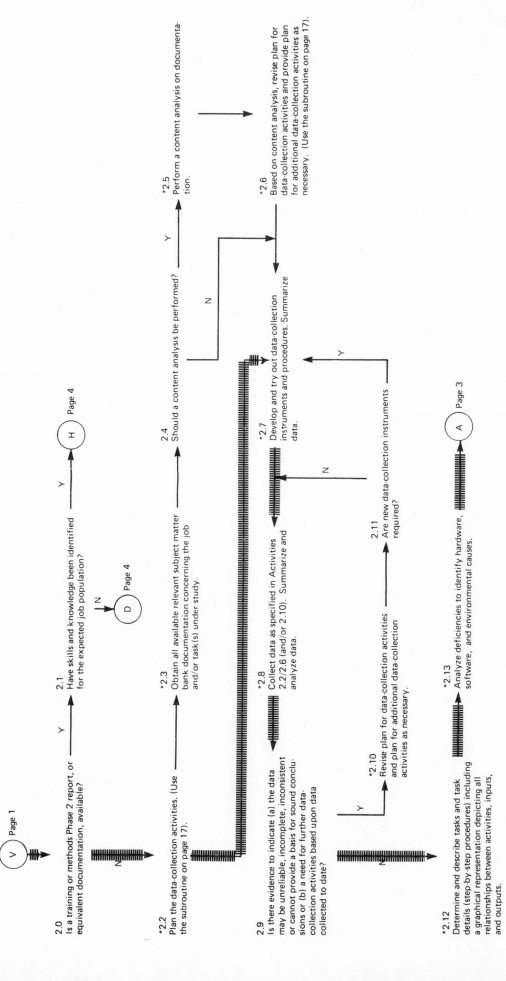

DEFICIENCY OF SPECIFIC OUTPUT ON AN EXISTING JOB, INITIAL TRAINING FOR AN EXISTING JOB OR CHANGED JOB POPULATION, NEW TRAINING TECHNOLOGY

V Page 1

2.0
Is a training or methods Phase 2 report, or equivalent documentation, available?

Y

2.1
Have skills and knowledge been identified for the expected job population?

Y

H Page 4

N

D Page 4

N

*2.2
Plan the data-collection activities. (Use the subroutine on page 17).

*2.3
Obtain all available relevant subject matter bank documentation concerning the job and/or task(s) under study.

2.4
Should a content analysis be performed?

Y

*2.5
Perform a content analysis on documentation.

N

*2.6
Based on content analysis, revise plan for data-collection activities and provide plan for additional data-collection activities as necessary. (Use the subroutine on page 17).

*2.7
Develop and try out data-collection instruments and procedures. Summarize data.

*2.8
Collect data as specified in Activities 2.2/2.6 (and/or 2.10). Summarize and analyze data.

2.9
Is there evidence to indicate (a) the data may be unreliable, incomplete, inconsistent or cannot provide a basis for sound conclusions or (b) a need for further data-collection activities based upon data collected to date?

Y

*2.10
Revise plan for data-collection activities and plan for additional data-collection activities as necessary.

N

2.11
Are new data-collection instruments required?

Y

N

*2.12
Determine and describe tasks and task details (step-by-step procedures) including a graphical representation depicting all relationships between activities, inputs, and outputs.

*2.13
Analyze deficiencies to identify hardware, software, and environmental causes.

A Page 3

* Indicates Activities Requiring Documentation

FIGURE 21-1.

STUDY CONSTRAINTS

The Training Development Standards procedure was developed largely through experience with job studies at the worker level, that is, with studies of technical or craft-type jobs. Few definitive studies had been made of jobs above the craft level. Not surprisingly, therefore, the procedure is oriented toward nonsupervisory jobs. Consequently, the study group under Charles Youngblood's direction had to accommodate the TDS to a somewhat different purpose—the development of a "mastery model" of generic managerial duties, tasks, skills, and knowledge which would serve as a pattern, and "ideal" profile, toward which to direct the training and development of supervisors.

Several constraints were encountered during the course of the Job Studies. The second-level study revealed a serious lack of documented standards for generic managerial skills and knowledge at this level. The earlier content analysis made in the Preproject Study had indicated that such information was unavailable in sufficient detail to be useful. Additionally, the mental standards used by higher-level managers to measure performance, as revealed by the interviews with the target population, were found to contain inconsistencies that cast doubt on their value. Accordingly it was necessary to conduct a full-scale data collection activity and construct a full-scale diagnostic test. Another additional step in the second-level study was to resolve discrepancies brought out in the review of job data by Subject Matter Experts.

FOCUS ON THE SECOND-LEVEL SUPERVISOR

It was noted in an earlier chapter that the company's advisory board on training, the Management Training and Development Advisory Board (MTDAB), decided to give initial emphasis to the job study of second-level supervision. Accordingly, the specific charge made to Charles Sherrard's Human Resources Training and Development study group was to:

Conduct a Phase 2 Job Study on the initial training needs of newly-appointed second-level managers (0 to 12 months) who have supervisory responsibilities. Examine these positions in 5 separate departments—Accounting/Controllers, Customer Service, Marketing/Sales, Network Services, and Operator Services.

Concentrate on surfacing job requirements and performance deficiencies resulting from being newly appointed, and identify as many deficiencies as possible which are continuing from the first level.

Objectives of the Job Study were further refined by the task force after some deliberation. For the second-level supervisory job, they were to:

- Identify all deficiencies
- Determine all tasks and all step-by-step details
- Derive skills and knowledge required to perform
- Identify skills and knowledge already possessed
- Determine skills and knowledge to be enabled

It should be emphasized that a Phase 2 Job Study is not intended to produce training or course materials. It is rather the *basis* for the *development of such materials*, as well as the source of deficiency data having nontraining implications.

SECOND-LEVEL JOB STUDY TASK FORCE

The Human Resources Development department responded to the charge by assembling a project task force of training and development people from System operating companies, supported by internal and external consulting specialists. Appointed to manage the study was Charles (Buck) Youngblood, a young veteran of the Bell System on rotational assignment from Chesapeake and Potomac (C&P) Telephone Company. Youngblood had moved upward through the C&P technical organization, from a line foreman in 1961 to foreman supervisor in the central office to district plant supervisor. In the early 1970s

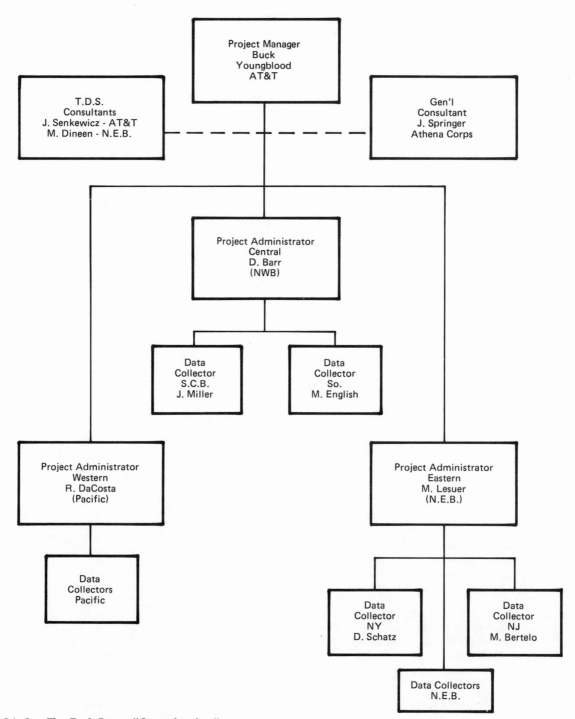

FIGURE 21-2. The Task Force "Organization"

he moved into the executive department of C&P Telephone as Affirmative Action/EEO coordinator and from there into management training and organizational effectiveness consulting.

Along the way, he received a degree in business administration from the University of Maryland, with strong emphasis on personnel management and industrial psychology. Youngblood also took advantage of the many educational opportunities inside the company—courses in supervisory skills, communications, human effectiveness training, job enrichment, MBO, the Managerial Grid, and others—in addition to a regimen of technical courses given by C&P.

As a result, Youngblood was well-qualified to take on project management responsibility for the second-level job study, operating out of the HRT&D department in Basking Ridge (now in Morristown), New Jersey.

Full-time members of the job study task force, in addition to Buck Youngblood, were three project administrators from System operating companies (OTCs), one in the East, one in the Midwest, and one in the far West—Maureen Lesuer from New England Telephone; Dale Barr from Northwestern Bell; and Bob Da Costa from Pacific Telephone. Assisting them on a local basis were specialists in training and development from four other operating companies, also geographically distributed.

Members of the task force were trained and experienced organizational consultants, management skills trainers, training course developers, and instructional technology subject matter experts (SMEs). All members had attended the Bell System Job Study Workshop, so were familiar with the AT&T Training Development Standards, the procedure that guided the job study.

The task force was also aided by several internal consultants—Moe Dineen of New England Telephone's Human Performance Division, and John Senkewicz and Myron Goff from AT&T's corporate Training Research Group. An external consultant, Judy Springer from the Athena Corporation, a specialist in human communications, also participated. At a later point, the group was assisted by two other outside specialists, Professor Ronald K. Hambleton of the University of Massachusetts and Dr. Leo Landa, an authority on the use of algorithms in training. Figure 21-2 is an organization chart of the second-level Job Study Task Force.

NEW TERRITORY FOR JOB STUDY

Because of the ground-breaking nature of this job study—generic managerial skills and knowledge had not been studied before in depth—no model existed on which to pattern the work. The task force, accordingly, was obliged to spend considerable time in defining the study process itself. This meant that the group had to ask some basic questions about its own role and the direction the study should take. The agenda for one early meeting is revealing.

Agenda, November 7

1. Background
    - Advisory Board
    - Project
    - Task force

    ● Why this Phase 2 study?

2. Focus of Study
    - Entire job
    - Parts of job
    - Hoped for outcomes

    ● What will we study?

3. Schedule for Planning Activities
    - November 11   ● How will we use this time?

4. Study Strategies
    - Concerns and issues   ● How will we study whatever we study?

5. Roles of Team
    - Manager   ● Who does what?
    - Administrator
    - OTC Resources
    - Consultant(s)

One would expect that in an organization as vast as the Bell System, with enormous resources at its command, simply giving the order or directive to perform the task is enough to launch it into immediate action. Not so. Even so large a company as AT&T has conflicting demands on its resources. Consequently, the job study got off to a slow start. It required a couple of months to assemble and convene the task force.

LEVEL 2 JOB STUDY OBJECTIVES

In accordance with good project management practice, the task force first set out to define the purpose and objectives of the study. Its primary goals, of course, had been prescribed by the Advisory Board in its charge to the HRT&D department. As restated by the task force, these were to:

- define the job requirements of second-level supervisors with subordinates reporting to them,
- identify the generic managerial performance deficiencies in the newly appointed target population, and
- gather data leading to empirical definition of a curriculum for management skills training.

The group quickly discovered that no clear and specific definition existed of the generic managerial functions of this level of management. Nor were there any clear standards by which to measure performance of managers at this level. Consequently,

the scope of the study was expanded to include several additional goals:

- To define performance standards for second-level supervisors
- To measure the characteristics of successful incumbents
- To define the role of the second-level supervisor

As it turned out, these secondary objectives became very important outputs of the job study.

In order to carry out the assigned mission and to accomplish all objectives, both primary and secondary, the task force decided to expand the study population to include supervisors who had been in the job longer than the 12 months specified in the assignment. This was done to observe remediation trends on the job, as well as to better define a training curriculum. Accordingly, the scope was expanded to cover second-level supervisors in the job up to 18 months.

THE JOB STUDY METHODOLOGY

The basic approach adopted by the task force was to construct a "model" of second-level managerial behavior, using selected *master performers* (highly competent supervisors) as a pattern. The resulting model is called the "Skill/Knowledge Mastery Model," or simply the "Mastery Model." The technique employed to build this model combined on-the-job observations and in-depth interviews. The Mastery Model, therefore, is not only performance-based, it is *excellence-based*.

The constraints of time and work pressures led to a decision to conduct complete interviews and observations with a selected group of master performers, then to confirm the data thus collected with a larger number of master performers using abbrevi-

ated interviews and observations. The data were also confirmed through interviews with selected managers on levels above and below these second-level members of the target population—first-level subordinates and superiors on the third, fourth, and fifth levels of the same organization "family."

After building the Mastery Model, the job study task force devised a comprehensive Diagnostic Test instrument to compare actual performance of newly appointed supervisors with the skills and knowledge specified in the Model. This served to identify significant deficiencies in managerial skills and knowledge upon which to base recommendations for remedial action.

STEPS IN THE JOB STUDY PROCESS

In brief, the multi-phase job study methodology was to:

1. Collect data on the managerial role, organizational goals, principal duties, and major tasks of

second-level supervisors through on-site observation of Bell System "master performers."

2. Confirm these data with associated managers at other levels through structured interviews.

3. Confirm the relevancy of second-level super-

visors' principal duties and rank them in order of importance to job performance and need for training.

4. Break down each of the principal managerial duties into tasks and subtasks (step-by-step procedures within each task), through on-the-job observation of master performers in actual work environments.

5. Construct a prototype "Mastery Model" containing 14 principal duties, 37 major tasks, 120 subtasks. Confirm this model through observations of an expanded population of master performers in other geographic locations and other departments.

6. Confirm the model further in terms of content, relevancy, logical sequence of tasks and subtasks, and criticality of each factor. This was done through an intensive review by Bell System subject matter experts (SMEs), specialists considered highly knowledgeable in their respective fields through long experience and demonstrated competence. The SMEs who participated in this review are:

1. Mr. W. L. Paullin
Corporate Personnel Manager
Mountain Bell

2. Mr. Emmett Smith
Supervisor-Personnel
AT&T

3. Mr. T. H. Lloyd
General Training Supervisor
New England Telephone

4. Mr. B. Lonbaken
Staff Director-Manpower Development
Pacific Telephone

5. Mr. D. C. Cohen
Supervisor-Operator Services Training
AT&T

6. Mr. L. C. Ombrello
Personnel Supervisor
AT&T

At this point in the job study, the task force developed *performance standards* for each of the 14 principal duties through interviews with third-level superiors of the target population.

7. Next, the study group detailed the prototype mastery model into the specific skills and knowledge factors associated with each major task and subtask. Subject matter experts in AT&T and operating companies reviewed this final Mastery Model for its comprehensiveness, relevancy, and responsiveness to the needs of the company.

8. Based on the final Mastery Model, the group developed a Diagnostic Test instrument and administered it to the target population of newly appointed supervisors. This diagnostic test was first given to selected master performers in order to determine whether there were deficiencies in the performance of highly skilled and experienced supervisors.

The final task of the study group was to develop a set of recommendations and prepare a Phase 2 Job Study report. The recommendations led to the development of a series of training courses and job performance aids, which are now being administered to second-level supervisors in Bell System companies. These courses are described briefly in Chapter 22.

THE FIRST-LEVEL SUPERVISORY JOB STUDY

The job study procedure just described was followed in its essentials later on, when the first-level supervisor's job was put under the microscope of the AT&T Human Resources Training and Development department. Several differences between the two studies are significant, however. For one, the first-level supervisor's job was studied in greater depth. For another, the study was conducted in a somewhat more structured fashion.

The later job study had the benefit, to be sure, of the study techniques developed and knowledge gained

through the second-level study, which had plowed fresh ground in the area of generic managerial skills and knowledge. As a result, the task force conducting the new study was enabled to move more rapidly into the main task by following a trail already blazed. The differences between the studies were to some extent, at least, a consequence of the different backgrounds and work experiences of the project managers and the project "monitors" responsible for the work.

The person chosen to "project manage" this job study was, like the manager who had headed up the earlier study, Buck Youngblood, brought in from the pressure-cooker environment of a Bell System operating company. Youngblood, it was noted earlier, is a manager who had worked his way up "through the ranks" in the best Bell tradition, taking advantage of opportunities to expand his educational and career horizons as he did so.

The choice of an operating company manager to lead these job studies served to keep them focused on the practical aspects of supervision in the "real world" of telephone operations, and avoided the danger of their becoming theoretical and academic. This decision also had the considerable benefit of broadening the managerial scope of the project manager, thereby enhancing value to the home organization on return.

For this job study of first-level supervision, a manager named Dale F. Barr, Jr. was brought in from Northwestern Bell Telephone Company on temporary assignment. Barr had been involved in the design and application of training and development programs for Northwestern Bell as staff manager of Training Technology. Northwestern Bell, headquartered in Omaha, Nebraska, and covering the five states of Iowa, Minnesota, Nebraska, and North and South Dakota, has a long history of emphasizing training and development of its people. Its first training center, set up in 1947, taught only three courses—basic electricity, installation, and toll instruction. Northwestern now has two large centers teaching 438 courses that cover every conceivable aspect of the telephone business.

Barr had actively participated full-time in the second-level job study as project administrator for the Central Region. He logged more hours—nearly 1500—than any other member of the task force. This experience, coupled with his background in instructional technology, suited him well for the job of managing the first-level study.

It was observed earlier that this study of first-level supervision tended to be done in greater detail and was more structured in its approach. The new study had a different project "monitor" from the AT&T Human Resources Training and Development department, one Kerry Glum, who had a marked influence on the study as it progressed. Glum is a young Bell System career manager with extensive research experience and orientation. She has been with AT&T for eleven years, most of them in management training and development. She followed up her undergraduate education in teaching with an MBA and has taken advantage of company in-house courses to broaden her management capabilities.

Kerry Glum's training in research methods and her reputed passion for detail have left an imprint on the first-level job study—and upon this book as well. I am indebted to her for a meticulous review of the manuscript while in progress, and for many thoughtful comments and suggestions for clarification and improvement.

The project manager's responsibilities in a job study of this broad scope do not end with publication of a Phase 2 study report. Kerry Glum has been involved with subsequent phases of the total project, to ensure that the Phase 2 study led to the development of training courses that are cost-effective and responsive to Bell System valid training needs. These training courses are described briefly in the final chapter.

22 First- and Second-Level Supervisory Training Courses

The essential purpose of a Bell System Phase 2 Job Study, it was noted earlier, is to define the valid training needs of the target population and to recommend training and other remedial action to correct any performance deficiencies revealed by the study (in this case, deficiencies exposed by application of a Diagnostic Test based on the Mastery Model).

The content of the Job Study is the foundation for the *design* of training courses (Phase 3 of the Training Development Standards), which are thereupon produced and developmentally tested (Phase 4), field tested (Phase 5), and introduced with adaptation to local circumstances as may be needed (Phase 6).

The recommendations made by the two supervisory job study groups resulted in a series of training courses that are now being administered within the operating companies of the Bell System. These courses, nine in number, are described briefly in the following "Generic Management Training Curricula" for first- and second-level supervisors.

It should be noted that the actual content of these training courses is proprietary to AT&T. They are intended solely for use within the Bell System and cannot be made available to others. The summary descriptions given here, together with the material presented in Part 2, should be helpful to non-AT&T training professionals as guides to the development of training programs tailored to the characteristics and training needs of their own organizations.

NOTE: Neither AT&T nor Bell System companies can answer inquiries or requests for information about these training courses or the job study. All inquiries should be addressed to the publisher of this book.

GENERIC MANAGEMENT TRAINING CURRICULA

A curriculum consists of a series of training courses that have been logically sequenced to provide managers with generic management performance training when it is most needed. The curriculum provides training in areas that will *ensure the new manager's* *survival* in the early days following his or her appointment to a given level.

Successful progression through the curriculum will result in the acquisition of the knowledge in a timely manner.

Performance-Based. The likelihood of high individual manager proficiency is possible because the training is performance-based. During the training, the conferees learn (based on deficiencies) to do what is actually done by high performing managers in the Bell System, or, as they are often called, "master performers." Identified by their organizations because of their competence and track records of success, hundreds of these master performers, representing all segments and Operating Companies contributed the criteria from which the courses were developed. On-the-job observations were conducted while these master performers were actually doing their jobs. They were interviewed extensively to determine and record even their thought process as they went about the business of managing.

These "hard" data have provided the basis for management training that is job relevant, directly linked to the conferee's real world. This, coupled with the method used in the design of the training, maximizes the potential for timely and effective back-on-the-job application.

Curriculum Design. Each course in each curriculum trains performance-based processes, which are general to all managers, and when applied, will improve their job performance in that area. A problem-solving model is an example of a process. However, learning the process is not sufficient in itself to maximize your ability to use it back on the job. As such, opportunity to apply each process in a job-relevant situation as it is learned is built into the training.

Course Sequence. The courses are sequenced in the curriculum based on three factors:

1. Process application and practice
2. Specific outputs from one course that are needed as inputs to another and are job-related

3. Timing, which spaces and positions the courses in terms of what the new manager needs the most and when

There are specific time frames when each course should be taken after an individual has been appointed.

These time frames were determined based on the skills, knowledges, and processes they address and how important these are to the manager's survival on the job, their relation to improved job performance, and their relative importance and application to each other.

Curriculum Prerequisites. The third factor in the curriculum design is course prerequisites. We use the term prerequisite here in a very specific context; i.e., the specific outputs (products produced) from one course are necessary inputs (working documents) for another.

In Summary. The curricula are:

Sequenced to provide:
● Timely learning relevant to job requirements
● Training applications and practice that will improve performance in a more efficient manner
● Reinforcement of skills, knowledges, and processes as relevant to the job situation

Performance-based:
● Built on "mastery" performance
● Derived from an analysis of existing *performance deficiencies*

Integrated:
● Avoid duplication of development and learning
● Unique, as appropriate, to a given level
● Available, as appropriate, on an individual basis

First-Level Curriculum—Course 1: Managing the Work and Problem Solving[1] (4 days, trainer-led)

At the end of this course, the manager will be able to:

● Evaluate information relative to a given problem to determine if a problem exists and if an existing problem is worth solving.
● Select the most efficient approach for solving a given problem, including determining what kinds of information need to be gathered and what areas of information gathering to emphasize.
● Organize the information relative to a given problem situation.

[1]Closely linked to Second-Level Problem-Solving Course

In addition, the manager will be able to use planning as it is specifically applied to their current job and to use methods to establish a plan, i.e.,

1. Define responsibilities
2. Define resources
3. Define constraints
4. Develop documentation

To define control, and develop specific methods that can be applied to their plan strategy:

1. Determine tracking method
2. Determine evaluation method

Course 2: Managing Performance (5 days, trainer-led)

At the end of the course on Managing Performance, the manager will be able to apply and implement the processes required of the first level for developing subordinates. This includes:

- Providing performance feedback
- Coaching a subordinate
- Career counseling
- Providing a motivative atmosphere

- Relevant facilities processes; i.e.,
  1. Informal oral communication
  2. Formal oral communication

At the end of this course, the managers will be able to respond to supervisory problems by developing alternative solutions for solving problems. This is accomplished by enabling managers to:

1. Effectively solve the problem
2. Enhance and/or maintain the employee's self-esteem
3. Maintain open communications with the employee

The strategies used to reach this objective are modeling, application feedback, and transfer of learning.

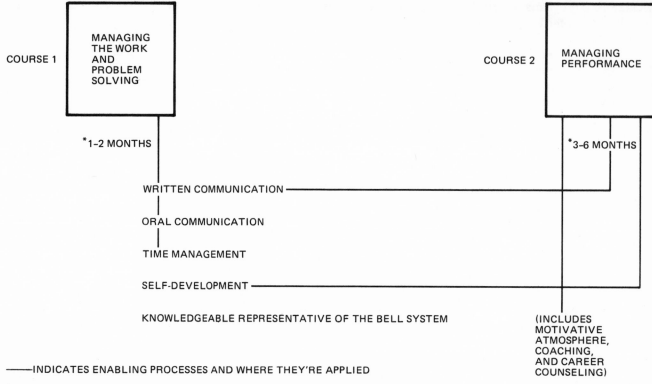

FIGURE 22-1. First-Level Generic Management
Training Curriculum

Second-Level Curriculum—Course 1: Managing the Problem-Solving Process (2 days, trainer-led)

Upon completing the *Managing the Problem-Solving Process* training course, the manager will be able to:

- Evaluate information relative to a given problem situation to determine if problem exists and if an existing problem is worth solving.
- Select the most efficient approach for solving a given problem, including determining what kinds of information need to be gathered and what areas of information gathering to emphasize.
- Organize information relative to a given problem situation.

Includes:

Future problem emphasis
Job aids for on-the-job learning application
Heavy case application and practice

Course 2: Managing to Write (2 days, self-paced instruction, trainer-assisted)

Upon completing *Managing to Write,* the manager will be able to use a job performance aid regularly as the means for writing effectively.
Includes:

Determining design *Based on Subject and Reader Profiles*
Writing effective openings
Creating the proper tone
Using a Pertinent, Release, and Close Language

Course 3: Defining the Job (1½ days, self-paced instruction, trainer-assisted)

Upon completion of *Defining the Job,* and given sufficient knowledge[2] about the job, the manager will produce a document that completely defines the job. This document will include:

- A job summary
- Responsibilities of the job
- Function statements for each responsibility
- Latitude and constraints in performing each function

The last part of this course will be completed on the job, where the manager will:

- Review and verify the output with the boss.
- Review what their work group, as a whole, is doing to verify or improve its effectiveness, by repeating the process with their work group.

Course 4: Managing the Job (2 days, self-paced instruction and trainer-led)

At the completion of this course, the manager will be able to:

- Plan, monitor, and control time expenditures by comparing planned versus actual expenditures and determining remedies for problem areas identified.
- Write acceptable performance standards and goals in conjunction with the job definition.
- Select negotiable and nonnegotiable goals and conduct an interview, negotiation and goal setting session.
- Includes enabling skills such as handling defensive reactions.

Course 5: Managing the Flow of Work (3 days, self-paced instruction and trainer-led)

At the completion of this course, the manager will be able to use a systematic process for planning, organizing, and controlling the work that flows through his/her work group.
Includes:

Identifying the nature of the item of work and its priority
Clarifying expectations
Determining work characteristics
Developing an implementation and monitoring plan
Monitor to its completion, including:
a. Giving constructive feedback
b. Providing coaching as a corrective action to improve performance

Course 6: Developing Subordinates (1½ days, self-paced instruction and trainer-led)

At the completion of the course assignment, the manager will be able to:

- Identify appropriate developmental activities for specific subordinates.
- Identify activities that can be utilized to develop subordinates who are rated satisfactory or higher and describe the components and their interrelationships in a subordinate development system.
- Write a developmental model for subordinates, which includes delegation stages that can be used back on the job, and a general developmental plan appropriate for their organization that can be used back on the job.
- Utilize an inventory system to provide information to establish a subordinate's entry into the participant's general development plan, including delegating for a chosen activity, appropriate responsibility, authority, and accountability for a selected subordinate.

[2]Sufficient knowledge is defined as participants having been at their present job for at least three months.

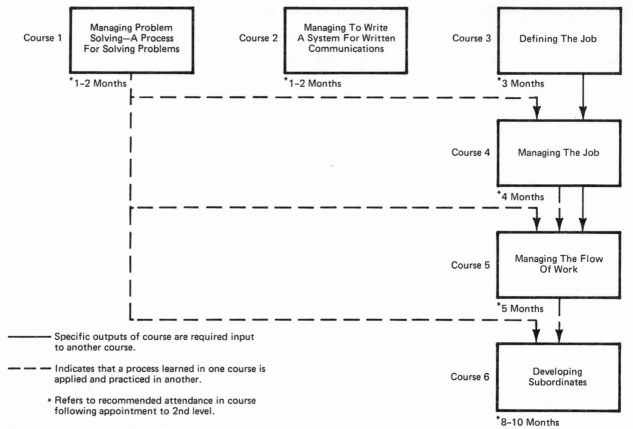

FIGURE 22-2. Second-Level Generic Management Training Curriculum

Other: Managing Your Time Management Problem (½ day, self-paced)

This course is offered to second levels and can be offered to third-level managers. It was determined in the third-level job study that a deficiency in time management was prevalent in the population of newly appointed managers.

Once again, focus and language will be common to both second- and third-level managers taking this course, resulting in enhanced communication.

23 A Behavioral Scientist's View of the AT&T Job Study

by Robert R. Carkhuff, Ph.D.
Carkhuff Institute of Human Technology

Robert R. Carkhuff is a recognized authority on human resource development. He is one of the 100 most cited social scientists and is author of 27 books, including the two-volume Helping and Human Relations.

Dr. Carkhuff is presently chairman of the Carkhuff Institute of Human Technology, Amherst, Massachusetts, and president of Human Technology, Inc., McLean, Virginia, a consulting firm specializing in improving human productivity in government and industry.

At the request of the publisher, Dr. Carkhuff has prepared the following brief review of the AT&T supervisory job study and the adaptation presented in this book.

IMPROVING HUMAN PERFORMANCE

When we analyze any area of human endeavor, three basic factors emerge: (1) people, (2) programs, and (3) environments (Carkhuff, 1981, 1982). The people factor represents interpersonal or facilitative dimensions. The program factor emphasizes substantive and systematic dimensions. The environmental factor involves follow-up support systems. This AT&T study of first-line supervision supports the significance of these factors.

The program factors that emerge as primary in this AT&T study emphasize planning and controlling the work as well as problem solving and providing performance feedback. These are labeled *survival* processes in the study.

The people factors, in turn, emphasize coaching subordinates and creating and maintaining a motivative atmosphere as well as various levels of communication, including informal oral communication. These are labeled *facilitative* processes.

The final processes emphasize the organizational context or environment within which the survival and facilitative processes take place. They emphasize the development of the supervisor and supervisee as part of the human environment, as well as written and formal communication and system content knowledge requirements that support the performance of essential supervisory tasks.

Together, these factors—people, programs, and environments—comprise the sources of effectiveness in individual task performance and agency productivity. When they are implemented and integrated at the highest levels, they contribute significantly to human productivity. When they are not implemented or integrated at the highest levels, they detract from productivity. The purpose of this Afterword is to explore further the assumptions and implications as well as the operations of these basic ingredients in human productivity.

PRODUCTIVITY ASSUMPTIONS

It is most efficient and effective to view productivity in terms of the basic inputting, processing, and outputting system (see Figure 23-1). As can be seen, static resource input is processed dynamically to produce static result output, the data of which is fed back as internal input to the productivity system (Carkhuff, 1982). The same precise stages are employed to assess productivity. Basically, productivity is a measure of results outputs against resource inputs:

$$\text{Productivity} = \frac{\text{Results Outputs}}{\text{Resource Inputs}}$$

The fundamental task over time is to increase results outputs by some increment while reducing resource inputs by some decrement:

$$\text{Improved Productivity} = \frac{\text{Results Outputs} + \Delta}{\text{Resource Inputs} - \Delta}$$

This basic productivity system applies to individuals as well as agencies (see Figure 23-2). As can be seen, the same inputting-processing-outputting system applies to the individual at his or her performance station within the agency processing system. Thus, the individual within the agency processing system processes resource inputs into results outputs. Indeed, ultimately, it is the skilled person who contributes the most to improved agency productivity by reducing inputs and increasing outputs at the individual performance station.

Improving productivity, then, involves improving the dynamic processing that transforms the resource inputs into results outputs. One of the essential levels of improving dynamic processing involves the first-line supervisory process. The improving operations of this supervisory process contribute to the reduction of resource inputs and the increase of results outputs. It is precisely these supervisory operations that the AT&T study of supervision has addressed.

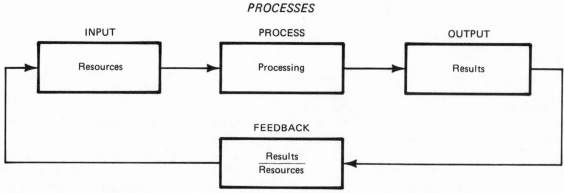

FIGURE 23-1. Basic Productivity System

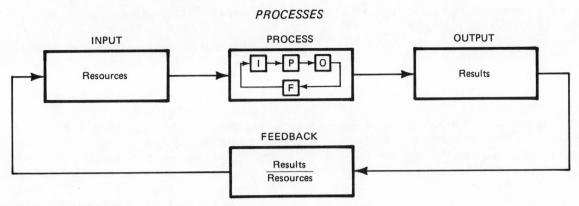

FIGURE 23-2. Basic Individual Performance System within Agency Productivity System

PERFORMANCE OPERATIONS

The essential task of supervisors, then, is to improve the processing within the agency by improving the processing that takes place within the individual performance station. In short, the essential task of supervision is to maximize individual performance by minimizing resource inputs and maximizing results outputs.

In order to maximize individual performance the employees must have the skills to analyze, operationalize, and technologize their task goals (Carkhuff, 1982). They must be able to analyze their tasks in terms of their components, processes, and functions. They must be able to operationalize their goals based on this task analysis. Finally, they must be able to technologize and implement the means to achieve these task goals.

The resources that the supervisor has for maximizing supervisee performance processing include the aforementioned people, program, and environmental factors. The people factors emphasize interpersonal skills that relate the supervisees' frames of reference to the tasks at hand. The program factors help to operationalize the tasks to be performed. The environmental factors support or reinforce the task performance.

People

The people factor emphasizes the interpersonal relationships that exist between supervisors and supervisees. The critical nature of the interpersonal relationship is seen in three stages of effective interpersonal supervision: getting the supervisee's image of the tasks at hand; giving the supervisor's image of the tasks; merging the images of the tasks (Friel et al., 1982). These three interpersonal stages occur at all of the stages of individual processing: analyzing, operationalizing, and technologizing. They relate the employee's frame of reference to the tasks and, thus, motivate the employee to perform the tasks at the highest possible levels. Clearly, the *facilitative* coaching, motivating, and communicating processes found in the AT&T study are discharged by this interpersonal factor.

Programs

To be sure, it is not enough to achieve interpersonal agreement on the tasks to be performed. Initially the supervisor and ultimately the supervisee must be knowledgeable and, above all, skilled in the substance of the tasks. It is precisely this substantive knowledge that works in conjunction with the interpersonal skills to facilitate analyzing, operationalizing, and technologizing of the tasks to be performed (Carkhuff, 1981). Clearly, the *survival* processes of planning, controlling, problem solving, and giving feedback are accounted for by this program factor.

Environment

Finally, it is not enough to converge interpersonally and programmatically in the supervisory process. The environment must support the programmatic achievement of performance goals. The key ingredient in environmental support is reinforcement. The environment must reinforce individual performance differentially by positively reinforcing improving performance, vigilantly observing unchanging performance, and negatively reinforcing decremental performance (Carkhuff, 1981). While the AT&T findings are less organized here, clearly self- and other development in a reinforcing communication context contribute to sustaining and improving performance gains.

Performance Integration

All of these factors—people, programs, and environment—must ultimately be integrated into a systematic performance improvement system. This means that the supervisors must be trained, followed up on, and supported for their supervisory gains in interpersonal, programming, and supporting skills. In turn, the supervisors must intervene in the supervision process, and follow up on and support the performance of their supervisees using their interpersonal, programming, and supporting skills. The agency must discharge precisely the same functions in improving the performance of the supervisors that the supervisors discharge in improving the performance of the supervisees.

PERFORMANCE DATA

The AT&T study is basically a naturalistic study that uses selected exemplary supervisors to prioritize and validate certain preselected supervision processes. We may call this a consensual validity study. What happens when we experimentally manipulate the independent people, program, and environmental factors and study their effects on employee performances? These experimental studies include two sets of studies: (1) those involving the effects of supervisors on employees; and (2) those involving the effects of directly training employees (Carkhuff, 1982a).

Supervisory effects

A selection of recent studies of agency productivity by Friel and his associates reveals significant productivity gains with the introduction of people, program, and environmental factors. All of the studies trained supervisors in a "get–give–merge and go" (GGMG) interpersonal skills approach rather than the traditional authoritarian "give and go" approach ("I give the task and you go do it"). Friel et al. used GGMG in conjunction with other systematically taught supervisory skills such as performance appraisal, employee development, and employee compensation programs. In various studies, they trained thousands of supervisors and managers and studied their effects on tens

of thousands of employees. There were positive results in the following areas: significant time savings ranging into the thousands of hours (Friel et al., 1982); significant money savings ranging to millions of dollars (Brillinger and Friel, 1982; Day et al., 1981; Feder, 1982; Friel et al., 1982); significant safety, idle days, and accident rate improvements (Brillinger and Friel, 1982; Day et al., 1981); and significant return on investment ranging up to 500% (Brillinger and Friel, 1982).

Direct training effects

Just as it makes sense to train supervisors, so also does it make good sense to train supervisees, not only to receive supervisor efforts but also to directly improve supervisee performance. Carkhuff and Friel (1982) directly trained government executives and significantly improved the quantity and quality of their interpersonal problem-solving, programming, consulting, and planning skill applications from 100% to 1,000%. Mullin, Quirke, and Chapados (1982) improved the goal attainment by more than 250% and the direct service to customers by more than 900% by training service employees in interpersonal and other program skills. Banks et al. (1982) trained an entire government agency in interpersonal and management systems skills and improved work quantity 7% and work quality 9%. Finally, Carkhuff (1982*b*) trained the personnel of a private corporation in interpersonal and program specialty skills with the following results: dollar output, +25%; personnel resources used, −16%; individual performance, +48%; and profit, +50%.

Clearly, there are two primary ways of affecting individual employee performance: (1) train the supervisors who have an effect on the employees and (2) train the supervisees directly. In the most effective productivity studies, both supervisors and supervisees are trained in the people, program, and environmental factors that affect their performance.

PRODUCTIVITY IMPLICATIONS

Perhaps the major implication of the AT&T study and the other reported work is the need for systematic intervention in the work of both supervisors and supervisees. Thus, supervisors are systematically trained, followed up on, and supported so that they can systematically train, follow up on, and support supervisees. Ultimately, both supervisors and supervisees must be trained in the skills that enable them not only to complement but to facilitate each other's contributions.

The implications for other functional levels— mid-management, management, and policy—are clear. Just as we train supervisors and supervisees in the people, program, and environmental factors that apply to them, so must we train higher levels of management in the skills that apply to them. Finally, all levels of skilled functions within all components of an agency must be integrated for maximum agency productivity.

Individual performance and agency productivity are both a function of dynamic processing that transforms resource inputs into results outputs. This dynamic processing is a function of people or facilitative factors, program or survival factors, and environmental or contextual factors. When present together

and at the highest levels, these factors converge to maximize human performance at all functional levels within an agency.

Any ultimate equation for productivity implies the expansion of results outputs to infinity (∞) and the reduction of resources inputs to zero (0):

$$\text{Productivity} = \frac{\infty}{0}$$

What this means is that we can create something out of nothing. While this outcome may or may not be achievable, it becomes our human mission. It is especially applicable to a world with expanding needs for results outputs and diminishing finite natural resources.

Perhaps most important, what improving human performance implies is maximizing human processing (see Figure 23-3). In order to maximize results outputs while minimizing resource inputs, we must maximize the human processing that transforms the inputs into outputs. We can see this most clearly in our equation for ultimate productivity. Indeed, it is in the process of actualizing human processing and, thus, human productivity that we become fully human (Carkhuff, 1982).

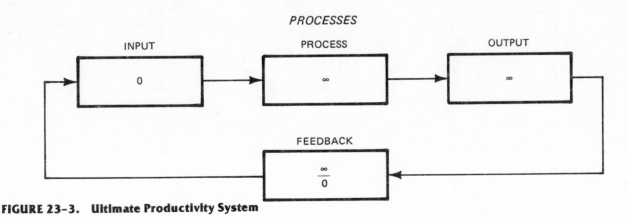

PROCESSES

FIGURE 23-3. **Ultimate Productivity System**

CHAPTER 23 REFERENCES

Banks, G., Cannon, J., Friel, T.W., and Pierce, R.M. Management by communication. *Research Reports, Carkhuff Institute of Human Technology*, 1982, *5*, No. 1.

Brillinger, R.H., and Friel, T.W. The PRIDE program: An interpersonal skills-based management system for productivity improvement. *Research Reports, Carkhuff Institute of Human Technology*, 1982, *5*, No. 2.

Carkhuff, R.R. *Beyond productivity.* Amherst, Mass.: Carkhuff Institute of Human Technology, 1981.

Carkhuff, R.R. Interpersonal skills outcomes. *Harvard Educational Review*, 1982*a*.

Carkhuff, R.R. *Productivity training.* Amherst, Mass.: Human Resource Development Press, 1982*b*.

Carkhuff, R.R. *Productivity processing.* Amherst, Mass.: Human Resource Development Press, in press.

Carkhuff, R.R., and Friel, T.W. The effects of inservice training in human resource development skills upon state education agency employees. *Research Reports,* *Carkhuff Institute of Human Technology*, 1982, *5*, No. 3.

Day, S.R., Matheny, K.B., and Megathlin, W.L. Training correctional personnel. In J.D. Blakeman (Ed). *Conference Proceedings: National Training Workshop for Master Trainers/Consultants in Interpersonal Skills.* Atlanta, Ga.: National Institute of Corrections, 1980.

Feder, E. The effects of interpersonal skills-based training of supervisors upon productivity. *Research Reports, Carkhuff Institute of Human Technology*, 1982, *5*, No. 4.

Friel, T.W., Cannon, J.R., Carlson, D., Feder, E., Holder, T., Pierce, R.M., and Shultz, J. Employees don't work for people they don't like. *Harvard Business Review*, 1982.

Mullin, T., Quirke, M., and Chapados, J. The effects of systematic *HRD* training upon organizational task completion. *Research Reports, Carkhuff Institute of Human Technology*, 1982, *5*, No. 5.

Date Due